HORATIUS BONAR

THE DESERT OF SINAI
NOTES OF A SPRING-JOURNEY
FROM
CAIRO TO BEERSHEBA

Elibron Classics
www.elibron.com

Elibron Classics series.

© 2005 Adamant Media Corporation.

ISBN 1-4021-8745-9 (paperback)
ISBN 1-4021-1846-5 (hardcover)

This Elibron Classics Replica Edition is an unabridged facsimile
of the edition published in 1857 by James Nisbet and Co.,
London.

THE DESERT OF SINAI:

NOTES OF A SPRING-JOURNEY

FROM

CAIRO TO BEERSHEBA.

BY

HORATIUS BONAR, D.D.

KELSO.

LONDON:

JAMES NISBET AND CO., BERNERS STREET.

1857.

PREFACE.

THIS volume is really what it professes to be,—" Notes of a journey."

The notes were all taken on the spot, generally on the back of the camel, and extended afterwards. A little practice made it easy to write in that position ; at least when the animal was not moving at more than its common rate of two miles and a quarter an hour. It was much more satisfactory to record every event as it occurred, and every scene as it came before the eye. In no case was memory alone trusted to ; but all was noted down, however briefly, at the moment. After-impressions, even of the most accurate and honest memory, are not always to be relied on, especially as to the *order* of events and scenes.

The two or three brief discussions, interjected in the course of the narrative, are hardly exceptions to this ; inasmuch as the materials out of which they grew were gathered on the spot. They are not so much after-impressions, as after-inferences from present impressions. The form of a journal has some disadvantages. It precludes classification ; and, by rendering selection difficult, involves unavoidably some degree of repetition. Yet it is the most accurate upon the whole ; nor is it by any means the least interesting.

I meant to have adorned the volume with several original illustrations from the photographs of one of the party. The "printing" from these "negatives" was, however, a work of some time and nicety ; and the cloudy skies of last summer were not favourable to the process. The design has been delayed, not given up.

This volume ends at Beersheba, embracing merely the desert, and the semi-desert outside Palestine. At another time, if God will, I hope to give "Notes of a journey through the land of Promise."

KELSO, *December* 10. 1856.

CONTENTS.

CHAPTER I.

CHAPTER VI.

CHAPTER VII.

CHAPTER VIII.

CHAPTER IX.

CHAPTER X.

CHAPTER XI.

CHAPTER XII.

CHAPTER XIII.

ERRATA.

Page 78, last line, *for* left, *read* right,
... 109, line 6 from top, *for* Eccl. *read* Exod.
... 141, ... 6 from foot, *for* Joel *read* Joab

THE DESERT OF SINAI.

CHAPTER I.

FRANCE—THE MEDITERRANEAN—MALTA—ALEXANDRIA.

THE last leaves had fallen when I left home, and were rustling under foot to the frosty wind. When I returned every branch was budding, and the May breeze, coming freshly down the river, brought good news of sunshine and summer. It seemed as if a winter had been cut out of the year, and that I had scarcely plucked the latest apple when I saw the trees again in blossom.

The journey occupied about five months in all,—five pleasant months, not soon to be forgotten.

Hastening up to London in a sharp December morning, I there joined the companions of my route, the Rev. Thomas Wright of Swinton, and two English friends, Mr Poynder and Mr Beddome. Our fellowship throughout was one of unbroken harmony and comfort. Scotland and England, Presbytery and Episcopacy, re-

A

presented by those who knew how to agree as well as
how to differ, held for months kind and agreeable com-
panionship together on sea and land,—in Egypt, in
Arabia, and in Syria. We embarked at Dover on a wintry dawn, under a
misty sky, upon a dull green sea. England soon disappears in the haze and France comes slowly into sight,
shewing a long low coast stretching to the right. Calais
soon makes itself known with its light-house, town-hall,
and old church. We come ashore in small boats, and
are met on the pier by half-a-dozen of blue-coated soldiers, who politely escort us to the custom-house, where
we produce our passports, tell our ages, professions, des-
tinations, and submit quietly to be treated as criminals,
or at least as conspirators come to overturn the throne.
We grumble at the annoyance, but congratulate ourselves on the difference between this country and our
own. Here everybody that lands is handed over to a
guard and dealt with as a villain, till he has cleared
his character and disproved the suspicions by means of
his passport. In Britain each stranger that comes, of
whatever nation, is bidden welcome, and is treated as
honest and good, till his own deeds shall prove the
contrary.

We soon start for Paris, which we reach in about
eight hours. We linger a day there amid sights of
beauty and wonder. Certainly man has spared no pains
to make his world fair. With scenes like these before
us, it is but too easy to forget that earth is a ruin, that

sin has eaten into its core, that death and sorrow lie all around, and that we need a " new earth wherein dwelleth righteousness." (2 Peter iii. 13.)

Dec. 18. 1855.—We left Paris at half-past eight in the evening. The frost was intense ; nor could the large bottles of hot water with which we were liberally supplied, keep out the biting cold. We reached Lyons at half-past seven next morning. The day was clear and sunny, but the air was keen, and the ground hard with frost. We would fain have lingered here for a little; but our faces were towards the East, so we pressed on. It was but a glimpse that we could catch of the strange old city, with its tall gloomy houses, its rocks, its quays, its churches, its avenues, its squares. Yet it was something even for an hour here to look upon the " arrowy" Rhone with its three bridges, and the more sluggish Saone with its seven. It was to the second century, however, with its rich martyr-memories, that our thoughts went back. Here the aged Pothinus suffered for Christ; here, too, Irenæus wrote, and taught, and died.

At half-past twelve we started for Marseilles, which we reached late in the evening. As we sailed out next morning we had a fine view of this noble city, with its wide harbour, its yellow rocks, its old forts, its six thousand villas spreading out over the valley. We were now on the waters of the Mediterranean ; but the breeze which met us as we sailed out of the Gulf of Lyons, proved too fresh for some of us, so that we were driven to our cabins, and kept there during the greater part of our voyage. Yet next day (21st), we enjoyed the sight of Corsica, with its rugged mountains, streaked with snow. On we went, through the Straits of Bonifacio ; then pushing southward, over a somewhat rough sea, and skirting the coasts of Sicily, we "sighted" Malta. It was a calm Sabbath evening when we entered the harbour. The sun had gone down ; but the moonlight threw its unclouded silver upon the yellow rocks and the fair blue deep. It seemed a night of summer softness to us who had just come from the land of the cloud and snow. The mingling colours of sea, sky, rock, and moonshine,—azure, gold, and silver,—gave to the scene a rich clear beauty such as one seldom sees.   .   .   .

Valetta, Dec. 24. 1855.—What a fair sunny spot this little island is ! It rises up out of the sea, like some yellow water-lily, spreading out its leaves to the sun ; or perhaps, it might better be called the golden clasp that knits together the two continents of the south and north, —Africa and Europe. In language, manners, aspect, buildings, it is partly European, partly Oriental, only with much more of the East than of the West about it. Its language is nearly Arabic, its boats are Egyptian, its churches are all after the model of Moslem tombs, and its costumes are Arabian, especially the female ; for the Maltese *faldette* is merely the Eastern head-dress loosened and brought over the shoulders, so as to become an ornament for the person, instead of a veil to hide the face.   Walked about the town for an hour or two.   Statues of "saints" frown over your head in every street.

Priests meet you at every turn, round and well-fed,—idly sauntering about from morning till night, as unlike ministers of Christ, or successors of the apostles, as can be conceived. It is said they are 2000 in number! As Malta contains about 140,000 inhabitants, there is a priest to every seventy of the people. Through the great kindness of Lady Pirie, we were enabled to see a good deal of the island; and in the company of our brethren Mr Wisely and Mr Tait, we surveyed place after place. . . .

St Paul's Bay, Dec. 26. 1856.—I have just been bathing in these calm tideless waters! The patch of white sand which I chose for my bathing-place was nearly opposite the spot where Paul was cast ashore. We climbed the slope above; and while Mr Wright was photographing we wandered about, gazing down on the placid bay. We read the last two chapters of the Acts of the Apostles, and then tried to note the scene in its different parts. Yonder the vessel came drifting onwards from *Clauda*, seeking some place of refuge. See, they are lightening the ship by casting out its freight. What despair is fixed in their faces as they look up to that sunless, starless sky! Mark how they are listening to the apostle as he exhorts them to be of good cheer. See, as they near yon small promontory on the right, they begin to take soundings, for they have heard the roar of the breakers. Then down go the four anchors to keep them from the dreaded rocks. Day breaks, and they descry an unknown country, where there is a creek

or bay "with a shore."* Up go the anchors, and the
vessel drifts before the gale to the land. Yonder to the
left, there seems a small island where two seas meet,—
there the vessel touches the ground and goes to pieces.
The sea is covered with the fragments, and on these, the
two hundred and seventy-six human beings find their
way to land,—all safe ! See (we may add) the apostle
gathers them round him on yon slope, and there kneeling down he gives thanks for deliverance to " the God
and Father of our Lord Jesus Christ." Having so done,
he kindles the fire, shakes off the viper, warms and dries
himself, and then, turning his steps to Citta Vecchia, he
is received by Publius, heals his father, and for three
months preaches throughout the island the glad tidings
of God's free love in the gift and death of His beloved
Son. . . As we sat gazing on the blue waters, several of the natives gathered round us. Children brought
us heath, lilies, carnations, of great beauty. A woman
came with water from St Paul's well. It was in an
earthen jug, dirty, and smelling with tobacco ; but we
drank of it, and found it good. The well was about a
quarter of a mile below us, on the road side. We visited
it, and found a neat little building over it, with this inscription in Latin :—" AD TE VENIENT OMNES NATIONES
ET TE GLORIFICABUNT"—(Ps. lxxxvi. 9) " All nations
shall come and glorify thee." An excellent inscrip-

---

* One of the company asks, "Has not every bay a shore?" No. A
shore or ἀιγιαλός is a shelving beach or level strand.—See Mat. xiii. 2, 48 ;
John xxi. 4 ; Acts xxi. 5.

tion, if meant for Jehovah and not for Paul; but why in Latin? Why not in the native tongue, that all might read it? The priesthood seem to think it no business of theirs to translate the word of God. On the spot where Paul is said to have kindled the fire there is a small church built, which, however, we merely looked at from the distance. It was the scene itself and not man's poor attempts to adorn it that fixed our eye. As we left, we turned round again and again to gaze upon a spot so beautiful in itself, and so rich in holy memories. But when shall Paul's "good news" be preached again here to all the inhabitants of an island, where every village and street and church contains some tradition of his visit and some memorial of his name?

Down from the well, and nearer the sea, is a small palm-tree, one of the few which Malta possesses; and in this neighbourhood grow the finest water-melons in the island. The chirp of the grasshoppers came up pleasantly from the short grass under our feet; and the little grey lizards darting from crevice to crevice, up and down the walls, gave life to the still scene. Here and there we saw the caper-plant growing out of the walls, and in different places the pepper-tree. We pulled some of the wild herbs that grew around, but on tasting them found them very acrid, leaving for a considerable time a disagreeable prickly sensation upon the tongue. The natives shook their heads on seeing us put them to our lips, and tried to stop us, crying *non bono*, "not good." I believe they are poisonous as well as unpleasant.

We drove slowly to Valetta, enjoying the mild sunshine of a December afternoon in Malta. It reminded
us of July at home. Blue skies, soft air, green trees, gay
flowers ! How could we call this winter ?

Thursday, Dec. 27. 1855.—We drove to *Citta Vecchia,* the old capital of the island,—said to be its centre.
It stands finely on a height, and the view from the roof of
the great church is splendid. No mountains indeed, no
cliffs, no forests, no streams ; but an endless succession of
sunny slopes and hollows,—villages without number,
churches, terraces,—rocks and green fields, with the
prickly pear and the Karub-tree, shooting up at intervals,
—more rarely the olive, and yet more rarely the stunted
palm. We visited the catacombs and the cave of St
Paul ; not finding however much to interest us in these, to
which we were lighted by a dirty monk, with a pair of
yellow candles in his hands. The names of the streets
through which we passed reminded us of the persons and
the events with which this old city is associated. It was
not unpleasant to read upon the corner of these streets
such names as " *Strada Paolo*" or " *Strada Publio,*"
for it was here that the apostle had healed the governor's
father,—it was here that so many miracles were wrought
upon the sick,—it was here that Paul and his friends
tarried three months, and when departing, were loaded
with honours by the grateful people. Here the good
news of God's free love were preached and received
eighteen hundred years ago. These glad tidings are the
same as ever ; but who in this ancient city preaches

them or receives them now? Rome's message to the people is not the same as Paul's; it is not of a work done by the Son of God, but solely of works to be done by the sons of men.

On our way home we visited *Tel-Macluba*, a curious square hollow of considerable dimensions, the sides and bottom of which were covered with shrubs of various kinds. It is deep, and the descent to it is on one side, by a rude flight of steps cut in a romantic chasm or ravine. Its name means the "overturned hill," and the tradition is that it was formed by a sudden sinking of the ground. It looks like a quarry, and yet in some respects it is very peculiar. No trace of the hand or tool of man is to be found on any part of it.

Friday, Dec. 28. 1855.—I strolled out to one of the forts and enjoyed the brilliance of a southern sun. Close under us lay the great harbour,—before us the blue ocean, without a wave to vex it or a shadow to darken it, all golden with the glow of noon. Far in the distance, seen but as a speck, lay Sicily,—a land not unknown in fable, or in history, or in Scripture. For here dwelt the Cyclops; here Ceres taught men how to plough and sow; here Aristæus taught the rearing of bees and the cultivation of the olive; here Hercules struck down robbery and built up law and government. Here had fought the armies of Carthage, of Greece, of Rome. We would fain have seen Etna, but even its eleven thousand feet had vanished in the distance. Still more gladly should we have got a glimpse of *Syra-*

cuse, not only because there Archimedes lived and died, but because it was there that the "ship of Alexandria, whose sign was Castor and Pollux," first touched after leaving Malta (Acts xxviii. 11, 12) ; and it was there that Paul landed and "tarried three days" on his way to Rome.

In the afternoon I went to the public library, and found there some rare and many excellent books, most of them patristic and Romish,—with not a few commentaries on Scripture. There was Walton's Polyglott Bible,—the works of Warburton and Tillotson,—Whitefield's Sermons,—and, what seemed rather curious, the Acts of the General Assembly of the Church of Scotland. In the adjoining museum there stood some stone idols taken out of the old Phœnician temple. They are small and unshapely, somewhat like the gods of India. They represent different ideas from the statues of Mary or Paul, which are to be found in the Romish churches ; but they exhibit the worshipper in precisely the same position. It is in both cases, man at the foot of a stone-image,—to which he bows because of the divinity which he fancies to dwell within. Such was Israel on the plain of *Er-Rahah* before the golden calf. Such is the Hindoo before his piece of brass. Such is the Romanist before his wafer or his crucifix. None of them really worship the metal or the stone ; yet God calls it *idolatry* (Exod. xx. 4 ; xxxii. 8).

Saturday, Dec. 29. 1855.—We drove this forenoon to the Phœnician temple, about seven miles from Valetta.

It is called *Jebel Kheim*, or the Old Hill. A vast massive ruin! It is not a mere circle of separate stones like Stonehenge, or such British remains of ancient worship. It is a regularly built temple, whose walls, gates, altars, are still visible,—composed of enormous blocks, without cement, some standing, some fallen, some whole, some broken, some in their original place, some tossed aside;—all of them well hewn and firmly set, and some of a peculiar composition, giving forth a shrill ringing sound when struck, not unlike a bell.* Close by the entrance is a small enclosure containing a curious collection of bones and skulls, said to belong to the original temple. The skeleton of a "giant" is reported to have been found here. The idols have been carried off to the museum at Valetta. Hard by is another structure of a similar kind. It is circular and built like the other, but of smaller size. Probably it was an outer court or porch to the former. There were no altars in it as in the other. These are by far the most ancient ruins in the island, and tell of the time when, in ages before Christ, the Phœnicians dwelt here,—carrying on at once their trade and their idolatry. Since they first held it, into how many hands has Malta passed! It was then under the rule of the great merchant-nation of antiquity; it is now in the

---

* These musical stones are not uncommon. There is a place called the Singing Valley, about three miles from Pottstown, in the United States, where there is a large number of misshapen stones, which look as if flung together by some great upheaval. The stones emit, when struck, all manner of tones; and it is said that the chimes of the finest bells cannot surpass in variety the sounds thus produced.

possession of the great merchant-nation of modern days.
There is only this difference. Phœnicia was in earnest
both as to her religion and her trade ; and she gave the
former as well as the latter to her colony.   Britain, intent on trade and heedless of religion, leaves the latter
behind her,—nay, through her governors and generals,
tries to hinder all efforts for giving the Bible and the
gospel to the Romanists of her dominions.   Under the
pretext of liberality, she wrongs both the Protestant
faith and the British name. An Englishman and a
Protestant has small chance of justice in Malta. The
Presbyterian governor of the island caresses the priesthood in a way such as his Romanist predecessor did
not, and receives, no doubt, in requital, their flattery
and their contempt.   By his urgent advice, though
without his countenance or presence, the foundation-
stone of the new Scottish Church was laid at night, by
torch-light, through fear of ruffling the temper of the
priesthood.

The temple commands a noble sea-view ; and, standing on the top of one of these old pillars, we gazed on
the Mediterranean.   Lying beneath us in the sunshine,
close at hand, was the small island of *Filfla*,—little
more than a bare rock,—but standing out finely in the
midst of the calm blue.

Monday, Dec. 31. 1855.—We left Valetta this morning about half-past eight, and were soon on board the
Alma for Alexandria, with a *gregale* wind and a rough
sea. We were loath to leave so hospitable and bright

a spot; but we had to press on. Often did the words occur to us, "the barbarous people shewed us no little kindness"—(Acts xxviii. 2). Farewell, sunny Malta!

The following sentence from a letter written on board ship contains all that is needful concerning the voyage:—" Wednesday night, on board the Alma.—Here I am, on the wide sea, where we have now been for about three days. I am trying to write a letter, but fear that it may not be quite legible, as the table shakes somewhat, even in this noble saloon. . . . I have been enjoying the quiet breeze on deck. Sea, sky, clouds,—all splendid; yet I have seen the like in old Scotland. Sunset was fine ;—a whole quiver-full of sunbeams seemed to shoot up and pierce a mass of overhanging clouds ;—then, amidst the radiance which he had thus thrown round himself, the sun went down, telling us to be content with an allowance of half an hour's twilight. Up sprang the silent stars, most of them old familiar faces, though not exactly in their old places. The Pleiades twinkled right above us, as if suspended like a silver crown upon our topmast. Orion took up his position in front, and our bow seemed to cut his belt asunder. The horizon had a girdle of clouds, but all above was clear. Several songs were sung by the passengers and officers ; and it was pleasant to hear these words, with their cheerful but solemn music, in such a scene;—

> What are the wild waves saying,
> Sister, the whole day long,

That ever amid our playing,
  I hear but their low lone song ?
Not by the sea-side only,
  There it sounds wild and free,
But at night, when 'tis dark and lonely,
  In dreams it is still with me.

    .   .   .

No, it is something greater,
  That speaks to the heart alone—
The voice of the great Creator
  Dwells in that mighty tone."

On Thursday evening we got sight of the light-house
of Alexandria ; but we had to " lie to " all night, as
the harbour can only be entered by daylight.   Next
morning, with the first streak of dawn, we made for
the port.   The sunrise was fine.   I had risen about
five ; and as I went on deck the moon was just coming
up,—in her last quarter.   Not a cloud or mist dimmed
the sky.   In a short time a pale whiteness spread over
the eastern horizon—

" The stars o'er the lighthouse set faintly and few,
  And the wave's level blackness was trembling to blue."

Then there seemed to rise up in the east a wall of dusky
red.   Gradually this grew brighter, till, like a solid
sphere of flame, the sun came up in his strength, behind the low, broad land of Egypt.   We had seen suns
as bright, perhaps, and mornings as calm ; but it was
our first morning in the East, and that sun brought with
it the memory of other suns, long set,—the suns of ages
past, that had risen over the same level sands, and
lighted up the same blue sea.   Sand, sea, sun, and sky

were all the same as in the days of the Pharaohs. One age had gone and another had come, but the land had altered little. The old race had passed away and a new one risen,—but here was Egypt still !

The pilotage is in the possession of one family, in which there are several brothers, who are said to exercise their monopoly in the way most convenient and easy,—refusing to obey signals from vessels till they have quietly finished their breakfast, however urgent the case may be. It is said, however, that death is the penalty when any vessel is wrecked in their hands. In Phœnician days, the office of pilot seems to have been one of honour,—" Thy wise men, O Tyrus, that were in thee, were thy pilots" (Ezek. xxvii. 8),—" the suburbs shall shake at the sound of the cry of thy pilots" (*Ib.* xxvii. 28).

We moved slowly into the harbour, with the old Pharos to the left, and shipping all round ; steamers and vessels of every kind from every land. It was a goodly sight. All was Eastern. Our pilot, with his red turban, long robe, and white stockings ;—custom-house officers superbly dressed in Oriental fashion ;—boats with lateen sails,—and smaller skiffs, whose boat-men rise with every stroke of the oar ; a boatful of Arab beggars ; the Pasha's palace,—all these told us how truly we were in the "land of Egypt."

CHAPTER II.

Friday, Jan. 4. 1856.—This is Egypt!—the land which, next to Palestine, fills the noblest niche in history. It contains greater wonders, both in its story and in its relics, than Babylon, or Greece, or Rome. It has a history twice as long, and quite as romantic, as that of the " Eternal City ;" and the ruins on the banks of the Tiber are a mere handful of stones in comparison with the ruins of " old Nile."

Rome is the type of force,—mere force, no more,— Egypt of genius,—fertile and gigantic in all its plans and works. In Rome everything is a copy,—her arts, her poetry, her oratory,—are all copied, either from Greece, or from the farther East. In Egypt all is original. Numerous nations are her debtors ; she is debtor to none.

She rises up at once a full-grown nation, without infancy or unripened youth. She comes in as heir to the wisdom and science of antediluvian ages. The dis- coveries of the men before the flood are preserved in her ;

and Ham, with his son Mizraim, transplants from the plain of Shinar to the valley of the Nile all the stores of ancient art and genius.

In Egypt all is great;—her temples, her palaces, her pyramids, her obelisks, her statues, her tombs. With nothing about her vast by nature, save her river, she has reared for herself monuments of greatness to which earth shews no equal. For what is the Coliseum or the Parthenon to the temples of Dakkeh, Kalabshi, Ibsamboul, or Karnak?

The region through which the Nile flows is the driest in the world. For nearly 4000 miles to the west, spread the sand-plains of Africa;—for nearly as far to the east, the similar deserts of Arabia and Persia. So that Egypt is a narrow strip of land reclaimed from utter barrenness by the waters of the Nile. The surface of this strip is round or convex, with a cut or furrow in the middle, through which the river flows;—so that its waters, when they overflow, cannot get back to their channel because of this natural embankment; thus making the provision for the watering of the land yet more perfect and wonderful. Egypt owes her whole existence to the Nile; and here was the great link between her and the God out of whose hand all the rivers of earth are poured. Her own hand, she might say, had given her the grandeur of her temples and pyramids;—but who had given her the river?—that wondrous stream whose course is one of four thousand two hundred miles, during one thousand of which it receives no tributary waters,—fit river

B

for a nation that owed nothing to any other kingdom of earth ! Hence the sin which God charges against her was that of calling this river her own ! Nebuchadnezzar's sin was a boasting of Babylon as his own (Dan. iv. 30). But Pharaoh's sin was greater. "Behold, I am against thee, Pharaoh king of Egypt, the great dragon that lieth in the midst of his rivers, which hath said, *My river is mine own, and I have made it for myself.*" (Ezek. xxix. 3-12.)

Yet for more than a thousand miles her river was truly hers,—in the sense of belonging to no other nation. Both banks of the majestic stream were hers. Few countries have either mountains or rivers which they can call wholly their own. The Rhine, to whom does it belong ? To Switzerland, or to Germany ? The Pyrennees, who calls them mine ? France or Spain ? Britain certainly can say of her hills, they are my own on every side ; and of her streams, they are mine, from the first drop trickling down the cliff to the full current that pours itself into the ocean. So of at least a thousand miles of the Nile could Egypt say, it is mine ; and had she said it in a becoming spirit, not boastingly, no sin would have been hers. But she looked on each side of her broad stream and saw no joint-owner, no rival upon earth,—and forgetting who had given her its waters and who had made them, she was lifted up in her pride ;—for what nation could tell of a river like hers ?

" On we passed to Alexandria (thus I wrote home at the time), where Apollos was born, and where long before the birth of Christ the Old Testament was translated into Greek. But all here is Egyptian (or I might say Mahommedan) darkness. Britain makes use of Alexandria for her commerce, but sends no message of grace to her multitudes. . . . Next to Palestine, Egypt is the most marvellous country in the world. The Bible is full of it. It was the seat of vile idolatry, yet God did more to shake it out of its wickedness than He did to any other Gentile land. From the time of Abraham down to the day when God's own Son was here, how many blessed feet have trodden it. Strange that Egypt should be the nurse of Christ, the refuge for his infancy against the wrath of Herod. 'He came to his own and his own received him not.' (John i. 11.) Even as a child it cast him out and 'would have none of him.' But a Gentile kingdom received him. A Gentile king gave him shelter. On the banks of a Gentile river, this tender plant grew up. What honour was thus given to Egypt! And for this there is yet to be a blessing in the latter day. For though for ages the 'basest of kingdoms' (Ezek. xxix. 15), it is yet to be lifted up and blest,—in that day when 'the Lord of Hosts shall bless, saying, Blessed be Egypt my people, and Assyria the work of my hands, and Israel mine inheritance.' (Isa. xix. 25.) So I thought as the eye rested on its varied desolations. We have so associated Egypt with darkness and idolatry, that we have forgotten the good things related of it, and the riches of grace yet to be manifested towards it in that day when the glory of Jehovah shall burst forth like dayspring for a benighted world."

I need not speak of the old obelisk, misnamed " Cleopatra's Needle," on which is written the history of other days long before the age of " Egypt's widow ;" nor of the curious old square limestone-blocks in its neighbourhood, over which the wave washes, and on which the sea-weed grows or rots; nor of Pompey's Pillar ; nor of Alexandria in general. All these are well known. The most interesting object which I saw, though I did not examine it till my return in April, was the ruin, or rather the large enclosure of ruins, lately dug up by the Pasha, about an hour's ride from the town, beyond the catacombs, close by the sea, and not far from the " battle-field" where Abercrombie fell. It is called " Cæsar's Camp,"—I know not why; for it is not a camp, in the proper sense of the term, but a regularly fortified suburb of the city. The ruins of some six or seven towers are visible. The foundations of villas are clearly marked with large hewn stones ; the remains of finely tesselated floors appear here and there. Altogether it is the place of greatest interest in this neighbourhood. In the town, too, are the remains of the foundations of the famous Library. At least some of the ruins recently dug up in erecting some new buildings are supposed to be the relics of the ancient Library. They lie scattered about in the shape of polished stones, broken shafts of pillars, and ornamented capitals. All round the town are immense mounds of broken pottery.

These may be said to extend for miles, and are curious as shewing the vast quantity of such materials formerly in use. Perhaps they are in part remains of the small brick cylinders commonly employed in building walls, or at least the upper parts of the walls. Not only in Egypt, but in Jerusalem and the towns of Syria, this is frequent. It gives lightness to the walls themselves and airiness to those parts which they inclose. But certainly at Alexandria the amount of these fragments is almost unaccountable. Yet we must keep in mind that Lower Egypt has no quarries. Its building-stones are from the far south, and in the Delta it is out of clay or mud that the materials for building are obtained. Hence in the ruins here you have just two kinds of debris,—large stone-blocks and earthen fragments,— with nothing between, in the shape of small stones, &c., as you have in Palestine. Brick-making must have always occupied a very large amount of native labour; and out of this the toils and miseries of Israel, in the day of their bondage, arose. (Exod. i. 14.)

Alexandria has now existed about two thousand two hundred years, and has seen many a change both in its circumstances and in its governors, from Alexander the Great to Said Pasha, its present miserable ruler, who by his cruelties has made himself vile in the eyes of his own subjects; so that to this day we see still in fulfilment the ancient word of prophecy, " The Egyptians will I give over into the hands of a cruel lord, and a fierce king shall rule over them." (Isa. xix. 4.) The

English of course he dare not touch, as he could not afford to lose the £150,000 a-year that flows directly into his coffers through their East India traffic. But the natives are made to smart, and especially the poor Bedaween of the Desert. They happened lately to provoke his anger, and troops were sent to subdue them. But who can track the paths of these sons of the rock and sand ? What army could find its way into their retreats, or hope either to capture or to conquer them ? You might as well chase the wild goat or the eagle. Accordingly the Pasha came to terms with them, made fair promises, and persuaded them to lay down their arms. No sooner is this done than they are in chains ! On they are driven, linked to each other,—scorched, starved, weary, thirsty,—till they reach Alexandria. There some are placed before the cannon's mouth and blown to pieces,—others sent to prison, there to starve and rot, the living and the dead together. The rest are kept for the hardest work that the Pasha can find for them ; and more than once we saw them passing to their weary toil in chains, through the streets. It was sad to see these free sons of Arabia,—thus torn from their tents and sands, and brought to pine in fetters, and die at length over-wrought and broken-hearted. Just the other day, too, one of the slaves of the same Pasha, in handing him a cup of coffee, spilt a drop upon his robe. In a moment the Pasha drew his scimitar and cut him down, leaving the carpet sprinkled with blood and brains. Poor Egypt! when shall thy bondage cease and the day of thy deliverance dawn?

But there are golden fetters for Egypt as well as iron. Alexandria is a great merchant-city for all nations; and here the thirst for gold prevails. To "buy and sell and get gain" (Jas. iv. 13)—this is Egyptian life.

Yet here learning once flourished; and the 700,000 volumes of the Alexandrian Library tell how vigorously it did so. Here, too, the Evangelist *Mark* preached the gospel, and here *Apollos* taught. Here *Origen* led the way, and *Dionysius* followed him, in perverting Scripture by a vain philosophy, finding figures and fancies in every verse. Here *Athanasius* held fast the belief in Father, Son, and Holy Ghost. Here, too, the unhappy Jews were persecuted, and 40,000 of them put to death to gratify the hatred of the "patriarch *Cyril*" —a man who in after ages was called a "father" and a "saint!"*

One evening Mr Brown and myself got hold of a small boat or cobble, in which was a father with his little boy. We made them row us round the island of Old Pharos, where Ptolemy Philadelphus, in B. C. 283, built the famous light-house, which was once reckoned

---

* In Egypt, as elsewhere, the Jew was to have "trembling of heart;"— and hence in the latter day, when on the eve of final restoration, it is written of them, "They shall tremble as a bird, out of Egypt" (Hos. xi. 11),—that is, they shall fly as a frighted bird, when escaping from the cage, to its own native skies and woods. This is when the Lord "sets his hand the second time to recover the remnant of his people .. from Egypt." (Isa. xi. 11).

among the seven wonders of the world. The night was calm but chill; and a cloudy sky, throwing shade over the sea, made the scene look bleak and sad. The small waves slowly breaking over the rocks in front of the light-house, and then finding their way past us to the peninsula on which it is built, threw up a dull and heavy sound,—not like the joyous "music of the waves." Yet the sea was quiet, and did not confirm Homer's epithet of *stormy*, which in describing Pharos he applies to it. Nor did we find it a day's sail from Egypt as that old poet affirms;—it took us less than an hour to go and return. It is no more a light-house, but a poor worn-out fort, yet in former ages it lighted many an "ancient mariner" to the harbour of the princely city, the second Tyre or Carthage. Its beacon-light is gone, and its white marble exchanged for yellow masonry and plastered ruins.*

On different occasions we saw several Arab funerals, on their way to the burying-ground, which is quite out of the town, near Pompey's Pillar. They use no coffin in the East; but the body, wrapped in its shroud, is placed in a sort of cradle, set on poles, and so carried on men's shoulders. The cradle is covered with a pall, if I may call it so, of red and yellow cloth. The mourners in one case were about twenty in number, in others less; wearing their ordinary dress, and moving briskly along at a considerable pace, singing lustily the Moslem creed, "God is great."

* "Albo lapide mirifice structa."—Pliny or Strabo, I am not sure which.

During our walks we saw something of the nature and produce of this fertile land. Palms, prickly pears, oranges, acacias, tamarisks,—all bore witness to the heat of the climate as well as to the richness of the soil. Though perhaps it is only the orange that blossoms and bears fruit at the same time, yet every month in Egypt has its flowers and fruits, all the year round.

> Some ripening, ready some to fall,
> Some blossomed, some to bloom,
> Like gorgeous hangings on the wall
> Of some rich princely room.

We marked with some interest the various *signs* above the shops, both in the great square and in the bazaar, some English, some French, some Italian, some Greek, some Arabic,—fit representatives of the various nations of which the city is composed. We were pleased to notice some turtle-doves flying about on some of the houses; but were rather discomposed at first by the howling of dogs at night. Yet what town, or fort, or village, or encampment in Egypt, Syria, or the desert, is free from this nuisance? It brought to mind more than one passage of Scripture. "Against Israel shall not a *dog* move its tongue." (Exod. xi. 7.) Often did we wish it had been so with us! "*Dogs* have compassed me." (Psa. xxii. 16.) Every traveller, passing by or through an Arab village, knows what this is, and knows also that a stone or stick soon makes them fly. "They return at evening, they make a noise like a *dog*, and go round about the city." (Psa. lix. 6.) How exact the picture! "Without are *dogs."* (Rev. xxii. 15.) Who ever saw a *dog,* in the East, within a house or tent? If not always without the walls of the city, they are always outside the dwellings,—a wandering race of prowlers whom no man owns, whom no man feeds, and for whom no man cares; yet each has his own quarter of the city, beyond which he dare not intrude, save at the risk of being torn in pieces by the dogs of that quarter into which he has intruded. One of God's sore judgments on the land was this, "the dogs to tear," (Jer. xv. 3), and how often did we see the dog tearing the dead carcase of the camel!

In passing through the bazaars we marked the different processes of eastern manufacture. Here were massive silver rings and chains, roughly cut and quite unpolished, yet of true metal,—exposed for sale on a small wooden table, by a poor Arab woman. Here was a coffee-pounding shop,—for in the East coffee is not ground but pounded. Three half-naked boys, with pestles as long as themselves, surrounded an immense mortar which could have held any two of them, and thumped away, with alternate strokes, till they had reduced the well-burnt beans to a fine black powder. Yet even out of such a mortar as this, and under such a pestle, the fool of which Solomon speaks would emerge with his folly all about him,—" Though thou shouldest bray a fool in a mortar, among wheat, with a pestle, yet will not his foolishness depart from him." (Prov. xxvii. 22.) Here, again, was a vermicelli merchant, busy both in making and selling his article. He stands before a large circular plate of copper, very slightly convex, and some three or four feet in diameter, under which is a small fire of charcoal. He then wipes the plate with a sort of towel, which seemed to have some olive-oil on it, which prevents the stuff from sticking to the plate. Then he takes a tin jug or dredging-box, filled with a thin gruel-like substance of flour and water, and pierced in its bottom with small holes ;—this he moves round the plate at a height of perhaps a foot or less, till the whole surface is covered with what appears to be fine white wire from the droppings of the box. As the heat of the plate not only prevents the falling drops from running together, but *bakes* them at once, the whole process is done in a single minute, and the layer removed and laid aside in a coil, to make room for another.

Various other eastern processes we used to mark,—curious and primitive, but they are too many to be noted.

One little shop I visited more than once. It is so little that more than two persons can hardly find sitting room in it. Its shelves are loaded with bibles and tracts, in some ten or twelve different languages,—Hebrew, Arabic, Greek, Italian, &c. A slight curtain is drawn across its entrance ; and within sits the unwearied missionary, Mr Brown, several hours each day, waiting to catch the passing Jew, or Arab, or Greek ; for though his mission is specially to Israel, yet no nation is overlooked by him. You draw aside the curtain and you find him dealing out his precious wares or sitting side by side with some inquirer, shewing him out of the Scrip-

tures that Jesus is the Christ.   Quietly does his work go
on in that obscure shop, day by day,—the stream of the
busy merchant-world running by, and few, few to cheer
him in his toil of patient love.   Issuing from his shop,
and locking its green door behind him, he accosts the
passers by.   He meets a Greek perhaps and offers him
a Greek tract ; but it is the merchandise of earth that
the man is in quest of, and though he receives the tract
civilly, he shews no interest in eternal truth.   Or it is a
Mahommedan that he falls in with ;—and he, when a
tract is offered, asks, " what is it about."   When told,
" it is about religion," he takes it, but intimates plainly
enough that there is no truth and no religion save in the
Korân.   Or he comes upon a Jew and asks him about
the Messiah promised to the fathers.   " Oh, you mean
the man that was hanged," he replies, and turns away
in scorn.

Yet no seed falls into the ground in vain, even in this
unfruitful world.   The lonely sower of the seed has his
day of joy in store.

One forenoon I was standing on the beach, looking
out upon the green sea with its " many twinkling "*

---

* Keble gives us " the many-twinkling smile of ocean " as the translation
of the well-known passage in the Prometheus of Æschylus.   But the epithet is not his own.   Gray had long before made use of the word, though
with another reference,—

" To brisk notes in cadence beating
Glance their many-twinkling feet "—*Progress of Poesy;*
and, thirty years before Gray, Thomson had written,—

. . . " The many twinkling leaves
Of aspen tall."—*Seasons: Spring.*

waves. The wind which had been blowing from the west for several days had just gone round to the east, and to the right, at the point of the Bay of Aboukir, the whole horizon seemed suddenly fringed with white clouds rising out of the sea. They were native boats in full sail, making for Alexandria. I stood watching them, and as they came nearer tried to count them, but in vain. I counted upwards of a hundred and then lost my number. It was as noble a sight as I had seen. Two hundred white *lateen* sails, filled with the fresh east wind and gleaming to the noon ! They appeared to form one continuous line, several miles in length, and rushed gallantly before the breeze as if contending for victory in the race, or hastening, like eagles, to their prey. They had been windbound at Rosetta, and were now set free.

When we were in Alexandria the Latin convent was busy with its *bells.* A fine set of these had just been put up ; and a grand festival was held in their honour. We heard more than enough of them. They seemed to be rung hour after hour, as if in triumph over their rival sects. The bells were sweet enough in tone, and made themselves heard at long-enough distances. But what does all this do for the thousands of the city ? The "vesper bell " sounds finely in poetry, but what is there in it to lead a human spirit out of the worldliness in which this city lies, or to say to one of its citizens, "Seek those things which are above, where Christ sitteth at the right hand of God ?" They do not summon men to hear the gospel which Mark once preached on these shores.

Worldliness and philosophy corrupted Alexandria's earlier faith, till Christianity under Origen or Cyril became little better than the heathenism which it had supplanted, and nothing but the ancient truth which Mark made known, and which thousands received from his teaching, will find its way through the indifference, the unbelief, the covetousness, the superstition with which such eastern cities are fenced round. Alexandria needs a Mark and it needs an Apollos too. Would that there were such now in it, to bear witness of a world to come, —such a witness as would lead men to seek treasure in an everlasting city.

CHAPTER III.

RAILWAY—ARAB VILLAGES—NILE BRIDGES—CAIRO.

Alexandria, Saturday, Jan. 5. 1856.—This morning at nine we left Alexandria for Cairo by railway. Some hours before this the morning had been chill, the thermometer at 50°, and the dew heavy upon the leaf; but ere we reached the station, we were warm enough, and were glad to find that the carriages (made at Birmingham, we observed) were wide and airy. Some brief notes of this journey may not be without interest, as it was one of the first runs which the railway had made. It was strange to be rushing at the rate of twenty-five miles an hour in such a conveyance through the land of the Pharaohs. Well might the camel and the bullock-cart and the Nile-boat stare at us! Which of them had ever made the journey to Cairo in seven hours? All of them together could not do it in less than three days.

The line takes its way at first on a long embankment through the lake *Mareotis,* so that we seemed to be shooting through water. Nile-boats and canal-boats,

with their lateen sails, moved quietly up and down, undisturbed by the rush of our engine.   Perhaps it is to
this sea-like lake that reference is made by the prophet
(Isa. xix. 5–10),—

    " The waters shall fail from the sea,"

for it is no longer what it once was, and looks more like
a very sluggish pool than a "lake" or "sea ;"—

    " The river shall be wasted and dried up,"—

for neither is "old Nile" what it was in Pharaoh's
days.

> They shall turn the rivers far away;
> The well-defended canals shall be emptied and dried up ;
> The reeds and flags shall wither, *
> The paper reeds (perhaps "meadows") by the river,
> By the brink of the river (where Moses was put).
> Everything sown by the river
> Shall wither, be driven away, and be no more.

The scenes through which we went in our journey
to-day seemed, each one, an illustration of these verses.
All has come to pass.   Egypt is now but the dried-up
skin of the great "Leviathan," the "flying serpent,"
the "crooked serpent," the "dragon," which Jehovah
has slain by his "sore and great and strong sword,"
(Isa. xxvii. 1), and left to wither upon the face of its
own sun-baked slime.

---

* Here the description of Shakspeare comes out, when he says,

        . . . the vagabond flag upon the stream
    Goes to and back lackeying the varying tide
    To rot itself with motion. . . .

. . . . . The fire
That quickens Nilus' slime,

is still blazing in the old sky, but the fruitfulness of the soil is decayed. What Egypt may become is not for us to say, but what it is, one may easily see by a journey from Alexandria to Cairo. We passed through immense swamps or flats, with occasional verdure where cows and buffaloes were feeding. In a little came to a native village,—its houses low,—built of mud, and roofed with turf, like a cluster of dirt-heaps,—not fit for stables. Like other Egyptian villages, it is built on a slight eminence or mound of mud, to prevent its being swamped or carried off by the Nile in its overflow. Out of one of the holes which were meant for doors came a little naked fellow, who, over-estimating his power of speed, tried to keep up with our train : and no doubt felt discomfited at his want of success,—for what animal had he ever seen that could have competed with him on a race along these sunburnt plains? As we halted at the first station, which is about half an hour's run from Alexandria, the natives gathered round us, looking on us with wonder and interest, but certainly not with awe or alarm. How unlike the station here to Euston Square or Newcastle ! Yet poor as its platform was, and ragged as was the crowd around,—station-master, guard, porter, bell, were all here ! Even an Egyptian railway must have these.

On we rush, passing one native village after another, very much alike in plan and architecture, as well as in materials and inhabitants. Ragged Arabs .. flocks of

C

buffaloes .. heath-like flats .. patches of green .. large
mounds, some of sand, others of earthenware .. burying-
places .. oxen ploughing .. small mosques and minarets
.. camels and boats .. sky covered with light woollen
clouds bringing coolness to the noon .. thermometer
nearly 70° in the shade, upwards of 90° in the sun ..
swamps of water .. large fields of fine black soil covered
with green crops*.. trees of various kinds in the distance .. reached the second station about eleven, a
pretty large village with a burying-ground .. hard by, a
shadoof or long pole with a stone at one end and a
bucket at the other for drawing water .. about half-past
eleven reached the steamer which crosses the Nile, the
bridge here not being yet built. We soon steamed
across the river of Egypt,—its dun waters gleaming in
the sunshine. In little more than an hour started again
on the other side .. trees more abundant .. strings of
camels .. two men raising water by swinging a sort of
basket-bowl between them, attached to two pretty long
ropes, by means of which it was alternately lowered and
raised .. Arabs pushing a railway carriage, about thirty
men behind and two runners in front, shouting and
laughing and dancing .. an Arab station-master ringing the bell .. tombs of Moslem saints by the wayside.
About two came to a richer and greener district,—perhaps Goshen .. struck with the width of the horizon,
the distance of the clouds, the lowness of the zenith ..

---

* " Et viridem Ægyptum nigrâ fœcundat arenâ," says Virgil, speaking
of the Nile. *Georg.* iv.

cattle and camels not at all alarmed at the rushing train, not even turning to look at it, save a little calf which stood staring with unutterable wonder. A little after two crossed the Nile by a railway bridge . . large villa . . fine willows . . rich fields. About three again crossed the Nile by a handsome bridge, at *Bennah* . . large palace . . immense flocks of pigeons and clusters of conical pigeon-houses. As we get towards Cairo villages larger and country richer . . white storks sitting silently on the ground . . got the first glimpse of the Pyramids from the carriage window, calm and venerable . . snatches of the desert visible with its yellow undulations . . not many miles off *On* or *Heliopolis* where Joseph dwelt, and where tradition says Joseph and Mary sojourned with the infant Jesus. As we neared Cairo crowds of people and animals of many kinds . . numerous trees for miles . . old bridge with pointed arches. Reached Cairo about four. Ourselves on donkeys and our luggage on a bullock-cart, pushed through the shrieking crowd of Arabs, and were soon at rest in Williams' Family Hotel. An interesting day, in which we saw a great deal of Egypt in its outward aspects . . a noble river moving majestically through vast plains of fruitful soil, a thin and scattered population, poor and ragged villages, little to fall in love with or admire . . yet were there the relics of a mightier age, the debris of the most wondrous empire that the world has seen.

About half-past five I set out to call for the American missionaries. Of course I took a donkey and a boy. I was led through narrow lanes and streets, with turnings and passages innumerable and inextricable. My guide brought me first to a large building, which turned out to be a Popish seminary. The priest who received me at the door, soon shewed me my mistake; but professed to know nothing about American missionaries, though I soon found that they were not far off. In a few minutes I reached their dwelling; and it was pleasant in the land of the Moslem to meet with brethren in Christ. They labour quietly, but in faith and love; not wearied in well-doing, though the door does not seem by any means an open one. Living in a city of 300,000 inhabitants, of whom only a few own, even in name, Christ Jesus as the Son of God, their instructions seem like "beating the air." Yet so was it with Paul when he stood in Athens and Corinth, surrounded with equal idolatry, sensuality, and worldliness; but the power of God shewed itself wondrously in these old haunts of paganism; and the hand that smote the temples of Greece can overthrow the mosques of Egypt. That this is the land where some of God's greatest deeds were done, and also the land to which a blessing is promised in the coming age, is a cheering thought to the weary missionary. It needs but a word, and the "glad tidings" find their way with winged speed through each of the two hundred and forty streets of this great city; the minarets of its four hundred mosques become the spires of Christian churches; the one true Book from heaven sets aside not merely the Korân, but the breviaries and liturgies of Latin, Armenian, Copt, and Greek.

Hurried through these narrow lanes, sometimes to the right, sometimes to the left, sometimes whirled right round, I was more than once in the act of tumbling, when caught adroitly by my donkey-man, and re-adjusted in my seat; for be it remembered that the animal is never *led*, but *driven* from behind by stick and voice, and sometimes when it was slackening its pace, it would be treated with a sudden blow which made it bolt forward in a moment, thereby nearly leaving its rider behind, at least when the voice had not forewarned you of the coming stroke. Often did we beckon for mercy to the animals, and soon taught our drivers the meaning of the word "gently," so that on pronouncing it, the response was heard in broken English "vurry wull," and the uplifted stick dropped,—donkeys, riders, drivers, lapsing into a quiet walk. It was only in this way that we could keep ourselves at times from riding down some tarbooshed Moslem in the bazaar, or being ridden over by some bullock-cart, or being knocked on the head by the projecting load of some gigantic camel, striding along, totally indifferent as to who or what may be in his way, or pushed rudely aside by the fore-runner of some great man's carriage, or crushed in both limbs by being forced into the centre of two long strings of loaded donkeys. The "driving" reminded us of the Shunammite, when in the day of her sorrow she set out for the Man of God, in haste, yet in quiet faith on the God of

Israel. " She saddled an ass, and said unto her servant, DRIVE, and go forward ; slack not thy riding for me, except I bid thee." (2 Kings iv. 24.) Here is the Shunammite with her donkey-boy behind her. It is *he* who drives ; it is *he* who carries the stick or goad ; *he* whips on the animal, or allows it to slacken its pace at the bidding of the rider.

I met, too, with an incident which shewed the meaning of Elisha's command to Gehazi, " If thou meet any man, salute him not ; and if any man salute thee, answer him not again" (2 Kings iv. 29), and of the Lord's instruction to his disciples, " salute no man by the way." (Luke x. 4.) With us, a brief, wayside salutation does not hinder. But in the East it does. As we were turning in by a narrow, dark, arched lane, my donkey-man suddenly sprung aside, with a loud shout of delight, and left me. Of course I halted, not knowing my way. Some donkeys were coming on in front, and my driver had seen in the foremost of the riders, a brother or friend, who was returning from a journey. My donkey-man was on foot, but this mattered not. In a moment he leapt up and seized his friend round the neck,—hugging him most strenuously, and kissing him first on one side of the face and then on the other. This mutual operation being over, they inquired after each other's health and then went on their way. I did not like the delay, even of the minute or two which the scene occupied, for it was getting dark ; but there was no use in saying a word. Besides, the scene was as interesting as it was novel.

In the great thoroughfares of London, such as Cheapside, crowded with riders, drivers, walkers,—drays, carriages, and gigs,—each one looks simply to himself; and this exclusive self-care, which some would call selfishness, is the best security for general safety, for order in the midst of confusion, and for the preservation of our neighbour's rights as well as our own. In the East no one deigns to look after himself, but reckons that everybody ought to look after him; and so each one marches on amid the crowds of the narrow bazaar, despising carriages, carts, camels, donkeys,—nay walls and pillars, not thinking it possible that any one would refuse to make way for him, or be so bold as deny him the sovereign right of way. One may imagine the confusion which results.

In our Western regions we plan wide streets and moderately low houses, to relieve the heat of summer. In the East they build streets as narrow as lanes, and houses like those of the High Street of Edinburgh as preservatives against heat! Nor can the success of this be doubted; for as there are some Highland ravines into which sun-heat and sun-light never find their way, so are there streets and lanes without number in Cairo, the recesses of which no sun has ever seen. But the fresh air, the pleasant breeze, the genial fragrance,— these are all banished with the heat and light.

In our far North-west, men put aside their hats or caps to let out the heat and let in the cold. In the warm East men carefully and closely cover their heads

to keep out the heat and to keep in the cold. Who sees
a bareheaded Arab or Turk? The *fellah*, though his
body is in rags has still the turban or cap for his head,
which sits there night and day, save when at certain
times he betakes himself to the public baths to get his
body washed and his head shaven. Day and night is
their head covered. I only remember one of our Arabs,
who occasionally trudged along in the desert without his
cap, and he was an odd sort of being, whose hair was
longer and shaggier than usual. Even when the tarboosh is laid aside for a little, the white under-cap still
keeps its place. With us the hat is taken off in worship, with them it is the shoe. The hat is never removed either when praying outside by the way, as we
often saw them doing, or in the mosque. In Jerusalem
we noticed that the converted natives retained their fez-
caps in church. Yet the Eastern idea in this case is not
the same as the Western. With us the removal of the
hat is an expression of reverence for the place we are
entering, or rather for Him whose presence is acknow-
ledged as there. With them the removal of the shoe is
not an expression of reverence, but a confession of personal defilement, and a recognition of the mosque as holy
ground. This idea had its origin in God's command to
Moses at the Bush, where the divine glory, or Shekinah,
appeared like devouring fire, as afterwards on Sinai.
Or shall we say that this command took for granted a
previously existing idea to this effect? " Draw not nigh
hither,"—that is, advance no farther, for this place is

the dwelling of the glory,—the holy of holies, that is only to be entered by the High Priest once a-year, and " not without blood." Nay, more, even the circle round is consecrated by the presence of the glory,—"*put off thy shoes* from off thy feet ; for the place whereon thou standest is holy ground." (Exod. iii. 5.) The Jews are as particular as the Mahommedans in this respect. Hence when we visited the synagogue at Nablous the old Rabbi insisted on our being unshod, just as when we entered the mosque of Omar. Yet elsewhere they made no such condition on entering their synagogues. They retain their caps however, like the Easterns,—and this even in the West. We once had a specimen of this in London. We went to St Paul's in the forenoon, and being somewhat forgetful, we did not take off our hats when we entered. In half a minute a verger was at our side, with " please take off your hats." In the course of the same day we visited the Jewish synagogue, and, mindful of the verger's word, we took off our hats as we entered. In a moment the Jew beside us called out, " put on your hats." We obeyed at once, wondering, however, at the difference of ideas between the church and the synagogue in the matter of worship. The difference was probably at first a simple matter of necessity. In the East you dare not expose your uncovered head to the sun without injury ; in the West it is safer to uncover the head than the feet. When the multitudes of Israel heard the voice of God " they bowed the head and worshipped," and Moses " bowed his head

towards the earth and worshipped." (Exod. xxxiv. 8.)
With us there would have been the uncovering of the
head as well. In the East the people bowed the head
to royalty as it passed by; in the West they take off
their hats while they shout forth their loyalty.

In the East men shave their *heads*, in the West their
beards. Yet the latter seems to have been an Egyptian
custom in former days ; for we read that Joseph, before
he went in unto Pharaoh, "shaved himself." (Gen.
xli. 14.)

In the West *black* is the emblem of grief in which
mourners wrap themselves; in the East there is no special colour. The attendants at funerals had on their
usual dress, and the pall was red and yellow. Sackcloth, with rending of the clothes, and ashes on the head,
was the proper sign of deep grief,—and "sackcloth
within, upon the flesh," (2 Kings vi. 30), the symbol of
more than common sorrow. Yet the mourners at graves,
at least the women, are in their usual white. Job gave
vent to his sorrow by adding to all the other expressions
of it that of "shaving the head." (Job. i. 20.)

In the West men wash their hands by dipping them
in water, in the East they have water poured upon them.
And often did we see our dragoman's little Nubian servant, Hamân, pouring water on his master's hands, as
Elisha did on the hands of Elijah. (2 Kings iii. 11.)
At one time he might be seen bringing a bason of water
for us to wash in, at another pouring water out of a jug
upon his master's.

We did not dine till half-past six, so that we had two hours to do what business our first afternoon in Cairo required. I noticed that while we were at dinner several persons came in and seated themselves on the divan behind us,—no one seeming to think them intruders. So the woman who came uninvited into the house of the Pharisee, was not considered as doing something strange or rude, but rather something quite common. She "stood at his feet behind him," and was neither removed nor wondered at. (Luke vii. 37, 38.) These visitors who had come in to the room where we were dining sat quietly till dinner was ended, and then entered into conversation with us.

In the course of the evening, we made inquiries respecting a dragoman for our desert journey ; but decided nothing. It is not easy to satisfy oneself, even with a score of excellent certificates. There are so many points to be considered,—fitness, experience, temper, cleanliness, obliging habits, and the like. For it is not merely comfort and safety that the traveller has to take thought for, but the accomplishment of his travelling aims,— seeing and hearing thoroughly all that is to be seen and heard. Very much depends on an *obliging* as well as *intelligent* and *communicative* dragoman.

Committing ourselves and our ways to that God who is not too great to care for each creature that he has made, and asking him to form all our plans for us, we lay down to rest, looking forward to the day of rest which was at hand. In spite of some noise in the street

and knockings at the door of the hotel, we slept in
peace. A week farther from our home on earth, a week
nearer our home in the kingdom of God !

Cairo, Sabbath, Jan. 6. 1856.—Rose between seven
and eight. Thermometer at 56°. The day is bright,—
the sky all sunshine and azure. Our hotel is in a sort of
square or open space. Fronting us is a large garden or
park planted with shrubs and trees,—lubbuks, acacias,
tamarisks, and such like. Our view from the windows
is pleasant though not extensive, and the ranges of
trees, so various in shape, size, and hue, would stand
out in fresher beauty, under so fair a sunshine, were it
not for the *dust* that disfigures every leaf and blossom
here. Egypt from the nature of its soil, as well as from
lack of moisture, is specially the land of *dust*; and
terrible must have been the extent of the plague sent
on her when God commanded Aaron, saying, " Stretch
out thy rod, and smite the *dust* of the land, that it may
become lice throughout all the land of Egypt," (Exod.
viii. 16) ; and how sore the calamity denounced against
Israel, whose land contains but little of this nuisance,
" The Lord shall make the rain of thy land powder and
dust : from heaven shall it come down upon thee, until
thou be destroyed." (Deut. xxviii. 24.) Getting so little
rain and at long intervals, the objects, both of art and
nature, take on a dusty hue, which sadly mars their
look. It is not merely the street or the low shrub that
takes on the dust ; but the tall minaret looks dingy too,
and the palm, in spite of well-watered roots, feels the

need of showers from above. No native feels this. He thinks that if he gets enough of water to *drink*, he does not need any for his hands or face; and so he thinks that if his palm-tree gets the Nile-stream for its *roots*, it can do without the rain of heaven for its *branches*. And we have not a few of such *dusty Christians* among ourselves,—men who, though they take heed to life and growth, forget the numerous little impurities which mar the symmetry and comeliness of noble character, and are like dust upon the leaves of those "trees of right-eousness" which are planted by the "rivers of water." There is something unpleasant in these unwashen palms, —either in figure or in reality. An Arab is watering the dusty street. He has a water-skin slung aslant across his shoulders,—and with its mouth in his hand he moves along squirting out the fluid in all directions. But he cannot reach the broad leaves of these branching *lubbuks*, or the thin wiry foliage of these slender *tarfas*. Nothing will touch or wash them but the rain of the firmament,—something higher than man, and less scanty than his water-skins.

We worshipped in the English Church in the fore-noon, and in the afternoon I preached in the rooms of the American Mission. Only a handful of Christian men,—English or American,—in this great city. Yet Egypt waits for the day of its light; and that day shall come. It is now the Korân; it shall then be the Bible. It is now Mahommed; it shall then be Christ.

The day has gone down in clouds, and there is a

slight shower this evening. The Sabbath-stillness is rudely broken in upon by a hurdy-gurdy in the square. Yet what stillness has there been throughout the day? None. Cairo has no weekly rest. Donkeys, camels, Arabs, men, and boys,—all crowd the streets as at other times; nay, shows and games of all kinds have been going on more noisily than usual. Yet thus it is both in East and West! The world needs rest, but takes none. Can it long stand this constant tear and wear of life? It will yet be found that God's demand for a seventh portion of our days was the most reasonable-of all demands. Man needs the Sabbath; and even were this age to throw it down, the wants of the next would call for its setting up.

As we were going to bed I looked out and found most of the clouds gone and the stars shining out. Orion, in his full eastern brightness, was right above our window, and seemed almost overhead. The hum of the day was over; and the Sabbath-calm had come at last, though not till the Sabbath itself was gone.

Monday, Jan. 7. 1856.—I rose before seven and went out for a walk. The morning was misty and the thermometer 55°. I walked outside the gate, on the road towards *Bulac.* Long lines of *lubbuk* trees, with their large thin pods drooping through their green leaves. Spent the forenoon in sketching our route and drawing out an agreement with the dragoman, *Haji-Ismael Achmet Siouti.* He was a native of Siout in Upper Egypt as his name imports, and took to himself the title

of *Haj* or *Haji*, because he had once been at Mecca,
though in what capacity we could not exactly learn.
Several with whom we afterwards met questioned his
right to the title of "pilgrim," inasmuch as it was said he
had only been to Mecca as a soldier, and the Prophet's
law forbade the name to be given to any one who had
been to the holy city merely in that capacity, Be this
as it may, he liked the title and took it; so we gave it
to him in our future journeys, as we found all our
Bedaween doing the same. We generally called him
merely by the title, *Haji;* but our Arabs always ap-
pended the first of his string of names, and often made
the desert-echoes resound with the name of *Hajismáel.*
If however, as Dr Wilson says, "its bearded possessors
are viewed as combining the character of the knight
and the saint," we are afraid that our dragoman could
not have made good any pretensions to the character
of either knight or saint. We do not doubt that he
had kissed the black stone of the Kaabah; but that
fact seems of small moment in our eyes, whatever it
might be in his or in the eyes of the Arabs. The contract was duly written both in Arabic and English, he
affixing his seal to it, and we subscribing our names, at
the English consul's office. For this we paid twenty-
seven piastres, or about five shillings and sixpence. He
engaged to be ready in three days,—providing everything
for us, at the rate of twenty-five shillings each, per day.

We found a shop, just at the entrance of the bazaar,
kept by an Englishman, where we got some articles for

our journey, such as white hats, white umbrellas, green or blue veils, but not at a very moderate price. Opposite to this was a shop of a native shoemaker, where we furnished ourselves with white or yellow boots; for the dust of Cairo and the heat of the desert make black ones a great discomfort. These boots, we found afterwards, suited well the dust of Egypt and the sand of the desert,—but the stones and rocks of Palestine called for something more substantial. Israel's wondrous story came to mind :—" I have led you forty years in the wilderness ; your clothes are not waxen old upon you, and thy shoe is not waxen old upon thy foot." (Deut. xxix. 5.) *Asher's* shoes of " iron and brass" suited his rocky coast from Carmel to Sidon, and no doubt Israel found in Egypt all that he needed, for his wilderness sojourn. Covering for both foot and head is needful, and rude as were the thong-stitched sandals of our Arabs,—made of fish-skin or some rude material,—still some attempt was made to protect the foot. Loose enough they often were, flapping to and fro upon the sole of the foot, as its owner scraped or shovelled his way along the sands ; in two cases it was *one* foot, or rather one sole only, that was thus shod ; but still no one liked to be shoeless ; though the sandal is not by any means so great a necessity as the turban, and, when running, it was generally put off as an incumbrance. I speak of the Bedaween specially, not the better classes of the Egyptian or the Syrian.

In the bazaars sat the " money-changers," with their

"table" or board before them, and their various rows
and heaps of silver. It would not be difficult to overthrow these "tables," (Matt. xxi. 12); but what a scene
would result from the "pouring out" of these heaps of
silver, especially along such a smooth platform as that of
the temple. (John ii. 15.) In no *mosque* do you find
any such money-changing or traffic of any kind. All
its courts, outer and inner, are held sacred. But in the
Latin and Greek churches there is no such reverence
nor restriction. Their outer courts are made precisely
what the temple was made by the Jews eighteen hundred years ago,—places of traffic in all kinds of wares.
Whether they are also "dens of thieves" I know not;
but this I may say, that no Moslem would carry his
market into his mosque, as Latins and Greeks do into
their churches. The Moslem admits neither the statue
of the dead saint nor the table of the living merchant.
The so-called Christians bid welcome to both. Some of
our party smarted sorely at the hands of these money-
changers. Indeed, unless you have a dragoman with
you when transacting business with them, you may
count upon being cheated.

In passing through one of the bazaars I was witness
of a sad scene. A father, in a rage, was beating his
child with a huge stick. He was a tall strong Arab,
and the child was a boy about ten. As he lay on the
ground, struggling and crying, the father kept striking
him on every part,—head, back, front, and foot,—without mercy. I never saw a dog at home so savagely

D

beaten. I was going to try my *hand* at interfering, as the want of language tied my *tongue*,—when some neighbours rushed forward and seized the man, who, after a struggle, allowed himself to be led away from his victim. I thought that the boy's every bone was broken,—for no European bones could have stood such a smashing; but he rose up in a moment, dried his tears, shook himself, and went away as if nothing had befallen him. It seemed quite a specimen of Eastern manners; yet the West need not boast. There are indoor scenes much worse than this at home, if our daily police reports are true. Let not the Londoner boast over the Caireen. A stricter police keeps these scenes from the public streets, but that is all.

CHAPTER IV.

PYRAMIDS—SPHINX—NILE—OLD EGYPT—CITADEL OF CAIRO—WALKS
THROUGH THE TOWN—PETRIFIED FOREST.

Cairo, Tuesday, Jan. 8. 1856.—Rose a little after
six,—just before sunrise ; and as I looked out towards
the east, citadel, mosques, minarets, came out in full
relief, like transparencies upon the reddening sky.
About eight o'clock we set out for the Pyramids,
having as our dragoman a most obliging Syrian, *Habeeb*
by name, from Beyrout. For some distance we rode
through an avenue of lubbuk trees. About half a mile
from the city we passed a palace of the Pasha's, at the
gate of which some dozen of his white-robed soldiers
were lounging. I happened to be walking on before,
and my donkey followed at some distance. On a
sudden I heard a shrill cry, and, turning round, saw
one of these soldiers thrashing my donkey-boy, as if he
would have beaten him to pieces. Immediately I in-
terfered so far as I could ; but not knowing how far the
boy might be the cause of the mischief, I was not very

energetic, especially as I could not understand the vociferations of the crowd or the explanations of the boy, who, half in Arabic, half in English, was uttering his complaint. Before I could make out the case, the soldier had mounted my donkey and was riding off. Up came Habeeb. In a minute the boy explained the matter, and off went the Syrian at full speed. He soon overtook the soldier and laid hold of the animal. The man of war resisted,—vociferated, and laid his hand on his sword. We soon came up and gathered round the combatants. Who was to yield? Not the soldier, we thought, well-armed as he was, and almost within hail of his comrades. Habeeb, however, was a man most determined in will and powerful in body. Not an inch would he allow the fellow to move. Off he must come from the seat he had usurped, or if he would not, he must be dragged or driven off. He got calmer,— looked at us and saw we were Englishmen,—looked at Habeeb and saw he was determined;—so there seemed nothing for it but to yield, which he did at last, dismounting in sullenness, and leaving me in possession of my charger. The donkey-boy was overjoyed,—crying out in his own way to us, "Bad soldier,—bad soldier." Habeeb was proud of his victory, and rode on at our head in triumph. We asked him if he was not afraid that the soldier would draw his sword. "What," said he, "a Syrian afraid of an Egyptian!" And, flourishing his stick, intimated that his wooden sword would have proved quite a match for the soldier's steel one.

I was glad that I had got back my donkey in peace,—
for had it been carried off, I should not have known
what to do, as the day was hot, and the way long, and
walking almost impracticable. The incident, however,
shewed us the oppression which these soldiers exercise
over all whom they can safely rob, or injure, or insult.

On we pushed through a continuous line or stream of
people and soon reached the Nile, where the hubbub of
embarkation was frightful. The island of *Rodah*, close
by which we sailed, is said to be the place where the
infant son of Amram was found by the daughter of the
king, in his bulrush-cradle. Here is a splendid palace
of the Pasha, and the famous Nilometer. As we crossed,
the pyramids of *Sakhârah* seemed to rise up in the far
south, while those of *Ghizeh* seemed to stand quite
near, and just in front. Our voyage was about fifteen
minutes in length,—and as we glided through the floating sunshine, the scene on each side was " goodly to
behold,"—for the river seemed lined with palms and.
palaces on both its banks, between which there crossed
and recrossed white-sailed boats without number. Landing, we rode on through villages, palm-forests, fields,
and sand-flats. We noticed (as often we did in Syria)
a man chopping up with an axe a field which had been
baked by the sun. He was literally " breaking up his
fallow-ground." (Jer. iv. 3.) We marked also how
carefully our Arabs avoided treading on the fields,—
keeping always to the sides,—illustrating Job's description of the violent man, who pays no attention to land-

marks or fences, " He beholdeth not the way of the
vineyards." (Job xxiv. 18.)

But a letter written from the spot will tell the story
as well. . . . " Leaving Cairo at eight, we reached
the Nile in less than an hour. Then 'rose from sea
to sky' such a hubbub as can only occur in Egypt.
We and our donkeys must embark. The latter were
pulled into the boat, some by the tail, and some by the
head, and some by the legs. The *jabber* of the Arabs
was horrific. They screamed, and shouted, and scolded,
and shook their fists ; they pulled, and pushed, and tore
at each other ;—such a mob ! The sail across the Nile
was lovely. The broad brown river (for its colour was
dusky olive), gleaming in southern sunshine,—the river
boats with their lateen sails,—the Pasha's palace,—the
little isle of *Rodah*,—the pyramids of *Sakhârah* and
Ghizeh, with a long range of white precipices as a background, to the west,—the forests of noble palms ;—here
was a scene of wonder, and greatness, and beauty, such
as one loves to look back upon through life. As soon
as we landed, the Arab shrieks recommenced. We
stepped quietly ashore, leaving our donkeys to follow,
which they did without delay, though whether with
head or tail foremost I cannot say. I am certain they
did not know themselves. Remounting them, we trotted
and gallopped away through a dirty Arab village,—a
mere cluster of dunghills, with holes scooped out of the
dried filth for human beings to crawl in and out by.
Then we passed out of human vileness into nature's

glory, riding along for above a mile through a wood of tall palms, whose stems were upright as an obelisk, and whose green crown of feathers no breeze shook. Then we rode through fields, whose fertile mud, scorched into hardness by the sun, was just beginning to be ploughed up. After passing two other villages we reached the sand of the desert, on the raised edge of which the Pyramids are reared as on a platform. The sand is fine and of a whitish colour, not flat but swelling into gentle hillocks, over which our donkeys went gallantly.* . . .

We soon reached the Pyramids; but here let me again quote a letter:—

" Under the Sphynx, Jan. 8, half-past 12. . . . I meant to have written from the top of the great pyramid, but my writing-case was left at the foot, through forgetfulness, so I scribbled a pencil note to——on the top, where I spent half an hour, and then came down to take shelter from the heat under the back part of the Sphynx's head. It is large enough to give shelter to a score of us. Right before me, as I sit with my back to the stony monster, is first the great pyramid of Cheops, which is about 460 feet high, or nearly 120 feet higher than St Paul's, London; next that of Cephrenes (or Belzoni's); then a smaller one, that of Mycerenus. Beyond these are smaller ones, some of them almost like conical mounds. We took about twenty minutes to ascend the great one." . . . .

* Tacitus speaks of the Pyramids as being " disjectas inter, et vix pervias arenas." The former of these epithets we found true enough, the latter not.—*Ann.*, L. II. § 61.

Some expositors of Scripture have written of the Pyramids as if they might be the work of the oppressed Israelites, in the days of their bondage! But the Pyramids (with the exception of two small ones at Dashûr) are built of limestone, not of brick. The limestone seems to have come partly from the immediate neighbourhood of the Pyramids themselves, and partly from the Mukattem ridge near Cairo. The red granite, which is found in the interior, and also in the surrounding tombs, is from Syene in Upper Egypt, 500 miles farther up the Nile.

The view from the top was no common one. Some travellers have written that they were disappointed both with the view and with the Pyramids themselves. We were not with either. Seated on the top we had to take breath for some minutes after the ascent, which tries every joint and muscle in your limbs. Then we began to look about us. To the east the yellow Mukattem cliffs, with the desert behind them and Cairo at their feet, gleaming in the fair noon. Between us and the city there flowed the mighty Nile,*—whose waters we could trace far north and south for many a mile by the long line of moving silver, dividing the vast waste of

---

* The Nile is certainly a most majestic river, especially when viewed from a height. In this respect it is quite different from the Jordan, whose high banks seem quite to swallow up the stream and prevent its being seen to advantage. No one who has looked on it would speak of Jordan " winding his *stately* march," or say " where *stately* Jordan flows by many a palm," (Keble). Jordan is not at all stately, nor does it flow by many a palm. The trees on its banks are many and various ; but we saw no palms among them.

dull unmoving sand. Along its banks rose numerous palm forests, and upon its bosom glittered the sails of a hundred river-boats, which, as they moved along, seemed in the distance like the white wings of sea birds. To the west there lay the Lybian wastes on which the blue horizon rested. To the south rose the fourteen Pyramids of Sakharah, some ten miles up the Nile, where is the lately discovered Necropolis with the mummy-pits of kings and gods.

There is no doubt that the Pyramids were the tombs of kings,[*] and the greatness of these structures shews how men strove to undo the humbling circumstances of mortality. To keep up the semblance of perpetual life, they caused themselves to be embalmed. To save themselves from the abasement of the " narrow house," they cased themselves in polished granite, and reared these enormous tombs. Faith, accepting the righteous sentence of mortality, as the wages of sin, and yet counting on a glorious immortality, in resurrection, said, " let me bury my dead out of sight," (Gen. xxiii. 4) ;

---

[*] It sounds strange to hear Cleopatra say,—

> "Rather make
> My country's high pyramidës my gibbet
> And hang me up in chains."

But it was the most expressive contrast she could have uttered. The honoured tombs of her fathers, where their dust was laid in sacred pomp, to be her gibbet, where she should be hung in chains ! *Shakspeare's* accuracy was great. Milton rather incongruously makes the *palace* of Satan to be based on or adorned with pyramids—

> . . . . . . a mount
> Raised on a mount with pyramids and towers
> From diamond quarries hewn.

but unbelief, rebelling at the punishment, and resolved to neutralise it, said, "let us keep our bodies from decay and cover them with mighty monuments,—that is all the life we know of." And thus "the kings of the nations, even all of them, lie in glory, every one in his own house," (Isa. xiv. 18) ; so that when God would threaten Babylon he tells her that she shall be "cast out of her grave" and "not joined with them in burial ;" and when he would warn Egypt he says, "they shall not lie with the mighty" (Ezek. xxxii. 27).

The prophets no where make the slightest reference to these works of Egyptian pride in their various predictions concerning Egypt, as if that which was the wonder of the nations was not worthy to be named. But perhaps it was to such structures that Job referred when he spoke of "kings and counsellors of the earth, who built *desolate places* for themselves" (Job. iii. 14.)

The whole place seems a cemetery of giants,—erected not merely to resist the overflow of the Nile or the still more destructive sand-flood,—but to defy time itself. What care men took to make themselves immortal ! First of all there was the embalming of the body. Then this embalmed body was placed in a marble coffin, fragments of which lie scattered here and there. Then this marble coffin was deposited in a granite tomb, of enormous strength. Then above was reared the Pyramid, like a mighty tombstone, securing the dead against all intrusion. Was all this to defy, not merely time, but judgment to come ?

But Egypt was not merely the burying place of Egyptians, but of Israelites as well. In the centuries of bondage how many thousands of the seed of Abraham were buried on the banks of the Nile ! In after ages too, when Israel fled to Egypt in the days of their last kings, what multitudes of Jews laid their dust in that strange land ; as Hosea prophesied (ix. 6.)

> For lo !
> They are gone before the destroyer !
> Mizraim shall gather them,
> Memphis shall bury them.

No country (their own excepted) contains so much of Israel's dust as Egypt.

In looking from the Pyramids, it is *old* Egypt that comes up before your view,—old Egypt on both sides of the river. Modern Egypt, both in its Christianity and its Moslemism, disappears. An old bridge seems to spring from the Pyramids, and to rest its first arch on the island of *Rodah ;* from that it springs its second arch, which spans Cairo and rests on *Heliopolis ;*—the Pyramids, the Nilometer, and the Obelisk, forming links of an unbroken chain. It is all *old Mizraim* everywhere, —a land that seems never to die,—or if it does, in its very death to rise up into a vastness that overshadows all modern grandeur. Gazing from the Pyramids, Cairo, fine as it is with its minarets and domes, seems but as a patch of mushrooms between two mighty oaks, or as a pile of white-washed houses between two old cathedrals. Greek philosophy had its day of greatness, but old Egypt

was still above it. Moslemism has had its era of grandeur, but old Egypt still towers above it. All the
changes of the last two thousand years are but as modern
additions to some old temple, which time after time
moulder away and leave the ancient structure more venerable and more marvellous than before.

But let me go on with the letter written under the
shaggy locks of the Sphynx. "Around me are vast hillocks of sand, the proceeds of the many diggings which
have taken place here, by Romans, Egyptians, French and
English. Amongst them are noble tombs, from which,
however, the sarcophagi have disappeared. There seem
to have been here at least a dozen of pyramids, great and
small. As I write, a half-naked Arab boy, from the
neighbouring village, sits beside me with his earthenware bottle of Nile water, out of which I must now stop
to drink, before rejoining my companions. . . After my
twenty minutes rest under the shade of the Sphynx, I
joined the party, and we all sat down to lunch in one of
the large excavated tombs. It had been unroofed by
some explorer and robbed of its contents, but its massive
walls of finely-polished granite afforded sufficient shade.
About twenty-five wild-looking Arabs, young and old,
male, but not female, are sitting round, wondering at us
as we uncover our heads and seek blessing on the food
set before us. We soon finished our lunch, and giving
the fragments to our hungry Arab boys, we rode about
200 yards off, where there is a knot of trees, two *der-
wishes* (as the boy called them) and three *palms*. Their

shadow was most refreshing, and the north-east breeze, which seemed then to spring up, was most pleasant. The sky was not quite cloudless. A thin sort of gauze seemed spread over it in the shape of light long clouds, which made its blue less deep, but which took off the trying heat. Yet I did not suffer from the heat but rather enjoyed it. One does not perspire so much in this dry climate as at home ; nor does one feel the fatigue of all this climbing, and riding, and knocking about so much so as in our native climate."

Our ride to and from Ghizeh was about twenty-eight miles in all. The Pyramids are not much above ten miles north-west of Cairo in a straight line. But our course, being at no time straight, made the ride some miles longer. We had more than once to make a long bend, that we might avoid some pool or ditch or slime-heap which had been left by the Nile, on the edge of fields that were rapidly throwing up from their moist soil the fresh verdure of spring.*

I noticed that the quay,—if one may call it so,—on the east bank of the Nile, was made of planks of the palm, shewing us another of the many uses to which that wondrous tree is put. The vine is for one thing

---

* Spenser's words are true enough,—

> As when old father Nilus 'gins to swell,
> With timely pride above the Egyptian vale,
> His fatty waves do fertile slime outwell,
> And overflow each plain, and lowly dale ;
> But when his later ebb 'gins to avail
> Huge heaps of mud he leaves . . .

Fairy Queen, B. i. C. i.

only, *fruit.* If it bears no fruit, it is useless,—fit only
for the fire (Ezek. xv. 1–5). The palm is serviceable
in an hundred ways. The palm and the camel,—who
can tell all their uses ?

As we rode slowly back, I noticed several illustrations
of Scripture,—women bearing children on their shoulders, which is quite common in the East (Isa. xlix. 22) ;
—a man staying his journey that he might "bow down
upon his knees to drink," instead of "lapping" with his
hand and passing on as one in haste and in earnest
(Judges vii. 5, 6) ;—a shepherd carrying a sheep in his
bosom (Isa xl. 11) ;—a runner, staff in hand and with
girded loins, running at full speed on some important
errand (Job ix. 25), "swifter than a post,"—(" one post
shall run to meet another," Jer. li. 31) ;—a vine with its
branches "running over a wall." (Gen. xlix. 22.) These
things we noted as we passed along, and then, about
sunset, found ourselves at rest for another evening.

Wednesday, Jan. 9. 1856.—Rose before seven,—
morning pleasant. At half-past eight set off for the
Citadel. In our way saw the mosque of Sultan Hassan,
—old and crumbling yet magnificent, from its size and
the noble simplicity of its architecture. The great court,
remarkable for its height and spacious dimensions, not
unlike St Paul's. We saw more than one mosque,
both outside and inside,—all of them simple,—unlike the
"churches" of the East and West. In a mosque there
is no object of idolatry,—picture, statue, or wafer.

Mahommedanism was the re-action produced by the worse than Pagan idolatries of Christianity in the fifth and sixth centuries. It was the reform of Eastern Christianity, a re-action from vile polytheism, which the worship of the saints and of Mary had produced. Few have a true knowledge of the enormous superstitions and idolatries which then went to make up what was still called Christianity. If they had, they would not indeed think better of Moslemism, but they would admit that it was some improvement upon the system which it supplanted. It was *man's* attempt to get rid of a gross religion, and to get back to something like *immateriality* of worship. A Moslem hates idolatry, and cannot bear to enter a Greek or Latin Church, because of the idolatries which defile every nook and stone. He would not bow before an image nor kiss the foot of a statue, nor burn incense to a picture. But he has learned of late that all Christians are not idolaters. And not long since, when the Pasha visited the Protestant Church at Jerusalem, he was struck with the difference between it and the other churches that receive the name of " Christian." " I could worship here," was his remark on coming out. He could not bear the idol-worship, of which he is often compelled to be a spectator, when called to act as preserver of the peace in the Church of the Holy Sepulchre, when Latin and Greek clamour and fight and riot, with their wafer-god in their mouths, and their idols looking down with complacency on the warfare. It is really a

relief to pass from one of these idol-shrines into the stern
simplicity of a Moslem mosque.

Soon reached the citadel . . situation lofty and view
fine . . close at hand the Mukattem cliffs . . Ghizeh, the
Pyramids, the Lybian Hills . . fields of green, forests of
palm . . the city of Cairo at our feet. We then visited
the Pasha's palace, and then rode to tombs of the Mám-
louks, most of them built on the sandy plain, some on
the brow of the Mukattem Hills, some cut out of the
precipitous rock, as in Petra,—all in ruins . . tried to
enter one of them less ruined, but it was barred. I put
my hand in at the large hole to unbar it in the inside,
but could not, which reminded us of the Song of Solomon,
" My beloved put in his hand by the hole of the door"
(chap. v. 4.) Down to the right as we went on, an
Egyptian regiment was drawn out for review . . the
echo of the cannon from the cliff striking. Returned at
twelve to the hotel, and after a little rest and food went
off to the *Shúbra* gardens, four miles off. These are
truly fine . . trees, shrubs, flowers of every hue and scent
. . long hedges of myrtle which the natives use for strew-
ing on graves . . sprightly acacias rising here and there
. . groves of oranges and lemons, gladdening the hot air
with their cool fragrance. In the midst was a most
gorgeous miniature palace, with a small lake in its
centre, to which, under a splendid arcade, all the cham-
bers open out. The inside all carpet and tapestry and
pictures, the outside all marble and flowers and divans,
—art seeming to copy nature and nature to study art.

" Thy plants are a paradise of pomegranates,
  With pleasant fruits ;
  Hennah with spikenard,
  Spikenard and saffron,
  Calamus and cinnamon,
  With all trees of frankincense ;
  Myrrh and aloes,
  With all the chief spices." (Song of Sol. iv. 13.)

One of the American missionaries gave us his company and guidance, which we much enjoyed. We returned about five, not sorry to rest.

Thursday, Jan. 10. 1856.—In wandering through different parts of the town, I saw and heard some more of the sights and sounds of Egypt. Among the sights was a native school, poor, dirty, and confused. The Eastern standard of education is low enough. Among the sounds was one of loud wailing coming out of a house in one of the narrow streets. It was " the wail above the dead," but it seemed quite an *uproar*. It brought to mind such words as these, " Teach your daughters *wailing*, and every one his neighbour lamentation, for *death is come up* into our windows" (Jer ix. 20, 21), and still more the words of another prophet, " Wailing shall be in all streets" (Amos v. 16). Still more exactly did it seem to resemble the scene at Capernaum in the house of Jairus, where the mourning is called a " tumult," and the mourners are said to have " wept and wailed greatly" (Mark v. 38). The sounds appeared to me quite inarticulate, but I believe they formed a regular lament, repeated again and again for hours or

E

days. If the deceased was a son, the cry of the parents is, " Ya Walladi, Walladi,—Ya Walladi, Walladi ! "—Alas, my son, my son !—just like David's bitter outcry over his dead, " O Absalom, my son, my son ! " (2 Sam. xviii. 33.)

Friday, Jan 11. 1856.—Went to the petrified forest, a curious place, where, on the surface of the sand, there lie scattered masses, great and small, of petrified trees. These extend over miles,—nay, afterwards we traced them all the way to the Red Sea. We would fain have gone to *Heliopolis* or *On,* the city of Pharaoh, where Joseph dwelt, and to which his brethren resorted,—the city which Herodotus and Plato visited,—the city to which tradition says the infant Jesus was brought, when Herod sought his life. But the distance is considerable, and our time was short. We could only turn our eyes in the direction of the mounds of ruin, and imagine that we saw the solitary obelisk, the very stone on which Joseph must often have gazed. On has had a strange and noble history,—a history for the Egyptian and the Syrian,—a history for the Gentile, the Jew, and the Christian. But no trace of its glory remains. The unspairing sand has swept through the forsaken city. Yet is it not of this that the prophet speaks, when pointing to latter-day blessing, " in that day shall five cities in the land of Egypt speak the language of Canaan, and swear to the Lord of hosts ; one shall be called *the city of the Sun."* (Isa. xix. 18, margin.)

CHAPTER V.

Cairo, Saturday, Jan. 12. 1856.—Rose before seven.
Thermometer 45°. Morning fine. Breakfasting at eight,
we began, immediately after, the business of removal.
It took upwards of two hours to get our camels loaded,
which was done in the public street, amid a crowd of
onlookers, young and old, of all nations. At a quarter
before eleven we moved off, going out at the *Shûbra*
gate, and soon after passing through an avenue of shabby
trees, which *lined,* if they did not *adorn,* the road. Leaving these trees, we came to what seemed the opening of
the desert,—undulating wastes of whitish sand on each
side, which soon became of a more rough and stony character,—the whitening skeletons of camels beginning to
appear. About five o'clock we halted and encamped,
not having advanced above eight or nine miles on our
journey. Our halting place was as tame and bleak as
can be imagined. But we soon shut out the solitude,
and sitting down to a comfortable meal, we forgot that
we were now in the Desert. It was strange to notice

how quickly the *tent* dispelled the feeling of loneliness
which does at times come down on one when he looks
round on such wastes.   The moment that the tent went
up, and was fairly drawn round us,—leaving us with bed
and table and *fenûss* (folding lanthorn), to our mutual
fellowship, the desert seemed shut out, the loneliness at
an end.   Having joined together in thanking God for
his gracious kindness, and committing ourselves and our
ways to his guidance, we lay down on our small iron
bedsteads, and well-wrapped, both in blankets and plaids,
soon fell asleep.   The thermometer was at 62°.   We
had not the murmur of the stream, nor the rustle of the
leaf to lull us ; but we had what was equally effectual,
—deep stillness,—a stillness to which for some time
past we had been strangers.   We had now gotten what
the prophet longed for,—" a lodging-place of wayfaring
men in the wilderness" (Jer. ix. 1.)   Our tent-dwell-
ings were exactly the " traveller's night-lodge," as the
word in that passage means.   But even in this sandy solitude, we felt no fear of evil by night or by day,—" thou
shalt lie down and none shall make thee afraid" (Job
xi. 18.)

As to this day's work and scenes, I wrote thus in a letter
dated " *Our Tent, Jan.* 14. . . We left Cairo on Saturday about eleven, taking our donkeys for a few miles, lest
we should make an exhibition of ourselves in the public
street in our first attempts at camel-riding.   We then
went on board the ' ship of the desert.'   The motion of
the camel is much less unpleasant than I had expected."

Another letter records the scene. "As we moved along I surveyed the whole retinue. There was our dragoman, Haji-Ismâel, mounted on one camel, with my two portmanteaus firmly roped to the side of the animal. He was dressed out for the start, with a goodly flowing robe and a head-dress, whose red and yellow stripes glittered brightly to the sun. On another camel were two large square panniers, of palm-branch wicker-work, filled with oranges and lemons, to the amount of at least 600 of the former and 100 of the latter. On another was our "canteen," that is, two immense wooden chests, containing our dining apparatus, such as plates, knives, forks, spoons, cups, not omitting candles and *fenûsses*, that is lanterns made of linen, apparently saturated with bees-wax or some such substance, which draw out to more than a foot in length when in actual use, but can be contracted or folded together into a very small space for packing. Above this apparatus was placed our kitchen-grate, a long iron box, pierced with a hundred holes in sides and bottom,—its four legs, like signal-posts stretched upwards to the sun. Then came another with an immense wicker-cage, which formed the prison-house of some 100 fowls, all alive, but quite willing apparently, to go to the stake for us,—as four of them are to be called on to do each day at sunset. Balancing these fowls is another cage, with half-a-dozen turkeys, which we are told are to be our "Sunday dinners." On another our bedding is mounted, on another our tents, on another our charcoal, on another our barrels of

Nile-water, on another sacks containing our camp-stools
and table,—our bed-steads, and the pins (*watt-watts*)
of our tents.   Most carefully was everything packed up
before it mounted the camel.   A tribe of wanderers
knows how to "pack," as indeed they have no security
for any part of their property in moving about save the
good packing.   They have bags for their money, and
sacks for other things.   Hence, in reference to God's careful remembrance of sin, Job says,—

> " My transgression is sealed up in a bag,
>   And thou sewest up mine iniquity."   (Job xiv. 17.

And Hosea also, alluding to the same custom,—

> " The iniquity of Ephraim is bound up,
>   His sin is hid."   (Hos. xiii. 12.)

On four lighter animals, which were said to be dromedaries, were the four travellers,—all of them in good
spirits, while one of them as the march proceeds, repeats
the well-known hymn,

> Guide me, O thou great Jehovah,
> Pilgrim through this barren land.

There were nineteen camels in all, and, including
dragoman and servants, about the same number of men,
—all of them swarthy Arabs.   Notable amongst them
is Sheikh Sulimân, the Sheikh or chief of one of the
Sinaitic tribes, who is our guide and guard.   He is a tall
erect Arab, beyond the middle age, with a happy face of
humour and kindness, which he shews every hour, in
every possible way.   His voice is shrill and cheerful, his

step as light as that of a *Wahâsh,* but he has one or two
front teeth knocked out, which mischance, however, does
not give him a sinister aspect, for through the vacancy,
the free Arab laugh seems to come all the more heartily.
He makes a most companionable conductor, though our
intercourse is by signs not words, for he knows even less
of English than we do of Arabic. His underdress is a
loose white shirt like a night-gown (*Kaftan*), over which
goes a brown covering or sackcloth cloak of camels-hair
(*Abyâh*). He wears a sort of sandals made of skin and
stitched with thongs; they barely protect the *soles* of
his feet. With these he trudges or skips or scrapes
along, according to his fancy, his gun (*baroudeh*) on one
side and his sword (*jambeh*) on the other. Our drivers
are like their chief, but each of them has quite a face, air,
and dress of his own,—one a fine Grecian profile, another
a pleasant round-featured Scotch visage, another wild as a
South Sea savage, another with a shaggy beard, another
without a beard, another soft-looking like a female,
another fierce as a bandit, another (my own driver and
valet) tall and vigorous, with an undressed sheep-skin
hung over his back, which sometimes forms a target for
orange-peel and such like. All of them are kind and
obliging." . . .

Sabbath, Jan. 13. 1856.—To-day we rest " according
to the commandment." Rose about eight. Thermometer 50°. Breakfasted at half-past eight. Went out
amid the sands while breakfast was preparing. After
breakfast " family worship." A quiet Sabbath fore-

noon! How deeply still,—save a casual interruption
from the voices of the Arabs or the growl of the camel!
After the uproar of Egyptian cities and villages, how
peaceful did this wilderness appear. We had regular service at twelve, though not summoned by the Sabbath-
bell. The tongues of the Arabs sometimes annoyed us,
breaking in upon our quiet, and reminding us of him
who said, "Woe is me that I sojourn in Mesech, that I
dwell in the tents of Kedar" (Psa. cxx. 5.) The heat
was great, and the thermometer stood at 79° in the tent.
Towards evening we saw our camels, which had been
allowed to wander through the day, sauntering back to
our tents. The moon rose in oriental brightness, shedding no inconsiderable light, though but in its first
quarter. Jupiter and Saturn shone out in spite of the
moonlight. The north-star seemed very low to us who
had been accustomed to see it far up in our northern
heavens. What peaceful splendour filled the wide blue
above, and covered as with a veil of transparent snow
the yellow waste around!

> How beautiful is night!
> A dewy freshness fills the silent air;*
> No mist obscures, nor cloud, nor speck, nor stain
> Breaks the serene of heaven.

* Southey's expression here, "silent air," has been remarked upon as
peculiarly expressive. So it is. But long before Southey, Ovid had spoken
of "muta silentia noctis,"—"alta quies,"—and had said—

> Nullo cum murmure sepes,
> Immotæque silent frondes, silet humidus aer;
> Sidera sola micant.—(*Metam.* vii. 187.)

and Lucretius had spoken of "pacati status aeris ille."—(iii. 294.)

In full-orbed glory yonder moon divine
Rolls thro' the dark-blue depths.
Beneath her steady ray
The desert circle spreads
Like the round ocean girdled with the sky.
How beautiful is night!

Monday, Jan. 14. 1856.—Our Sabbath-rest greatly refreshed us, and we all started this morning about 8, quite invigorated and braced either for heat or cold. The day was fine, and the thermometer at 56° in the tent. We had to be patient witnesses of some clamour and strife among our men, arising not so much from the adjustment of the loads, as from some new Arabs, who had arrived last night and insisted on being taken into service. We left the dragoman to fight the battle and walked on for a mile or two.

We were now in the direct road for Suez. There are others,—one specially, farther south, through Wady *Tawarik*, by which some have supposed that Israel went, resting their supposition on the name said to be given to this valley,—viz., *Wady Et-Tih*, or, "the Valley of the Wanderings." It is not likely, however, that Israel came so far south before they struck eastward. It appeared to us that their route had lain more eastward all along, so that to have got round the extremity of the ridge that forms the northern wall of this Wady, would have been very far indeed out of their way. They appear rather to have come nearly straight south, along the vast sandy plains, and to have pursued their way till they suddenly found themselves locked in by the promontory which projects into the sea, and forms an acute angle with its western margin.

The road lay through dreary flats of sand, with occasional undulations. It is marked off by low *walls* of sand, about two feet in height, thrown up on each side to indicate the proper track, which otherwise must have been hard to find in such a monotonous plain. The only relief to the eye to-day was a desert tree, on a small sandy mound. It was just shewing its leaves, no more. It stood like life in the midst of death. It looked somewhat like a thorn to us, but we did not see it in leaf. The Arabs called it *Sayâleh*, and it is supposed to be the shittim-wood of Scripture. It is a kind of acacia. To the left rose some sandy peaks as we advanced, and about mid-day we saw *Jebel Atâkah*, or the mountain of deliverance, towards our right. We pushed on till six o'clock, and encamped under the lee of the Transit Company's eighth station, as the wind was beginning to blow strongly from the west. The day went down amid clouds and gloom. We had some hard work in pitching our tents, and securing them from the desert-blast, which seemed to increase every hour, and which sung through our cordage while it shook our dwelling furiously, putting pole and canvas to the proof. Disregarding these assaults from without, we made ourselves comfortable within, and employed the evening in writing letters which we might post at Suez.

Tuesday, Jan. 15. 1856.—A bleak cold morning after a stormy night of rain. Thermometer 51°. Unmoored

about nine, though the day promised ill. The blasts
swept bitterly along, bringing with them sometimes
rain and sometimes sand. We had started for a walk,
but found it difficult to face the storm. At one time
we sat down at a break in the low wall of sand, which
was high enough to afford some shelter. The words of
the prophet seemed vividly real; and we felt that we
needed not only a "shadow from the heat," but a
" covert from storm and from rain." (Isa. iv. 6.) Ours
was a poor enough covert, but we were thankful for it,
as both "storm" and "rain" kept driving on. We
stood the buffeting, however, much better than our
Arabs and their camels. The former shivered and
cowered, the latter stood still, as if afraid of the wind,
and benumbed by the cold rain. We made but little
way, yet still kept moving upon the whole, till we came
to the next "station," where we all took shelter, men
and beasts, hoping that the tempest would go by. When
resting here for upwards of an hour, we paid a visit to
a curious-looking hillock of sand about half a mile off.
There we found an enormous shaft sunk in the sand,—
the memorial of a vain attempt to discover water in this
desert. Its diameter was upwards of twenty feet; but
of its depth we can say nothing. We came as near to
the edge as the crumbling sand would allow us with
safety, in order to look down; but in vain, we could see
no bottom. We heaved in huge stones,—the debris of
huts built doubtless for the diggers,—and judging from
the interval ere the sound came to us, the depth must

have been very considerable. Many of the "pits"
spoken of in Scripture may have been, like this, the result of a fruitless attempt to dig for water, as it is difficult otherwise to conceive for what purpose they were
digged. Whether "the pit in the wilderness" (Gen.
xxxvii. 22) into which Joseph was cast was such, we
know not, but we know that "the pit was empty, there
was no water in it" (Gen. xxxvii. 24). Yet it would
appear that these pits were sometimes dug for shelter,
as in the case of that one "which Asa made for fear of
Baasha king of Israel" (Jer. xli. 9). Sometimes they
were made for the execution of criminals,—"bring them
to the pit of destruction" (Psa. lv. 23); "they have hid
for me their net in a pit" (Psa. xxxv. 7). Sometimes
they were used as prisons, "they shall be gathered as
prisoners are gathered in the pit" (Isa. xxiv. 22); "I
have sent thy prisoners out of the pit" (Zech. ix. 11).
Sometimes they were employed for the burial of the
slain (Jer. xli. 7, 9).

As we lingered at the station, sheltered and safe,
we watched the fury of the storm, which swept past
us, and which seemed now at its height. Blast after
blast rushed eastward, bearing before it miles of sand-
drift, which surged, and whirled, and eddied, as if the
soil had broken loose from the rocks beneath it. The
whole plain seemed to writhe beneath the scourging
wind. One grey wave after another came rolling past
us, scattering the sand-spray as it went by, and dashing
round the corner, under the lee of which our camels lay

sheltered. Now it rose and fell in cloudy wreaths; now it poured itself along in divided streams over the slopes of the hillocks; now, in one wide torrent, it scoured the whole breadth of the waste; now, in hasty volumes, it rose up and mingled its yellow with the black of the rain-clouds above, giving to the sky a peculiar tinge of dun and purple, altogether indescribable. Then at last came a fierce hail-shower, with the discharge of which the storm all but exhausted itself.* We moved off at once without delay, as the sky began to clear and the wind went down, giving us only now and then a reminiscence of its former vehemence,—a parting token of overspent fury. As we went along the landscape became finer, the wild hills coming sharply out on each side, in the clear air. *Atâkah*, to the right, skirted our way,—hollowed and indented at every part; and one or two Sayalehs at different places took off the tameness of the scene. But, as a whole, the day

---

* The old poet's description of a sand-storm is true and vivid:—

> " Behold these needlesse banks of sand, which have
>   No seas to bound but this vast ocean
> Of barrennesse; where, when the windes conceive
>   High swoll'n displeasure, and to battell run,
>   Bandying their mutual blasts a thousand waies
>   At once, a drie and parching storm they raise.

> " For the wilde soile, impatient to be plow'd,
>   At Eolus' pleasure flies full in his face,
> And, climbing up into a tawny cloud,
>   With smoking rage torments its new-gain'd place;
>   Whilst blinded passengers amazed stand,
>   And all the aire is nothing else but sand."

Beaumont's Psyche, Canto viii.

was a disagreeable one, and we were not sorry to pitch our tents and shut out the remains of the storm.

Yet one thought relieved the dreariness of the day. It could not be far from this that the desert-pillar first came down and rested over Israel. These peaks had felt its glow; these sands had known its brightness. Our route was now that which Pharaoh took in his pursuit of Israel, till arrested by the fire of the mysterious cloud, which, more effectual than a wall of cliffs or than troops of chariots and horsemen, barred his way, till his victims were beyond his reach.

Desert, Wednesday, Jan. 16. 1856.—A cloudy dawn after a sad night of rain, which soaked all belonging to us,—tents, clothes, &c. Thermometer at 50°. We struck our tents about nine. The wind had gone low, and the rain had quite ceased, so I walked on before, for a solitary saunter. The sky looked heavy, but the sunshine was not lacking altogether. It came out through the masses of cloud in brilliant bursts, like fiery columns, calling the pillar-cloud to mind,—for through that very sky the glory of Jehovah had passed. The hill-range on the left came out beautifully in the sun,—brown in its general hue, but everywhere streaked with sand in long strata, like belts of snow. Not far off to the left, was the Pasha's deserted palace. Soon the plain widened and grew more thoroughly desert, the road quite ceasing, and the sand getting rough with stones. The hills on the left (*Awabeit*) were speedily left behind, and the *Atâkah* range, on the left, came out magnificently.

During the whole afternoon we kept in sight of it. What a relief to the eye were its brown peaks and its gloomy hollows ; while its long serrated line seem to cut the half-cloudy, half-azure sky. Towards evening, this range took a bend southward, as if retiring to leave room for a larger plain, round one side of which it swept in a semicircle, while it left the other to be bounded by the sea. This noble semicircle of preci-pices is *Ras Atâkah,* " the head of *Atâkah.*" It main-tains its full height for some twelve miles, and then drops right into the sea, eight or ten miles down from Suez, leaving not a foot of land for passage. Into this *angle* formed by the sea on the one hand, and *Ras Atâkah* on the other, Israel marched ; and here they were " shut in," (Exod. xiv. 3) ; while Pharaoh coming from the west, in the route which we had taken, marched upon their rear, and cut off all retreat. It is worth remembering, that *Ras Atâkah* is not the name merely for the abrupt headland which shoots into the sea ; it is the name for the whole twelve miles of precipice which form the ter-mination of the range. More than once I asked the Arabs about this, to make sure of it. Pointing to the one end of it, I inquired its name,—" *Atâkah.*" Pointing to the other end, I inquired its name,— " *Atâkah.*" Then passing my finger along the whole line, I put the question again ;—" *Kûl Ras Atâkah,*" replied my camel-driver, rather amazed at my igno-rance, and, waving his hands impatiently, as he pointed to the whole headland, from end to end,—" *Kûl Ras Atâkah,*—it is all *Ras Atâkah.*"

In the course of the afternoon we came within sight of the sea,—a mere gleam of blue amid the yellow sand,—yet bright and beautiful. We could discern three large vessels riding at anchor; but, saving these, no signs of humanity or of life. Yet across that blue stripe, and probably just at the point where these vessels were lying, moved the hosts of Israel, those very waters rising up on their right and left to form a liquid wall, and the pillar-cloud moving before them to lead them through. Each part of the scene seemed sacred, —desert, mountain, sea, and sky.

The rapidity with which the sun sinks down, when once it begins its descent, struck us. Instead of taking a long slanting curve as with us, it drops almost right down " in western cadence low,"—" hasting with prone career,"—not indeed to " the ocean isles,"—but to the desert hills. The speed, too, with which the shadows lengthen is very much greater than with us; and to this, no doubt, is the allusion of Psalm cii. 12,—" My days are as a shadow which declineth,"—or more truly, " My days are as the shadow which is *inclined;*" that is, which has begun to lengthen, and which goes on rapidly lengthening till it has vanished wholly.

About six, the sun set brightly behind *Ras Atâkah,* whose summits continued to glisten with the soft purple radiance, long after its eastern slopes were hung with shadows. We paced on in the cloudless moonlight, for every cloud had disappeared, and the moon, almost right above our heads, hardly cast the shadow of either man or beast upon the sand. It was a splendid scene, —just such a night as we could have wished to be our first upon the shore of such a sea.

As we came nearer, we joined in singing first the Hundredth Psalm, Mr Beddome leading the song, and filling the desert air with the old melody. We then sung together,

> Sound the loud timbrel o'er Egypt's dark sea,
> Jehovah has triumphed, his people are free.

I shall say nothing as to the performance, save that at such an hour and in such a scene, it could not fail both to stir and to solemnize.

Had the light allowed, we ought to have seen before this, on our left, the Castle of *Ajrûd*, an old fort upon the pilgrim-route,—or as it is called the *Haj-road*,—to Mecca. But all in the distance was invisible. Even *eastern* moonlight cannot throw back the veil of night. The sun of Egypt and the sun of the desert seemed certainly to widen the horizon of day, but that of night, under the brightest moonshine, was no wider than our own. The "desert circle" in which Thalaba and his mother are made to wander, did not spread to any greater breadth than upon our own brown moors.

We stopped a few minutes at a great public well called *Bîr-Sueiss*, the well of Suez, a little way from the town of Suez, to give our camels drink. Most of them drank greedily; but one or two did not, though

F

they had been without water for nearly five days. The
well looks like a large fort, with water-troughs outside
the walls. It was a strange moonlight scene,—the old
walls above us,—camels and Arabs clustering under
them upon the yellow sand. The whole cavalcade soon
moved off along the plain. We encamped about eight,
hard by the town, and still nearer the sea.

We had now reached the shore of that sea up to
which God led Israel. This was our direct route to
Sinai, but it was not *theirs*. Had it been a straight
road to that mountain that they were seeking, they
would have kept more to the east, and there would have
been no need of crossing the sea at any point. In coming up to the sea at all, they were taking a circuit,—a circuit which, without any compensating advantage, threw
them upon their enemies, and made their position most
perilous. But in going south along the western margin
of the sea for miles, as they did, they were doing more
than taking a circuit. They were *deliberately* interpos-
ing the sea between them and Sinai,—and voluntarily
imposing upon themselves the necessity for crossing a
gulf which they could easily have avoided, thereby
making their extrication almost impossible. Had any
general done so with his army, he would have been
declared either mad or utterly ignorant of the country.
But Moses knew the region well. He had more than
once gone to Sinai, and was fully acquainted with the
way. He could not but know that he was misleading
Israel, unless he was conscious of divine guidance all the

way,—guidance which superseded and overruled his own judgment.

Suppose that, in the time of Rome's early invasion of our country, the Roman army under Agricola had been compelled to retreat from the Grampians upon Perth, intending from that to fall back on Edinburgh, what should we have thought of Agricola, had he led his troops eastward to the shores of Fife, and set them down on the sands of Burntisland, with eight miles of sea between them and the city, when by pursuing a more southward march he would have secured as near a route, without a sea to cross or an enemy to face? It would have been accounted the most thorough blunder that was ever committed by a general. Moses was precisely in these circumstances. His object was to reach the Sinaitic desert, yet he turns away from it and throws a broad sea between himself and that desert! Only one thing can account for this, and acquit him of the greatest folly ever manifested by the leader of a people. That one thing is, that it was at the direct command of God that all this was done. God's purpose was to shew his power both to Israel and to their enemies. For this end he led them by a way which *required* the special and supernatural forthputting of that power. What is the cleaving of the sea, or the levelling of a mountain, or the drying up of a river to Him? *Man* is not entitled to lead others into difficulties in order to shew his skill and power in their deliverance; for he cannot calculate upon being able to effect his object in any circum-

stances. But it is otherwise with God. And Israel's
march down the western shore of the Red Sea is one of
the most striking examples of such a procedure. There
was need of a stupendous miracle for many reasons. It
was needed to overthrow the last remains of Egypt's
pride, as well as to overawe them in all time to come.
It was needful in order to strike alarm into the nations
around ; and it was needful in order to give Israel
one proof more,—the crowning proof of all,—of what
Jehovah was ready to do in their behalf. By this was
Israel in after ages furnished with matter of thankful
song to all generations,—

> To Him who divided the Red Sea into parts;
> For his mercy endureth for ever.
> And made Israel to pass through the midst of it;
> For his mercy endureth for ever.

Such were some of our speculations as we were skirting the spacious plain that stretches down from *Ras
Atâkah* to the sea. We seemed to trace the whole
march of Israel up to the point where the mountains
stayed them,—and looking at it in all its parts, we came
to the conclusion, that either there was in this case a
most enormous blunder or a most signal miracle,—a
miracle deliberately fore-intended,—a miracle which
owes its magnitude to the peculiarly circuitous march
which Israel was commanded to take. Deny the miracle,
and you make this circuitous route a piece of reckless
folly, or pure ignorance on the part of Moses. Dilute
the miracle till you have brought it to a minimum by

means of an extraordinary ebb tide, and you still have the march to account for,—and to account for in a way which brings no glory to God, and allows small credit to Moses for anything but incapacity. It is only by admitting the miracle in full that you clear up all mystery, and make the narrative as consistent and intelligible as the event is marvellous and divine. How little is gained by assailing one miracle in a book which relates a thousand! What a poor thing it is to clip and pare off all the edges of miracle in order to make it look like a natural event! And what a cowardly state of mind is indicated by the attempt to reduce a miracle to its minimum before consenting to believe it, or to avow your belief of it. The admission of the smallest amount of the supernatural is in truth the admission of the greatest amount, for the direct interposition of the divine arm to raise or to smoothe a ripple, which would not othewise have been raised or smoothed, is as truly a miracle, as to cleave the broad ocean in twain. The question of the miraculous is not as to the amount of power put forth, but as to the direct interference of that power. Why should a man who believes in a God be afraid to believe in a miracle? The Bible is a narrative of miracles, and you can only drive out the supernatural from its events by thrusting the non-natural into its words.

CHAPTER VI.

Suez, Thursday, Jan. 17. 1856.—Rose about seven
and went out for a walk and a survey. Strolled among
the sandy hillocks and by the edge of a small arm of
the sea which went up beyond our tents. The sun was
just rising in the clear east, with nothing to intercept
the brilliance of his beams, as they came down over the
level breadth of as calm a sea as ever bid welcome to an
eastern dawn. No scene of morning could better illustrate the figure of Zophar the Naamathite, when speaking of the righteous passing out of tribulation into gladness—" Thou shalt shine forth, thou shalt be as the
morning." (Job xi. 17.) The sky was just parting
with that soft purple which in these climes is peculiarly
its tinge before the sun has risen. The bold cliffs of
Atâkah, just fronting the East, were coming slowly out,
revealing the innumerable precipices, and ravines, and
steeps, which darkness had hidden. What a rich blaze
of sunlight it was, that seemed to be flung against that
noble headland ! Just such a blaze as Israel must have

seen from the opposite coast in that morning when they found themselves safe from the pursuer, and with this same *Ras Atâkah*, this "mountain of deliverance" full in view, they sang the song of thankful gladness to their Almighty Deliverer.

> " Oh, welcome came the cheerful morn to shew
>   The drifted wreck of Zoan's pride below ;
>   The mangled limbs of men, the broken car,
>   A few sad relics of a nation's war." *

The Indian steamer was now in sight, and the rude telegraph (not electric) of the Transit Company was working to send the intelligence to Cairo. Our dragoman quite lost his temper with the dogs of Suez, which had eaten his mutton and carried off his fowl during the night. This was no great loss to us, as the sand-storm of the preceding day had so impregnated everything with sand that we were not sorry to have our teeth spared the pain and the risk of chewing these articles,— especially as it seemed of little consequence to dogs or Arabs what amount either of sand or dirt might be mingled with their food. Our tents were spread out to dry in the sun, as they had got thoroughly soaked with

---

* Heber's " Passage of the Red Sea." In a previous line he had spoken of the sun's "latest ray" fading upon " Edom's hills." The hills of Edom, properly so called, are at least 150 miles off, and could not have reflected the sun to the Egyptian desert. In a famous German picture of Israel's triumph, Moses, Aaron, &c. are represented as standing on a lofty *precipice* overhanging the sea, while the *Pyramids* appear in the background ! There are no such precipices on the eastern shore, and the Pyramids must be about 90 miles distant !

two nights' rain. Life in the "tented field" does well
enough in fine weather, but wet tents, wet clothes, wet
bedding, make one glad of a more substantial roof than
canvas. After breakfast our dragoman got his temper
ruffled again by our cook, a poor ignorant creature, half
French half Arab, both in language and in race, who
could do nothing but blunder his master's orders and
break his dishes. Haji Ismâel beat him severely with
a large stick,—the first thing that came to hand. "I'm
in the desert now," said he to us, "and I must be
master; when I'm on business I don't know my own
father or mother." There was some truth in this, though
we half pitied the poor Frenchman; and the latter part
of the speech reminded us of Deut. xxxiii. 9, "who said
unto his father and to his mother I have not seen him,
neither did he acknowledge his brethren, nor know his
own children."

We soon made the discovery that these beatings were
common things,—quite the usual appendages of a reproof when the dragoman had lost his temper. After
vociferation and gesticulation, enforced by the furious
flashes of Arab eyes, had exhausted themselves, he would
rush upon his victim with any implement of wood or
iron that might lie in his way. Nor was there any re-
sistance or apparent resentment; the assault seemed
counted on as a matter of course. "Beating with
stripes" seems strange to us; but an eastern thinks
little of it; the frequent allusions to it in Scripture as
the punishment of servants, shew how ancient the prac-

tice is. "If the wicked man be worthy to be *beaten*,
the judge shall cause him to lie down to be *beaten* before his face," (Deut. xxv. 2 ; see also Luke xii. 47).
As the beating is the legal mode of punishment in the
east, so it is the method adopted by those who take the
law into their own hand. It certainly was effectual, so
far as we could judge. The Bedaween would dispute a
matter with our dragoman, and return all his angry
words with vociferations equally emphatic ; but the
stick never failed to stop their mouth, and it was with
this that he generally silenced all obstinate disputants.
He boasted that he had beaten one of our tallest and
strongest Arabs three times in the course of our first
fortnight in the desert. I may notice that he carried
no sword, which was perhaps well ; but his companion
was a thick, though short, black staff of ebony, carved
at the head, and grooved along its length. He was not
a "man of war," though he was a "man of strife."
Though the Arabs were armed,* yet they drew no sword
against him at any time, but submitted to his beatings
quite peaceably.

We spent some hours in Suez or *Suweis*, a huge
market-depôt for the goods of the east and west. Without water and without harbour it can never be a city.
A great *Khân* it has been, and it is likely to be greater

---

* "They all hold swords,
Expert in war :
Every man his sword upon his thigh,
Because of fear in the night."—(*Song of Sol.* iii. 8.)

yet ; but nothing more.   No Alexandria nor Cairo will
ever rise here.   The unceasing sand-drift filling up the
sea may possibly force it down the sea-coast in quest of
better harbourage, for no craft of deeper draught than
a lighter can at present touch at its quay.   It would
certainly be better to anticipate this and turn the railway from Cairo downwards to the south-east point of
Atákah, erecting there a harbour round whose deeper
waters a city might gather.

We watched the landing of the passengers from India,
—many of them pale and scorched,—but bright with
the prospect of home.   The scene was just the reverse
of what we had witnessed in the Mediterranean.   There
the faces were fresh with the glow of the north, but there
seemed sadness over them, in the remembrance of home
left behind, and we saw tears dropping from the eyes of
mothers, on the letters which they were writing to children from whom they had just parted.   After the passengers came their luggage, and after it followed the
vessel's cargo, consisting of all India's varied stores,
chiefly bales of raw silk on its way to Marseilles and
Lyons.   Two or three hundred camels were waiting to
convey these across the desert.   In them we had the
finest specimens of the camel that we had seen, beyond
anything that the streets of Cairo or the plains of Egypt
had furnished.   The camel has a peculiar look of meek-
ness and melancholy about his face, specially in his mouth
and eye.   He has no touch of dry humour or demure
drollery about him as the donkey most certainly has, all

over his face; yet he is not dull and unintelligent. Mute patience is his characteristic, though we have been witnesses of the angry look and the surly growl. His abundance of bone and sinew does sometimes make him look gaunt and shabby. But each one of this great herd now waiting for the freightage of India, was, though as meek as ever, noble and stately, in good condition, and fit for any amount of work,—very different from ours, which looked meagre, both in size and appearance, when compared with these well-fed burden-bearers, which, in spite of wind, or rain, or heat, were to pursue their journey of eighty miles, night and day, without the stoppage of an hour. The scene in the yard where they were loaded was quite peculiar. The confusion, the strife, the uproar, the noise of Arab tongues, are quite indescribable. Yet the patient camel stands in the midst of it,—not at all disconcerted or frightened. He kneels and rises at the *word* or rather the *sound* of command, for it is by a peculiar guttural sound that the command is given. In less than half an hour the sounds have ceased, the yard is empty, the crowd has separated, the camels are on their way to Cairo.

In the course of the forenoon I bathed in the Red Sea, a little way from the town. The water was shallow, but cool and pleasant.

Embarked about three, in a clumsy Arab boat capable of holding a dozen. We moved down, but neither by sail nor oar. There was no wind for the former and no depth of water for the latter. We advanced by pushing

with a long pole,—which process was accompanied by
some peculiar song, which, though repeated fifty times
in the course of our voyage, we could neither pick up
nor understand.   It seemed an unmeaning chant.

We went slowly down, keeping *Jebel Atâkah* on one
side, and *Jebel Er-Rahah* on the other,—getting a nearer
view of the point of the former, where Israel must have
entered the sea.   We were sailing over the debris of
Pharaoh's host, over chariots and chariot-wheels; might
we not see gleaming from under these shallow waters
the gilded horse-trappings,—the helm, the spear, the
shield, the torn banner, with its soiled and broken staff?

The shoals all seemed to run up and down the gulf,
not *across* it.   The *lie* of the immense sand-banks is
pretty nearly north and south, with channels of deeper
water between them.   This struck me as another objection to the *shoal* theory of Robinson.   For though
the shoals and sand-banks are frequent, yet they do not
run *across* the sea, so as to have formed a highway for
Israel to tread.   Speaking in usual phrase, it would be
a thousand chances to one that there should be any long
and continuous sand-bank running across.   Even though
these had been left dry by the ebb, there would be deep
water between.

The great triangular plain on which Israel was caught
as in a net by Pharaoh, stretched to our right, walled
in by the mountains on one side and the sea on the
other.   Pharaoh is represented as saying, " they are entangled in the land, the wilderness hath shut them in,"

(Exod. xiv. 3). Knowing as he must have done, their belief that they were the heirs of Canaan, he expected that they would have marched straight into it by the short desert, so that they would have been soon beyond his reach. When he heard that they were not marching northward " by the way of the Philistines " (Exod. xiii. 17), but southward, he immediately concluded that they were within his grasp. " They are entangled in *the land*," (literally " they are perplexed with the land ") " the *wilderness* hath shut them in " (literally " hath imprisoned them.") It seemed as if they could not escape him ; for he thought it impossible that they could march far south, knowing the mountain-range that was before them, and he deemed it equally impossible that they could attempt the desert. As soon as he learned that they had not gone northward into Canaan, he felt sure of their being his prey. His object was to get between them and *Canaan*, not between them and the wilderness. He did not suppose it possible that two millions of people would march into the wilderness ; for that, according to the calculation of any Egyptian, would just be to perish with thirst and hunger. On the ground of this passage alone we should be inclined to object to the theory which makes them turn the western flank of Atâkah and march down Wady Tawârik. In this case it would not be the *wilderness*, but the *land* alone that would " imprison" them.

Our Arabs called the sea not the " Red Sea," but *Bahr-Malak*, the *Salt Sea*, in contrast to the *Bahr* of

Egypt, that is, the Nile. Every few minutes varied the
scene,—the clouds altered as the sun got low, and put on
a darker tinge; the sky took on a silky softness richer
than anything we had seen at home; the ridges of the
hills came sharply out, with all their dark ravines; till
at length the sun went down behind *Atâkah*, and the
reflection of the last rays went and came, with a dull
purple brightness, quivering for miles over the still face
of the passive blue. Blue, I have called the sea,—yet
not strictly so, save in the far distance. It is neither a
red sea nor a *blue* sea; but emphatically green,—yes,
green, of the most brilliant kind I ever saw. This is
produced by the immense tracts of shallow water, with
yellow sand beneath, which always give this green to the
sea, even in the absence of verdure on the shore or sea-
weeds beneath. The *blue* of the sky and the *yellow* of
the sands meeting and intermingling in the water, form
the *green* of the sea,—the water being the medium in
which the mixing or fusing of the colours takes place.

At length about seven o'clock we reached our land-
ing-place, and were carried ashore on the backs of Arabs.
Our camels had been sent round the head of the sea,
early in the day, and were to meet them at Ayûn
Mûsa. So after satisfying our boatmen, we set off to
walk along the sand, with our dragoman and two or
three of our Arabs as guides.

The walk was fine. There was the bright light of a
moon now in her second quarter, with broken drifts of
cloud that coursed along, and for a moment obscured its

face. These changes from moonlight to shadow, and from shadow to moonlight, give fine effect to the desert scene,—for it was one vast plain of level sand that we were now traversing. I have seen moonlight on the mountains ; I have seen moonlight on the moors ; I have seen moonlight on the sea ; but I never saw anything so vividly yet so mildly brilliant as moonlight on the yellow sands of Arabia. There were just three great breadths or masses of colour,—the sky, the moonshine, and the sand, without anything of intermediate or contrasting hue to mar the effect of these,—no rock, no tree, no patch of dark soil. These three, the blue, the yellow, and the white, had the whole scene to themselves, without a rival above, or beneath, or around. Their unbroken fusion into each other, seemed to throw out a sort of intermediate brightness, belonging to all, yet distinct from each, and to produce an atmosphere of the softest and most mellow splendour I had ever seen. The blue was softer yet darker than usual, the white was more intense, the yellow purer yet more vivid in its tinge, while, apart from these, there was a restless lustre filling the whole air, as if, in the braiding of these colours into one, their various threads were giving out their peculiar glow, which as the big clouds hurried across, alternately lost and regained its richness.

We reached our tents about nine. The night-breeze was stirring among the palms and tamarisks,—taking away the loneliness and lifelessness of the desert. A few lights were visible, a few inhabitants of the village were moving near our tents. The sky was clear and a silent dew was falling. Everything looked pleasant ;—and we felt how much we had to give thanks for to our loving God, who had thus far brought us on our journey in peace. Our tents were pitched perhaps in the very spot where Israel's were, when they sang the song of Moses and of Miriam :—

> I will sing unto Jehovah, for he hath triumphed gloriously :
> The horse and his rider hath he thrown into the sea.
> Jehovah is a man of war, Jehovah is his name.
> Pharoah's chariots and his host hath he cast into the sea ;
> His chosen captains also are drowned in the Red Sea.
> The depths have covered them :
> They sank into the bottom as a stone.

On these sands were strewn the wrecks of Egypt's chivalry. Israel indeed waited not to gather the spoil. They needed it not, for their trembling oppressors had at once conceded their just claims, and sent them away with wages and with gifts.* But we could imagine the scene presented by these sands for many a day, as robes, and girdles, and gems of the costliest kind (for it was the peerage of the land that perished there), with fragments of the various furniture of war, were washed ashore to become the spoil of the Ishmaelite. God's people were not to be the gatherers of Egypt's fragments. There were " wreckers" at hand for these, as it is written :—

> Thou hast broken the heads of leviathan,
> Thou hast given him for food to the dwellers of the wilderness.

---

* Exod. xi. 2, the transaction is not one of borrowing but of demanding a right.

As to the passage of the Red Sea by Israel at low tide, and when the waters were driven back by the wind, I may add a few remarks which, especially to a spectator of the scene, may come with some force. The lowness of the tide is a mere gratuitous assumption, intended to supersede the necessity of a miracle, or to reduce it to its minimum of the supernatural. There is no hint of anything of the kind given us by the historian, and to assume this is not merely to *invent a fact*, but it is to say that Moses has given us such a narrative as would imply a miracle, when there was no miracle at all. Now had Herodotus done such a thing, what should we have thought of his veracity ? If he stated a thing as a miracle which turns out to be a common natural phenomenon, and which he knew quite well to be no miracle,—what opinion should we have of his *honesty ?* If, then, Moses narrates a thing as a miracle,— or even if he narrates it *ambiguously,*—when he knew well there was no miracle at all, —is he writing honestly ? Is he a narrator or an inventor ? Now Moses has certainly narrated the passage of the Red Sea in a way such as to make all his readers in every age believe that he was relating a miracle. If he meant no miracle, there has seldom been a narrative so fitted to deceive,—a narrative which has been so successful in deceiving millions for more than three thousand years,—and that in a matter of the most solemn kind ; for the question is not one as to the depth or breadth of water, it is one as to divine agency,—it is the same question as has been raised by neology, as to

G

whether Christ's healing of the sick was the result of supernatural power, or of superior skill in medicine.

So explicit is the language of the narrator* that it has
led all subsequent writers, down *almost* to our own day,
to believe that a supernatural event actually took place.
It is certain that all Israel at the time believed that a
vast miracle had been wrought for them ; and it was
of no *ebb-tide* that Moses and Miriam and Aaron spoke
when they led the mighty song of Israel's happy praise,
lifted up within view of those waters through which a
way had been cut for them :—

> Pharaoh's chariot and host hath he cast into the sea :
> His chosen captains hath he drowned in the Red Sea.
> The ABYSSES have covered them,
> They went down to the DEPTHS like a stone.
> *   *   *   *   *
> By the blast of thy nostrils STOOD UP THE WATERS,
> Gathered as a mighty heap were THE FLOODS,
> Congealed were the ABYSSES in the heart of the sea.

What sort of man does Dr Robinson take Moses to be,
who could thus declaim about an ebb-tide and shoal-
water, uttering big words which meant nothing.   But I
forget.   It was not Moses who spake these words ; it
was the Holy Ghost.   It was easy for Rosenmuller to
say, " every body knows that this expression was by no
means to be taken in their proper sense ; they are merely
the description of an ebb-tide ;"† but it was hardly to be

* " The waters were A WALL unto them on the right hand and on the
left."—Exod. xiv. 21, 22, 29.
† Scholia in Exodum.

expected that a man so reverent towards Scripture as the American traveller should have spoken much in the same way.

Joshua, too, must have been deceived, or lent himself to deceive others ; for he speaks of this event forty years after, as a miracle, nay, as a miracle precisely of the same kind as the division of the Jordan. In the case of the Jordan there were no shoals nor ebbs to do the work, for the crossing of that river occurred when it was deepest, broadest, and most rapid. If Joshua speak the truth, in very deed there was a miracle of no ordinary kind, as every one must know who has tried its depths or looked upon the rush of its headlong waters. Israel crossed it at the time when it overflowed its banks, at which time it would be impossible to cross it. No swimmer could breast it, no boat could stem it. Yet Israel's myriads walked calmly through ; for as soon as the feet of the priests touched the stream, the waters were cut off and stood up as an heap.* Surely any one who believes the Bible must admit the literality of this miracle. Nay, whatever be the extent of his faith in inspiration, he will at least admit that *Joshua believed the miracle.* Well,—this very Joshua, who was witness of both scenes, makes mention of both, and declares that the passage of the Red Sea and the passage over Jordan, were both of them miracles *precisely of the same kind ;*—nay, he commands Israel to tell it

---

* " They shall stand up in one great heap," or wall—the same word as is used by Moses in reference to the Red Sea. (Josh. iii. 13, 14, 16.)

to their sons and to their sons' sons, that these were two stupendous miracles, wrought in the same way by the hand of God. "Then ye shall let your children know, saying, Israel came over this Jordan on dry land. For the Lord your God dried up the waters of Jordan from before you, until ye were passed over, *as the Lord your God did to the Red Sea, which he dried up from before us*, until we were gone over." (Josh. iv. 22, 23.) This is explicit enough. Joshua believed both events to be miracles, and miracles *the same in kind*. Joshua sought to make all Israel, to the latest generation, believe the same. Could Joshua have known anything of the "shoals" and "the ebb-tide?" If he did, where was his truthfulness?

But there were others at this time who had heard of the miracle, and believed it too. Rahab of Jericho and her fellow-citizens received the tidings of it, and took all literally. "We have heard how the Lord *dried up the water of the Red Sea for you*, when ye came out of Egypt." (Josh. ii. 10.) The inhabitants of Jericho would certainly not be disposed to give Israel the credit of greater miracles than they could help; yet they believed the supernatural division of the sea. They do not seem to have got the hint about the ebb-tide. How it would have comforted and soothed them in their terror!

But there were others still who believed the miracle in all its greatness. These, too, were Israel's enemies, who would gladly have denied it and been truly thank-

ful for the theory of the " ebb-tide." From several
notices in the book of Joshua, we learn that the whole
inhabitants of Palestine were filled with fear because of
what they had heard of God's doings for Israel at the
Red Sea. Would any such terror have possessed them
had they not fully believed the miracle?

In latter ages, too, we find that men were equally deceived as to this occurrence; so that even if Moses
description does not necessarily infer a miracle, it certainly led them to suppose that he meant it to be so
understood. David so understood it :—

> Come and see the doings of God :
> Terrible of deed is he towards the sons of Adam.
> He turned the sea into dry land :
> Through the flood they passed on foot.—Ps. lxvi. 5, 6.
>
> Thou hast divided by thy strength the sea.
> Thou hast broken the heads of the dragons in the waters.—
> Ps. lxxiv. 13.
> He cleft the sea;
> And he made them to pass through;
> Yea, he made the water to stand as a heap (or wall).—
> Ps. lxxviii. 13.
> He rebuked the Red Sea also,
> And it was dried up.
> Yea he made them walk in its depths.
> As in the wilderness.—Ps. cvi. 9.
>
> To Him who divided the Red Sea into parts :
> For his mercy endureth for ever.—Ps. cxxxvi.13.

Not only were David and Asaph thus misled and made
to mistake a journey across sand at ebb-tide for a mira-

culous cleaving of the waters ; but Isaiah equally mistook the matter, and magnified into a miracle what must have been an everyday occurence to the dwellers on that coast.   He thus spoke :—

> Where is He who BROUGHT THEM UP OUT OF THE SEA.
>   *   *   *   *   *
> Leading them by the right hand of Moses
> With his glorious arm, CLEAVING THE SEA before them.
> To make himself a name everlasting;
> Leading them IN THE ABYSSES,
> As a horse in the plain.—(Isa. lxiii. 11–13.)

Nehemiah, too, evidently believed it to be thoroughly miraculous, " Thou didst divide the sea before them, so that they went *through the midst of the sea* on the dry land ; and their persecutors thou threwest into the deeps, as a stone into the mighty waters," (ix. 11).

In like manner it is evident that the Apostle Paul was misled to speak in the same strain as psalmists and prophets had done before him,

> " They all passed through the sea."—(1 Cor. x. 1.)

Nay, he singles out this passage through the sea as a thing which only *faith* could have effected, " By faith they passed through the Red Sea as by dry land." (Heb. xi. 29.)   Surely it was no very marvellous act of faith to walk over sands which the ebb-tide had left dry.

Were all these " holy men" mistaken ? Did they magnify into the supernatural what was one of the most natural of all events ? Had they actually the hardihood to construct a stupendous miracle out of such a common thing as an ebb-tide? And did the God of truth allow them to write in his Book of truth words which were either wretched bombast or a vainglorious lie? Most assuredly Moses, and David, and Asaph, and Isaiah believed the cleaving of the Red Sea to be one of the greatest miracles ever wrought on earth. They had no idea of an ebb-tide and shoals. Dr Robinson and others may say that they were mistaken in their belief of the miracle.* If that position be taken up, then I understand the state of the question,—and cer-

---

* I hardly know whether I might not couple Mr Stanley's name with that of Dr Robinson and other deniers of the miraculous cleaving of the Red Sea. Mr Stanley is brief and cautious, and has balanced his statements with such care that one is at a loss to understand his precise opinion. Yet a reader of his volume is made to feel that, in believing the miraculous passage far down the sea, in opposition to the more natural one far up, at the ebb of the tide, he is not taking the philosophical view of the subject, and that he is also adopting a modern theory in preference to ancient opinion! Why Mr Stanley both here and elsewhere should quote the authority of the Septuagint when it *contradicts* the Hebrew, one is at a loss to see. He refers to it in order to *neutralize* the express statement of the Hebrew. The Hebrew gives *east* wind, and the Septuagint *south*,—which are we to believe? Mr Stanley has not *said* that we must give up the former; but he has so written that we are left to conclude that, in the absence of corroboration from the latter, the former is not to be depended on. He refers also not seldom to the traditions of the Greek Church, and without telling us exactly what weight he attaches to them, he takes great pains to place them upon record, and so to colour them that they win the reader's favour by a beauty of complexion and a grace of form altogether fictitious and deceptive. I do not suppose that Mr Stanley believes them, but I feel some difficulty in knowing whether he wishes his readers to receive them or not. He himself does not found any argument upon them; but he so introduces them that many of his readers will do what he has not ventured upon doing.

tainly, *it is the only real question before us,* viz., whether the opinion of the sacred writers as to such a matter of fact *is to be depended on?* It is impossible to explain away their language, or to evade it by pronouncing it the exaggeration of poetry or the license of oriental figure. These holy men believed in the literal and miraculous cleaving of the depths.

Nor is this a question as to *verbal* inspiration. I confess that I do not see how we can have the *thoughts* of God if we have not his *words;* so that I might say " these are the words of God himself regarding this miracle, and he could not be mistaken, nor employ ambiguities of expression, of the most deceptive kind." But this is not after all the question. Suppose that the very words are not infallibly inspired,—suppose that they are the mere words of fallible men,—still they are words *which were evidently meant to express a miracle.* The *thought* or *opinion* of the writers in the above case was that there had been a miracle. Attach what *value* you please to their words,—still the *meaning* is as obvious as any meaning can be; and it is with the *meaning,* not with the *value* or *quality* of the words, that our argument has to do.

The only answer to all this is that the words are inaccurate and exaggerated. But what authority has any one to pronounce the language of another inaccurate? If a man is prepared to *prove* them inaccurate by personal observation, or by other history, or by their involving an impossibility, let the evidence be stated in full. The advocates of the non-miraculous have not attempted this line of proof. So that, in the absence of such evidence, we must avow our belief in the entire accuracy of the language employed in the statements cited above. Respecting this there can be little doubt. These writers *believed* in a miraculous division of the Red Sea, and *they have said so.* Let Rationalism step in here and shew that Moses, and Joshua, and David, and Isaiah, and Paul were wrong in their *belief.* Their language is explicit enough. It is upon the matter of their *belief* that the question must turn. And that question involves in it not the fallibility of men, but the untruthfulness of God. For if God has spoken through them *in any sense*, then *he* certainly meant us to understand that the passage of the Red Sea was altogether supernatural. *He* surely would not himself speak, nor would he allow his servants to speak, in a way that would convey a totally false impression of the facts. He would not, as the God of truth, have told us that the sea stood up on either side of Israel as a wall, if he wished us to understand that the ebb-tide had swept away every drop of water on the right hand and on the left.

The denial of verbal inspiration to the Scriptures may seem a light thing, but let it be remembered that it is founded on the assumption of their *verbal inaccuracy ;* and it is almost superfluous to say that inaccuracy of words involves inaccuracy of thought and of statement, so that, according to the deniers of verbal infallibility, the Bible, though its author is God, contains inaccurate language, deals in inaccurate statement, and utters inaccurate thought. Other books are admitted to speak correctly the words and sentiments of their authors, but this alone does not convey either the words or thoughts of its author, but many things inconsistent with truth, and at variance with the author's mind! The denial of verbal inspiration may facilitate the rationalist in evading all that he is not inclined to believe, and may free him from certain trammels which are felt to be oppressive, but, founded as it is upon the assumption of inaccuracy in word and opinion, it can only lead to an utter denial of the whole book itself, if not to a denial of Him whose revelation it professes to be.

If the Korân does not contain Mahomet's words, and does not accurately represent his sentiments, of what value is it as an exposition of Mahommedanism? If the Bible does not utter the words of God, and if it does not accurately represent his mind, of what use is it as a revelation from God? And what must be his character, who could give to his poor blind creatures a volume professing to come from himself, yet awanting in that most essential of all things in authorship,—a true statement of facts and an accurate representation of the author's mind.*

---

* In the above argument I have kept to one point, which I think has not been sufficiently taken up,—viz., the *veracity* of the language of Scripture. But besides this, one cannot but ask (1.) How could an ebb-tide secure a passage for two millions, seeing they would require much longer than six hours to cross? (2.) How could they be shut in with the mountains if they were ten or twelve miles from them, as the Suez passage implies? (3.) How could the flow of the tide account for the destruction of

Ayûn Mûsa. Friday, Jan. 18.—Rose between six and seven. Though there had been rain during the night, which awoke us more than once, the morning was clear and the air pleasant. The east was beginning to be streaked with the pale red, which betokened immediate sunrise. I walked for some time in various directions on the undulating sands, noting the different views and trying to reach the sea, which, however, I found to be too far off. I visited the group of palms spoken of by travellers, and marked a considerable variety of trees in the gardens beside where we were encamped.

I tried to mark the passage of Israel to the sea from the point of *Atâkah,* and could not help observing how exactly an *east* wind would cut the sea just in this very line. (See Exod. xiv. 21.)

The east wind was one of God's instruments for the division of the sea, just as was also the rod of Moses. (Exod. xiv. 16.) No one thinks that the rod of Moses divided the waters, and that, therefore, there was no miracle, so it is no less idle to maintain that the east wind did so, and that, therefore, there is no need of a greater miracle than a strong east wind could perform. We

the Egyptian army ? By the time that Israel had crossed, the tide must have flowed, and if their enemies followed, they must have deliberately plunged into deep water, knowing that they would be drowned. Nothing is really gained either by denying the miracle or trying to reduce it to its minimum. To sustain and carry out the disbelief in the *one* miracle, so many other miracles are required, that only the more credulous class of minds will abandon themselves to the singular delusion.

might as truly reason that there is no intimation of a greater miracle than the rod of Moses could effect. Nay, and we might as well argue that there was no greater miracle in Christ's opening the eyes of the blind than the skilful use of clay could accomplish, and no greater miracle in the raising of Lazarus than a loud voice could work. The voice, the clay, the rod, the east wind, are not the standards by which to measure the miracle. The divine power that went along with them did the work; *they* were but signs pointing the eye to the thing done, and connecting it with the Infinite doer.

The villagers brought us some Turquoise from *Sura-bit*, for which we gave them a piastre or two. The stones were in the matrix,—of a bright green—genuine enough, but too small to be of any value. One man was busy grinding meal for the day, in the handmill,—that is, two flat circular stones, very much like what was once common enough in Scotland, where the remains of the *Quern* are often to be met with still. It is at sunrise that the operation begins, and it is the sound of new awakened activity and busy life begun. The "sound of the grinders" was "low" certainly, yet the "grinders" had not altogether ceased." (Eccles. xii. 3, 4.) The one "grinder" whom we saw at his work took away the utter silence, and made music of his own kind to us, in no unpleasant way. There was not the utter desolation elsewhere described by Jeremiah, when he says, "I will take from them the sound of the mill-stone" (Jer. xxv. 10); and by John when he says, "the sound of a mill-stone shall be heard no more at all in thee." (Rev. xviii. 22.) We did not see *women* at this work, though they seem to have been the chief grinders both in Egypt and in Palestine in other days. We read of "the *maid-servant* that is behind the mill" (Eccl. xi. 5); and also that "two *women* shall be grinding at the mill," (Matt. xxiv. 41). It seems, however, to have been a menial office, performed only by the lowest servant in the house; for when Isaiah would paint the degradation of the daughter of Babylon, he says, "take the mill-stones and grind meal." Samson was set to "*grind* in the prison-house." (Judges xvi. 21.) Job says, "let my wife *grind* unto another," (xxxi. 10). Jeremiah complains, "they took the young men to *grind.*" (Lam. v. 13.) A mill-stone, from its having a hole in the centre, would be more easily, than any ordinary stone, fastened on to a person or object in order to sink them in water; and hence our Lord's reference, "it were better that a mill-stone were tied about his neck and that he were cast into the depths of the sea." (Matt. xviii. 6.) The mill-stones which we saw in the desert were small ones; but elsewhere we saw very large ones four or five feet in diameter, reminding us of Rev. xviii. 21, "a mighty angel took up a stone like a great mill-stone, and cast it into the sea;" and yet even in such passages the point of the figure does not seem to be so much the size of the stone as its crushing and grinding power,—"on whomsoever it shall fall, it will grind him to powder." (Matt. xxi. 44.)

There are some well-cultivated gardens here, with fruits and vegetables, watered by "the wheel."

This *Sakieh*, or water-machine, which we often saw in Egypt, is turned by an ox, or by a small horse. We noticed that these animals, when engaged in turning the wheel, had their eyes bandaged, and we were told that this was to prevent their becoming *blind* by the motion. The water is raised out of a deep well by a wheel, whose revolution turns a rope to which earthenware buckets are attached at small intervals. It is probably to this wheel and these pitchers, which are necessary appendages to every large house, that Solomon refers, when he compares man to a noble palace falling into decay :—

> Ere the silver *cord* be loosed,
> Or the golden *bowl* be broken,
> Or the *pitcher* be broken at the fountain,
> Or the *wheel* broken at the cistern.—Eccl. xii. 4.

These jars empty themselves into a trough or small reservoir, out of which the water is conveyed in conduits or trenches through the garden or field. In an eastern garden each bed or compartment is surrounded with such a conduit, whose sides being made of earth, can easily be opened at any part to let in water. This is done generally by a hoe, or some such agricultural implement, but occasionally, though rarely, by the hand or foot. I never saw the foot so employed ; but I was told it sometimes was. It has been thought that this is the allusion in Deuteronomy (xi. 10), " the land, whither thou goest in to possess it, is not as the land of Egypt, from whence ye came out, where thou sowedst thy seed, and *wateredst it with thy foot*, as a garden of herbs." It may perhaps be so,—but the foot is so seldom used in this operation that we suspect the allusion must be to some means of raising water, in which the foot of man was used instead of the ox. The *Shadûf* is used for raising water out of the river to a less height and from a less depth than the *Sakieh.* It is merely an upright pole fastened in the ground, over the top of which, as on a hinge or fulcrum, there is a crosspole, with a rope and a bucket at one end, and a corresponding rope and a heavy stone at the other. Two men, one at the bucket and the other at the stone, work the machine. Another water-machine has been already noticed as used on the Nile. It is simpler than either of the above, and used for less heights and depths than the *Shadûf.* It is a kind of basket swung between two men, sitting opposite to each other, at an interval of five or six feet. This looks like *skimming* the water up, and is a clumsy as well as inefficient plan.*

We examined the " wells of Moses," out of which all the water comes, but found them brackish and not remarkably clear. They are dug in the sand, but not regularly built. Of these Israel drank,—or at least of wells in this neighbourhood, for no where else could

---

* Dr Robinson refers to Niebuhr as giving a description of a *Sakieh* at Cairo, which was turned by the *foot.* This seems the best illustration of Deut. xi. 10.

they get water for many miles round.   The whole region
about is truly what our Lord speaks of,—"dry places," or
more literally "unwatered places." (Matt. xii. 43 ; Luke
xi. 24.)

We rode off about nine, through a fine large plain ;
but quite a plain of the desert,—no stream, no verdure ;
—at first soft sand, then hard gravel, then stones, and
all these generally of a white colour.   *Ras Atâkah*
towered upon our right, full in the morning sunshine.
No trace of a road appeared ; for though the camels do
form a track, or rather a number of parallel tracks, yet
the drifting sand obliterates them, or the rain washes
them out.   Still the way-marks are preserved everywhere,—consisting of small heaps of stones set up on
each side, which are carefully preserved by the Bedaween ; for even *they* might at times be at a loss as to
the way, so great is the sameness of the region, for miles
on every hand.   Jeremiah's words came into mind,
" Set thee up *way-marks* ; make thee high heaps, set
thine heart toward the high way, even the way which
thou wentest," (xxxi. 21).   The sand does not seem to obliterate these, or if it does they are renewed from time
to time.   They were always a welcome sight to us, assuring us that we were in the right track, for at times we
almost began to ask whether even our Arabs were sure
of their way ; so waste did the desert appear, without a
mark or foot-trace of any kind whatsoever.

About four miles from *Ayûn Mûsa,* we crossed
Wady Marazah, at least so our Arabs called it, though

I observe other travellers speak of crossing *Wady er-Reiyâneh*, or " *the wet*," at this point. Then we passed *Wady Kurdhiyeh*, about two miles farther on. The Red Sea still continued in sight, sometimes before us, sometimes at our right hand, bright with the gleam of noon, while the piles of Egyptian mountains beyond threw up a background to the view, which gave a *finish* to the scene, and took off the monotony of the desert.

The way for some time became very stony, while round us there rose an amphitheatre of sand. About four o'clock we got into a spacious plain of hard sand and stone, of which there must have been four or five miles on either side of us. Then came *Wady Sûdhr*, and in the distance on the left *Tâset Sûdhr*, or cup of *Sûdhr*,—a somewhat lofty mountain, peaked and slightly flattened at the top.* *Sûdhr* and *Shur* are possibly the same ; and, if so, then it took its name from the desert, of which we read, " Moses brought Israel from the Red Sea, and they went into the wilderness of *Shur*." (Exod. xv. 22.) A little way on we crossed a small hollow, like the shallow channel of a stream, from which but recently the rain had been dried up. Here, as well as elsewhere in the desert, that passage came up before us,—

> " My brethren have dealt deceitfully as a brook,
> As the stream of brooks they pass away ;
> What time they wax warm, they vanish :
> When it is hot, they are consumed out of their place."

* An old traveller speaks of Wady Sûdhr as noted for its *serpents ;* but we saw none.

As we were not counting on rain nor depending on the pools, we were not in the condition painted in the well-known engraving of " the dried-up well." But we could imagine the awful despair of those who were reckoning on such supplies by the way and were disappointed.

> " The troops of Tema looked,
> The companies of Sheba waited for them.
> They were confounded because they had hoped ;
> They came thither, and were ashamed."—(Job vi. 19.)

And yet we could see at the same time the aptness of the figure,—

> " Thou shalt forget thy misery,
> Thou shalt remember it as waters that pass away."—
>
> (Job xi. 16.)

About five pitched our tents in *Wady Wardân*, with a tame and barren scene around us, which our canvas soon shut out.

More than once we had noticed in our early mornings dull masses of cloud in the sky. As the sun got up and gathered strength these all vanished. They did not drift away or pass to a different region of the heavens,— but they *vanished* on the spot ;—such was the absorbing power of the desert-sun. Clouds that would have brought a whole day's rain in our climate, disappeared. We were reminded of that figure in Job, " As the cloud is *consumed and vanisheth away*, so he that goeth down to the grave shall come up no more " (vii. 9).

Wady Wardân, Jan. 19.—Rose about six, and went out to walk upon the broad plain of sand stretching on every side of our tents. It was nearly dark, and all was silence ;—our Arabs were still asleep, and not a breeze was up to ruffle the still air. There was nothing to see, but there was enjoyment in the solitude, and buoyancy in the fresh dry atmosphere of these boundless sands. The sun rose in splendour, burnishing the rugged peaks in the distance, and coming down with his gay gleam upon our canvas. Returned from my walk before eight. Stood listening to the echoes of a pistol which one of our party was firing. A pistol-shot may seem a poor thing to listen to,—not so its echoes,—its echoes in such a desert ! Each far-off cliff took up the sound,—and sent round the response,—as if the Sinaitic peaks and the western ranges of the Red Sea mountains were answering each other across the quiet waves.

How quickly an encampment breaks up,—men, camels, tents, with all appendages, great and small, disappearing, and leaving only some indentations and fragments and ashes behind. One could understand the ease with which the invader of a land might sweep all such away.

> " Suddenly are my tents spoiled,
> My curtains in a moment."—(Jer. iv. 20.)

And how true the picture given of the spoiling of the sons of the desert by the king of Babylon,—

> " Arise ye, go up to Kedar,
> And spoil the men of the East !
> Their tents and their flocks shall they take away :
> They shall take to themselves their curtains,
> And all their vessels, and their camels."—(Jer. xlix. 28, 29.)

Might it not be of this sudden departure at dawn that
Job speaks,—

> " Thou shalt seek me in the morning,
> But I am not."—(Job vii. 21.)

Yet one can trace the places of encampment by their
relics, and in the case of such a multitude as Israel, it
would be very plain. What a beaten track must they
have left behind them. But the one great mark by
which they would be recognised, would be the ashes of
the altar and the blood of the sacrifice. Their path
through the desert was sprinkled with blood ; and this
they left as the way-mark,—bearing testimony to all
who should look upon it, of the great truth to which
their whole service bore witness, that " without shedding
of blood was no remission." But this thought is rather
one of anticipation, for though, no doubt, Israel had their
altar both in Egypt and when they went out of it ; yet
when they passed through this region where we then
were, their full service was not given.

We set out about half-past eight,—the morning fine,
though with a haze of cloud thrown over the sky. On
we went across *Wady Wardân*, whose flatness was soon
relieved by a lofty peaked cliff to the right,—with the
Red Sea and its farther mountains as the background.
For hours we traversed a track of stony sand, when one
of our camels fell, though with no injury to any one.
It is seldom that a camel slips or falls in rough places.
His broad spongy foot grasps all the roughnesses, nor do
they seem to incommode him, however sharp. But in

moist clay he cannot move a step, and trembles all over
as a horse when attempting to move upon ice. We
passed sandy channels, newly dry, intimating a recent
fall of rain. Then *Jebel-Areghal* with its huge slopes,
about one o'clock,—then about two, *Hor-Es-Sûdhr*,—
then *Wady-El-Amârah.*

And now begins "the great and terrible wilderness"
in reality. It is indeed horrible to look upon. There
came first towering mounds of rough sand ; then stupendous precipices of unformed half-baked rocks in awful
confusion and dismay, like the lava of some infernal
volcano ; while in the distance shot up wild brown spec-
tral mountains, which neither pen nor picture can rightly
represent.

Moving through these horrors we came to the great
"stone of the rider," or *Hajir-er-R'kab,*—to which tradition assigns some niche in the history of Moses. The
Bedaween seem to reverence it and make it a resting-
place. It is an immense fragment of rock which has
fallen from the heights above into the plain, but beyond
this it has nothing very notable about it. One sees as
rugged boulders in similar positions everywhere among
our Scottish hills. All that it did was to illustrate Job
xiv. 18, " the rock is removed out of its place," and to
remind us of Bildad's scornful question, " Shall the earth
be forsaken for thee, and shall the rock be removed out
of its place ?" (Job xviii. 4.) We examined the " Hajir "
pretty closely on all sides, and in spite of the horizontal
lie of its strata, thought that it was a fallen fragment,

and not a rock in its original situation, with its softer parts wasted away.

Soon after this we saw somewhat in the distance a figure like a stunted palm making its appearance upon an easy rising ground. We were told it was *Howârah.* We soon reached the spot and found two bushy or rather shaggy palms of low stature, with no visible stem, and a bitter well, not remarkable in any way, and of which neither man nor beast could drink. Somewhere in this neighbourhood was the *Marah* of Scripture, where the bitter waters were healed by the power of God. (Exod. xv. 23.) I do not say so merely because the waters are bitter, and because the Arabs call them *Murrah* and *Mushtaib.* The water of Ayûn Musa was also called *Murrah* or bitter, and no stress can be laid on this. Besides, seeing the waters were sweetened, might we not expect to find not bitter but sweet waters at *Marah* if we do come upon the ancient wells? But the " three days " from the time of crossing the Red Sea, would bring them to this neighbourhood. (Numb. xxxiii. 8.) It took us but two days to reach it; but they, with their flocks and their little ones, could not move so fast as we did.* Besides, the time required to reach again the

---

* Yet the statement of Moses in Deut i. 2, would indicate a rate of travelling quite as rapid as ours,—"there are eleven days' journey from Horeb, by the way of Mount Seir, unto Kadesh-Barnea." Let *Kadesh-Barnea* be placed on the most southerly of the sites which have been assigned to it, still it would take eleven days' hard travelling to reach it. We doubt if any dragoman would undertake it in less than twelve.

Red Sea after they left Marah and Elim corresponds to this ; for from the statement in Numbers (xxxiii. 10) it would appear that one day's journey brought them from Elim to the Red Sea, on their way to Sinai, which corresponds exactly with the distance between the two points. The *Marah* of Scripture could not be much farther on than *Howârah*, else Israel could not have reached it in three days, so that it must have been not far from this very palm-crowned hillock of sand, if not actually here. I cut off a palm-branch in memory of the spot to exhibit at home as a relic of Marah,—a remembrance of Israel's murmurings and God's unwearied love.

Lepsius (with others of the same class) sets aside the miracle of Marah, and tells us that it was by means of some fruit, or peel of a shrub, that Moses, quite in a natural way, made the bitter water drinkable ; and as no such amount of peel could be got at Howârah, he gives this chiefly as his reason for placing Marah at Ghurandel. But at this day, many as are the shrubs of the green Ghurandel, there are none that will sweeten bitter water ; and certainly it would take an enormous amount of peel to sweeten water for two millions. As to the recipe of the *Ghûrkûd* berries, on which some rely for their escape from the miracle, it is a mere traveller's invention, unknown to Arab or any one else in the desert. All Lepsius' peel and Burckhardt's berries would do little for such a multitude. One wonders at Dr Robinson's favour towards such childish

credulity. (Vol. i. p. 98.) Mr Stanley keeps silence.
He mentions the place but not the miracle. Yet the
miracle was no common one, and the narrative is one
of singular simplicity and beauty,—summed up in these
solemn words, which are mere mockery, if not founded on
a mighty miracle, "There he made for them a statute
and an ordinance, and there he proved them and said, If
thou wilt diligently hearken to the voice of the Lord
thy God, and wilt do that which is right in his sight . .
I will put none of these diseases upon thee which I have
brought upon the Egyptians, for I AM JEHOVAH THAT
HEALETH THEE." (Exod. xv. 26.)

Soon after this we came to an immense plain of hard
rocks. The mountains which bounded it were truly
magnificent. Their numerous summits seemed not so
much peaks as spikes or tall spires of rock, which neither
Arab nor *Gazellah* could climb, and which even the
eagle might fear to alight upon. Their vast sides,
which sloped down at a considerable angle to the plain
through which we were passing, were all furrowed and
cut up,—not by ravines,—but by enormous quarries,
which seem to have been dug, side by side in succession
for miles. Horrid splits appeared in all directions, as if
something more terrible than gunpowder had been employed to blast the rocks. It was well named a "terrible
wilderness" (Deut viii. 15), a "land of deserts and of
PITS," (Jer. ii. 6). I thought that, often as I had
looked upon the wild mountains of Scotland, I had
never before seen "ragged rocks." (Isa. ii. 21.) The

" raggedness" of Almarah is far beyond anything in Glencoe, though the heights of the mountains may be much the same. The whole scene is one of the most magnificent desolation and unmingled terror.

More than once we had seen (not to-day only, but on other days) our Arabs looking for the *shadow*, and glad when they saw it beginning to lengthen. Their desire was not like ours, to see, and note, and learn by the way, but simply to get their day's work done.

" As a servant earnestly desireth the shadow,
    And an hireling looketh for the reward of his work."—(Job vii. 2.)
" Turn from him that he may rest,
    Till he *shall accomplish as an hireling his day*."—(Job xiv. 6.)

Since leaving *Wady Sûdhr*, yesterday, the ground has continued gradually to rise, hour after hour ; but towards sunset to-day we began to desend into *Wady Ghurandel*, which is a sweet oasis in the desert,— covered with trees of all kinds, and fertilized by a stream, which retains the falling showers longer than most similar ones, and raises enough of verdure to feed some Arab flocks. About seven we pitched our tents, in the midst of the tarfa-trees, under a bright moon. We could not see the extent of the valley, but we saw verdure waving round us. It was a relief to pass out of a land of horrors, such as we had been all day traversing, into a spot of milder aspect,—and withal, so rich and green.

Wady Ghurandel, Jan. 20.—Went out about seven for a quiet hour. The birds were chirping in the tarfa-

trees, some of which were fifteen or eighteen feet high,
and were giving out a pleasant fragrance. These birds
were not the desert fowls called quails, which we frequently met with in small flocks,—not among trees, but
in the more barren plains of the desert. The palm-
trees were without number. I began to count them,
but having reached the eightieth, I desisted. They extend for more than a mile and a half down the Wady;
and must amount to several hundreds, at the lowest esti-
mate.* Most of them have four or five stems shooting
up from one root. They have been goodly trees, as the
prostrate trunks shewed, but have been cut down clean by
the ground, and the present forest is made up of shoots,
which gives a stunted and shaggy appearance to the whole.
The palm, like the olive, seems, when cut over, to send
up new shoots or suckers, so that we saw several stems
coming up from one root. Often were we reminded of
the words of Job,—

> " There is hope of a tree,
>   When it has been cut down,
>   That it will sprout again,
>   And that its shoots will not cease.
>   Though its roots wax old in the earth,
>   And its trunk die in the ground ;

* Mr Stanley writes,—" In 1853, I counted twenty at Useit and *six* at
Ghurandel." (*Sinai and Palestine*, p. 27.) If so, he must have merely
skirted the Wady ; he could not have *traversed* it. I counted the palms
with some care more than once, and noted down the numbers ; nor did I
stop till I had gone beyond the "three score and ten." Those that I
counted were all within a quarter of a mile of each other.

Through the scent of water it will bud,
And put forth boughs like a (fresh grown) plant."*—

(Job xiv. 7–9.)

From a pretty deep cutting in the channel of the
stream, (which the Arabs call a *Júrf*), effected by
the rush of the torrent, it would seem that the soil is
gravelly for many feet beneath the sand.   I thought I
was alone ; but suddenly, at the opening between some
palm-trees, came upon a Bedaween encampment, consisting of about half-a-dozen men and camels, with one
or two women and children.   The morning was quite
one of Sabbath quiet.   Yes ; it was Sabbath in the
desert,—Sabbath among the palms of *Elim !*   For there
seems little doubt that this is really *Elim.*   It is a stage
beyond Marah, and a day's journey from the Red Sea,—
just as Scripture represents.   It lies in Israel's route.   It
is just a spot for them to encamp in.   If this be not
Elim, there is no other spot on which the name can be
fixed, which so exactly suits the distances, or to which
the peculiar features so well apply.   If this be not
Elim, then Elim must have vanished from the desert,
and this new oasis risen since the days of Israel.   The
threescore-and-ten palms have multiplied into hundreds ;
but the twelve wells have diminished, and the shallow

---

* " Hope of a tree " is literally " expectation," and may probably refer
not so much to man's hope about a tree, as, by a figure, to the tree's
hope about itself, corresponding to Rom. viii. 19, 20, " the earnest *expectation* of the creature," and " subjected the same *in hope.*"   This resurrection of the tree is accomplished even by the " scent of water ; " and
truly most of the desert-trees seemed to live upon nothing more.

excavations, which now get the name of wells, are scanty and brackish springs. There is a considerable amount of running water at one part, which calls up verdure all along its margin, though it is not altogether fresh. This small stream winds along among palms and tarfas for some miles. It flows westward, and falls into the Red Sea.* In Israel's days the water was probably sweeter, though nothing is said in Scripture as to this. It is only implied that it was sufficiently sweet and copious to furnish drink to the thirsty multitude. Pleasant beyond measure must have been this valley, after so many days of weary travel; for though the pillar-cloud sheltered them from the scorching sun, still it did not make up to them for the want of verdure and fresh streams.

Marah and Elim! How near they lie to each other! Thus near to each other are the bitter and the sweet of life, the sorrow and the joy of time! Both in the same desert, and oftentimes following each other in the progress of one day or hour. The bitter too is first,—and

---

* The curious old journal of the Egyptian Prefetto, published by the Bishop of Clogher in 1753, speaks of Ghurandel (or *Garondo* as it is there called) as being Marah, not Elim. The testimony to the beauty of the Wady is very explicit. It is called a "delicious place;" and the following description is given :—"There are in this place *many palm-trees*, and in the bottom of the vale is a rivulet flowing from the aforementioned mountain, the water of which is tolerably good and in sufficient plenty, but is *not free from some bitterness*, though it is very clear." P. 15. Indeed, it would seem that when water comes up from or in any way percolates through the desert sand, it becomes unpleasant. It is only when it comes fresh from the rock as in Sinai that it is altogether pure.

then the sweet. Not first Elim and then Marah ; but
Marah first and then Elim,—first the cloud, then the
sunshine,—first the weariness, then the rest ! In token
of this we broke off a small branch of palm from one of
these Elim trees, and laying it on the similar branch
which we had brought from Marah, we tied them
together, to be kept in perpetual memorial, not merely
of the scenes, but of the truth which they so vividly
teach.

After breakfast and prayers I sat for an hour or two
in the tent reading, comparing passages, and noting
down texts for friends at home. The heat, however,
was great, and the noise of the Bedaween tongues broke
the Sabbath-calm ; so we went out about twelve to the
palm-trees for shady quiet and also for worship. A
prostrate palm-log was our first seat ; but the shade
was insufficient. So we removed to another spot where
two bushy palms, forming a sort of angle and waving
their long feathers over us, gave us complete shelter.
There we worshipped together the Lord God of Israel,
in the place where his people had done so, more than
three thousand years ago. We sang the hundredth
psalm, " All people that on earth do dwell ;" we read
the 35th of Isaiah, " the wilderness and the solitary
place shall be glad for them, and the desert shall rejoice
and blossom as the rose ;" the subject of our discourse
was Isaiah xlviii. 21, " they thirsted not when he led
them through the desert." Often did the words of the
prophets respecting the days to come recur to us while

musing here,—surrounded with some tokens of verdure in the desert. These palms and tamarisks are but the earnest of the promised fruitfulness. God will yet clothe these sands, and rocks, and naked hills. The "times of the restitution of all things" (Acts iii. 21) will do great things for these wastes. The wilderness shall become a fruitful field, and the fruitful field (such as Elim) will be counted for a forest, and esteemed as nothing in comparison with the far fresher verdure which shall cover the whole scene. Then shall come to pass what is written,

> "I will plant in the wilderness
> The cedar, the shittah-tree, and the myrtle and the oil-tree;
> I will set in the desert
> The fir-tree, and the pine, and the box-tree together."
>
> (Isa. xli. 19.)

This scanty stream and these poor wells may suffice for the wandering Bedaween or the passing traveller now, but they shall be as mere drops in the day when God renews the earth and fulfils his old promise to the desert,

> "I will open rivers in high places,
> And fountains in the midst of the valleys;
> I will make the wilderness a pool of water,
> And the dry land springs of water."—(Isa. xli. 18.)

And again,

> "In the wilderness shall waters break out;
> Yea, streams in the desert."—(Isa. xxxv. 6.)

Looking on a scene such as that before us, it seemed altogether natural to understand these words literally.

No doubt it *may be* allegorized (for what is there in Scripture that may not be subjected to this process, seeing the first chapter of Genesis and the first of Matthew have been turned into *myths ?*) ; a *natural* change may be the apt figure of a *moral* change ; but it is so only because it is itself *a real thing.* The physical restoration must be literal, *in order that* it *may be the figure* of a spiritual renewal. Adam was the *figure* of Him who was to come because he was a *real* man,—*literally* what Scripture says he was. So the renewing of the barren sands may be a figure of man's regeneration to God, but it is so in virtue of itself being literally true. And why should it be thought an incredible thing that God should literally restore creation ? Why should it be counted unlikely that Arabia should become like Syria, a region of streams and showers, a land of roses and myrtles,—that the wilderness should flourish as the garden of the Lord ? Who shall hinder that

> .   .   .   . " this earth
> Shall all be Paradise, far happier place
> Than that of Eden, and far happier days?" *

For " He turneth the wilderness into a standing water, and dry ground into water-springs ; and there he maketh the hungry to dwell, that they may prepare a city for habitation, and sow the fields, and plant vineyards, which may yield fruits of increase." (Ps. cvii. 35.)

* Milton's Par. Lost.

CHAPTER VII.

WADY GHURANDEL—WADY SALMEEN—JEBEL HAMMAM—WADY USEIT
—SERBAL—WADY THAL—WADY SHUBIEKAH—WADY TAIYEBAH
—WADY BUDRAH—WADY SIDREH—WADY MAGHARAH—WADY
MUKATTEB.

Wady Ghurandel. Monday, Jan. 21.—Awoke at
five, and looked out through the flaps of the tent. The
moon was shining in its strength, and the shadows of
the *Tarfas* lay in patches along the sand. It soon set,
however, and for half-an-hour there was darkness. Then
the sun came up without a cloud over the low sand-cliffs.
There was no mingling of the two " great lights ;" two
hours ago it was all moonlight ; an hour ago it was all
starlight ; now it is all sunshine ! On we move, starting about eight. Passed along the valley. To the left
stands an immense square block of stone, such as we
had seen on Saturday, called *Hajir-el-Gibbor*, the great
stone, being the outstanding remains of the stratum,
which happening to be harder than the rest, has resisted
the influences to which the softer parts have yielded.
Soon turned to the left through a rugged defile, and

left Wady Ghurandel behind. The defile has no name so far as we could learn; but is notable for its level stony ground, and for the flat isolated peaks on each side, produced by the abrasion of the softer sections of the rock. The morning was hot; but in this narrow pass, a breeze met us which brought down the heat, though the sun had lost none of its brightness. Moving eastward, we got up to higher ground, and came to a large piece of table-land. On each side rose hills of the boldest ruggedness,—on the left of a light brown, and on the right dark brown,—forming an amphitheatre of awful desolation. No verdure, no life, no springing seed, no budding leaf, no blithe blossom, no fragrant herb, no summer incense;—nothing to soften or to animate the scene. Woods, streams, and flowers,—what is earth without you! And *with you*, what a land would this be! But its dead scorched nakedness is terrific, though sublime beyond conception. No sunshine could make it joyous, though the cloud and the blast would certainly make it more dismal and appalling.

The heat was excessive,—reminding us of the words, " the sun beat upon the head of Jonah, that he fainted" (Jonah iv. 8). In about half an hour we descended into a lower level,—a sort of shallow basin, less rocky in itself, but girt with the same ruggedness,—

"Nothing but grey infinitude around."

Down we came lower still into a small valley, with a

I

bare, rough cone of white sandstone rising in the centre, and a smooth piece of white rock, almost level with the ground, on whose surface were cut the names and initials of travellers, ambitious of desert-fame. We stopped a few minutes to read the names, but not to carve our own. We had already refused this honour on the top of the great pyramid, when an Arab boy produced a long knife for this purpose; and it was hardly worth our while to give our names to the sand or the Bedaween, when we had already declined placing them above Pharaoh's haughty dust.

We then passed into *Wady Salmîn*, a little before ten, where we found some stunted *tarfas* and a solitary *sayâleh*, already noticed as probably the shittim-wood of Scripture, from which exudes the gum-Arabic used at home. We saw nothing, however, but the rough stem and the bare thorny branches. It hardly deserves the name of " towering" which has been applied to it, yet it is by no means meagre or dwarfish. It is bushy and branching, spreading out considerably on all sides, and at the same time rising sometimes to a height of perhaps twenty feet or more. On the right rose up *Jebel Hammâm*, " the mountain of the warm-baths," at whose base flow out the hot salt springs, like those of Tiberias; on the left *Jebel Useit*, savagely rugged. A little way on, another vast amphitheatre of sand; then, as we turned, *Jebel Hammâm* stood right before us, whose lofty brown slopes, curiously streaked with white and grey,—surmounted with fantastic peaks,—furrowed

from head to foot with ravines, and pits, and hollows,—
are quite beyond description.

Since we left Ghurandel, vegetation has been but
scanty,—no tarfas like those of that Wady cheering the
waste. This makes the rationalistic theory as to the
manna the more unlikely and untenable. If manna
were the exudation of the tarfa, certainly it would be
found where that tree most abounds, as in Ghurandel.
But it was not till Israel were two or three days beyond
this that the manna appeared. The region where that
tree is scantiest was the region where manna was first
found !

About half-past ten we crossed a dried-up water-
course running west, and then came suddenly down on
Wady Useit at eleven. It is a pleasant valley, though
much inferior to Ghurandel, with about twenty palms,
and ten or fourteen little wells,—if one might call them
by that name.* We tasted the water, but it was salt-
ish,—" murrah,"—and we noticed here, what we had
found on some preceding days elsewhere, salt incrusta-
tions all along the edges of the furrowed or broken sand.
The mountain panorama of this wady is very fine ; it is
a region of boundless desolation and hideous grandeur ;
the enormous *notches* in the hills, as if they had been

---

* How Mr Stanley has made the following statement, I do not understand :—" No one who was guided by the wish to choose the larger palm-
grove could hesitate to select *Useit*," (p. 27). I examined both with some
care, noting down everything at the moment, just as I saw it,—and I am
far under the mark when I say that the palm-grove of *Ghurandel* is ten
times the size of *Useit*.

tossed up by the shovel of some huge giant, and then pinched and kneaded all over by his fingers into the most grotesque yet grand deformities, are features of this range of which only the photograph can give any idea. The artist's pencil is at fault in the desert; and the engraver wholly fails to represent the uncouth and savage emaciation of these hunger-bitten hills,—the "looped and windowed raggedness" of their gaunt peaks and unearthly ravines. One could fancy them the scoriæ from the lake of fire,—and in their dark recesses one could think they saw the very gates of hell.

We stood for some minutes under a palm, which comforted us with its shadow,—for the heat was great. A pleasant breeze, however, from the north-west came along behind us, bringing coolness and refreshment. Not far off was another of the acacia or sayâleh trees.

At half-past eleven we reached a wide plain two miles across,—flat, and covered with small stones. Sand-ridges rose on each side, and beyond these a precipitous range of whitish brown. Far before us to the eastward rose *Sarbût-el-Jemel*, with its towering gloomy peak, while more to the south is *Jebel Serbâl*, near to *Wady Feirân*. All here is splendid desolation. At one we came to *Wady Thâl*, a pretty spacious basin sprinkled with tarfas and a few meagre palms; at the head of it is the mountain *Ras-Wady-Thâl*. At two o'clock we came to *Wady Shubeikeh*, a dried water-course, winding in a southerly direction. It has many branches and off-sets, and hence its name *Shubeikeh* or "the net."

The thermometer was 92° ; and the hot sun was beating on us, when suddenly we passed under " the shadow of a great rock." It formed a precipitous wall on our right for about a hundred yards, and gave grateful shelter in this " weary land." (Isa xxxii. 2.) But our camels seemed to love the heat, and staid not in the shade but moved on, and brought us out into the broad sunshine.

We were traversing a scene of grandeur as varied as it was matchless. First we passed through what can be called nothing else than a long succession of stupendous quarries. Then the valley takes a noble sweep, and presents a similar succession of huge terraces, overhung with scowling precipices. Then we come right upon a vast towering semicircle of rocks that seem to bar our exit, till a sudden turn to the right brings us into a more open way. The yellow cliffs give freely out their echoes to the songs or shouts of our Arabs, who seem to take a childish joy in making each rock respond to their music or their laughter. This is by far the most tortuous and singular valley we have traversed. At one place the harder parts of the vast white slope, not abraded by the rain, come out in full relief, like a row of Egyptian gods sitting in state with their hands upon their monstrous knees. At another, scores of Gothic buttresses seem planted against the walls of some enormous cathedral. Then before us a fine large tarfa-tree rises out of the sand. Then a vast semicircle of sheer precipice, some hundreds of feet in height, and which might contain a city in its noble

sweep,—with a few poor palms at the foot. Then
beyond this some twenty or thirty larger palms, above
which rises a most singular peak, first tawny sandstone, then red, then white, then red again, then black,
—till the summit pierces the blue sky with a dark yellow
spire. It must be at least six hundred feet high. This
is *Wady Taiyibeh* or " the good,"—so called from
its tarfas, palms, and water, which latter, however, we
did not taste nor see. This valley winds for about a
mile ; then the great white mountain-wall gradually
lowers itself,—notched and cracked all over as by some
superhuman axe or hammer,—leaving solitary peaks in
the valley, and ridges, like camels' backs, abutting against
it. A bright green plant or shrub inserts itself into
the crevices, and adorns the yellow rock with its fringes
or tassels of fair green. *Lussuff*, my guide called it ;
and probably it is the *hyssop-plant*, as the likeness of
the words seem to indicate. If so, it illustrated the
expression, " the hyssop that groweth on the *wall*."
(1 Kings iv. 33). In leaf it resembled the *Portugal
laurel ;* but in size it was much smaller. Israel would
have access to it, as they passed through the desert ; and
would have sufficient supply for the performance of the
ceremonies appointed for the cleansing of leprosy. They
were to take " cedar-wood and scarlet (wool or cloth)
and *hyssop*" (Lev. xiv. 4, 6, 51, 52), and dip them in
the blood of the slain bird. For such a purpose the
lussuff would suit well. The shrub, however, which is
called hyssop by the monks, is not the lussuff at all,

but a sweet-scented plant of a much smaller size which they call *Jadheh*, which we often plucked among the sands and rocks.

Suddenly at an abrupt bend rises a promontory eight hundred feet high, all scooped, notched, and hammered as before, forming itself curiously into a semicircle, and dipping to the south-west, its slopes powdered with debris, and rough with the fallen splinters of the cliffs above. Under its mighty shadow we passed about four o'clock ; and greatly were we refreshed by its shelter as well as struck by its wild echoes. The road now becomes good, as if it had been macadamized. Half a mile on, at another bend, up shoots another bold promontory, somewhat like its fellow, only it seems to rest itself upon yon long masses of outstanding rock. Suddenly at another turn, some dozen of tall white cones shoot up ; next rises a dark row of grim peaks, presenting their precipitous fronts to us, and then dropping away in the distance to the setting sun.

The road here is so excellent and regular, that it seems as if made by the hand of man. Could it be Pharaoh's highway to the quarries and mines of Maghârah ? Very possibly : certainly, it was no Arab that engineered or formed a road like this. Here the sea bursts on us, less than a mile off. The moment we come within sight of the sea, each Arab runs up to his camel and rubs something into its nostrils with the palms of his hands. It was said to be gunpowder and oil,—meant to prevent the camels from becoming sick, which they are reported to do when first coming upon the sea. The bluff rocks, not unlike St Abb's Head in form, but half red, half white, looked nobly down upon the blue deep. The peaks on the right, as we turn southward, are the blackest I have ever seen,—yet looking blacker perhaps from being intermixed with a few streaks of white and yellow.

We reach the sea about half-past four; I bathe, and sprain my ancle for the third time upon the stony yet soft sand of the beach. Reach our halting-place at half-past five;—the mouth of *Wady-el-Markhâh*, the "valley of rest," hard by the sea, and within sound of its soft ripple. Our dragoman tells us that the water there is good. The night comes down on us:—and such a night! Full moon, cloudless sky, calm sea, and shadowy cliffs! We enjoy the scene around,—but still more the remembrance of the wondrous magnificence through which we had all day been passing.

Wady-el-Markhâh, Tuesday, Jan. 22. . . Went out between six and seven. The dawn-streaks were few and faint. The moon was still unclouded, though far down the west, clearing the sky of all lesser orbs save the morning-star, which whatever it might lose in lustre by the presence of its rival, seemed to gain in soft beauty by its reflection upon that placid sea! How profoundly still! Coolness, and balm, and twilight gentleness,— how lovely! One could almost forget that they were dwellers in this hot and stifling world.

Refreshed myself by bathing in the Red Sea. The

water, within two or three feet from the shore, was much colder than farther out, and the sand felt cold. I remembered what Herodotus tells about the crocodile,— that it takes to the river at night for the sake of warmth, —the land cooling more rapidly than the water. While swimming about I watched the moon's broad path across the sea, as it gradually narrowed and grew dim with the brightening dawn, till, as the sun came up, it passed away, though the moon itself still kept its place in the sky. The silver floor thus partly overlaid and partly mingled with gold, looked strangely brilliant.

At eight we started. Our way led along the shore. Not a ripple on the sea, not a cloud in the flaming firmament! The coast-cliffs were wild and precipitous,— seamed and scarred,—split into spikes, and wasted into cones, as if by the joint action of rain and lightning.* The road lies over a broad platform of flat rock. In rounding one of the points we touched the water, so that the tide-ripples, for there were no others, washed round our camels' feet. I had bathed in the morning moonlight; but my companions, more wisely preferring sunshine, now took to the sea, with some two or three of our younger Bedaween, who enjoyed the sport of swiming and splashing amazingly. Soon we began to turn inwards in a south-easterly direction, and to move away

---

* Some travellers have maintained that the idea of the pyramid was suggested by the conical hills which occur in Egypt and the desert. But though this is possible, yet after all, the pyramids are the *natural* form which any solid structure must take that seeks both height and stability.

from the sea. The road from Ayûn Mûsa had receded from the sea, so that for nearly three days we had lost sight of it. Yesterday it suddenly brought us to the sea again, and our morning ride had been along its margin. All this strikingly shewed the minute accuracy of the Scripture narrative regarding Israel's march,—"they removed from Elim, and encamped by the Red Sea," (Numb. xxxiii. 10). To one that does not know the exact geography of this region this might seem unaccountable; but one who has been upon the spot knows that this is, if not the only practicable route, at least the best one.

From the Red Sea Israel proceeded to "the Wilderness of Sin," (Numb. xxxiii. 11), and in the narrative of this we have one of the many proofs of the difference between Horeb and Sinai. Israel had left Elim where they had water. They then came to the Red Sea, where we now were, and where also there was water. They then left the Red Sea, and after two stages, Dophkah and Alush, they came to *Rephidim,* (Exod. xvii. 1 ; Numb. xxxii. 14), where there was no water. All these three places were not in the Wilderness of Sin, which they had now left behind, and which lay between the Red Sea and Dophkah (Numb. xxxiii. 11, 12). From the same passage it is clear that Rephidim lay between the desert of *Sin* and the desert of *Sinai ;* and from Exod. xvii. 6, it is also plain that the smitten rock of Rephidim was in *Horeb,* at some considerable distance from Mount Sinai,—a day's journey at least, if not more.

The traditional rock of the smiting, shewn by the monks at Sinai, *could not* be the rock which Moses smote ; and Sinai the *mountain* is thus explicitly distinguished from Horeb the *region*, though it is quite possible that the desert of Sinai and the region of Horeb might be much the same, or at least adjoining,—the Horeb district lying westward of Mount Sinai, and the Sinai eastward, their *march* or border being the mountain or some of the wadys running by its flanks. The " deserts " of " the desert " seem to be very numerous,—just like the moors of Scotland; and like them named from any known spot near them. There is (1.) the wilderness of Beersheba at the extreme north, with the wildernesses of Paran and Zin to the west and south-west of it ; (2.) the wilderness of Etham (Numb. xxxiii. 8) ; (3.) the wilderness of the Red Sea (Numb. xiv. 25) ; (4.) the wilderness of Shur (Exod. xv. 22) ; (5.) the wilderness of Sin (Numb. xxxiii. 11); and (6.) the wilderness of Sinai (Exod. xix. 12). Such are some of the *provinces* of the great desert. It is not at all unlikely that were more minute inquiry made by Arabic scholars, living for some time in these deserts, many of the lost names would be recovered, and the places identified. But travellers hurrying through can do little towards the accomplishment of this.

It is into the wilderness of Sin that we now turn— bending inwards and eastwards. Before us rises a range of rugged black precipices, like a fortress to guard the entrance. But our obliging sheikh is making his way

up to us, with a twig in his hand and a smile on his
face. He has something to tell, or shew, or give. He
presents the twig, with a sign that we should smell it.
We do so, and find it strongly aromatic. Its name is
Shia,—a low shrub very common in the desert, most
acceptable to us as an article of fragrance, as it is to the
camels as an article of food. The heat is barely tolerable ; but a pleasant breeze is springing up from the
east, to our great relief. But here comes a caravan of
some eight or nine camels, from Mount Sinai, carrying
charcoal, perhaps, or fruits to Cairo. The hand-shaking
between this party and ours is curious. There is no
hearty grasp of the hand, but little more than placing
the palms together. The energetic part is the kiss ;
but here this is awanting ; probably they are only dis-
tantly acquainted.

The granite now begins to appear in pieces of a foot
square or smaller. It increases as we get on, for we
are moving towards the primitive rocks of the Sinaitic
group. We enter a narrow defile, *Nakb-el-Leghûm,*—
the *lussuff* hanging its fresh green leaves out of the
crevices, and a small palm, with a few tarfas at the
base. The cool sea-breeze follows us, winding through
the tall precipices. On the left, white peaks shoot up,
on the right, dark ; in front there is a black mass of
wall, and towering high above it, close behind, shoots
up another sable mass of peaks. But here comes
another caravan, of twenty camels at least. Such a
shaking of hands ! Foremost is our sheikh, who ad-

vances to the old grey-bearded (I cannot say grey-
headed, for who can see an Arab's bare head?) Sheikh
Beshârah, from Sinai, probably the same who was Dr
Robinson's guide. The sheikhs take each other by the
right hand ; then, throwing the left round each other's
necks, they kiss five times on either cheek. They then
inquire after the health of themselves and their friends.
How like does this seem to the sons of Isaac,—"and
Esau ran to meet him, and embraced him, and fell on
his neck and kissed him." (Gen. xxxiii. 4.) Here are
the same four things :—they run to meet, they embrace,
they fall on the neck, they kiss. So in the case of
Laban, "when Laban heard the tidings of Jacob, his
sister's son, that he ran to meet him, and embraced him,
and kissed him." (Gen. xxix. 13.) Still more does the
meeting of Sheikhs Sulimân and Beshârah remind us of
Aaron and Moses,—"he went and met him in the mount
of God and kissed him,"—for this is the region in which
the two brothers met, and their mode of salutation was
the same. It was in token of intimacy and affection
that David kissed Barzillai (2 Sam. xix. 39); and it
was to indicate *equality* as well, and to win the people's
hearts, that Absalom kissed all that came to him, (2
Sam. xv. 5). When Joel kissed Amasa, he took him
by the beard with his right hand, whereas in the case of
these sheikhs here, their right hands clasp each other.

But now we are in a large basin, girt in with yellow
rocks and fronted by a towering mass of cliffs, black,
red, and brown ; all, as usual, excoriated and bare from

top to bottom. There is hardly a shrub in this wady, not a fragment on the cliffs, even of the dull green of desert shrubs. The hills seem wearing down, more so than do the pyramids of Egypt. Fallen stumps of palms and withered branches of that tree, mingled with granite boulders, lie strewn through the basin. What with the soft nature of the rock and the want of vegetation, the torrents have had their will with these mountains, and they have used it in a way which one can have no idea of save by seeing it. Job must have been among scenes like these when he said—

"The mountain falling cometh to nought;
The rock is removed out of its place.
The waters wear the stones:
Thou washest away the produce of the dust of earth,
And thou destroyest the hope of man."—(Job xiv. 18, 19.)

At one o'clock we turn to the right and enter *Wady Shellâl*, with its black cliffs. The approach of another caravan of ten camels, from Mount Sinai, tells us that this is the highway of the desert. The rocks are getting harder, and basalt shews itself in several places. Hitherto we had passed through arid hills and plains of sandstone, which do not retain water; but as we advanced southwards the primitive rocks begin to shew themselves, which, as they detain the showers longer than the others, are better able to nourish at least some shreds of vegetation here and there. Here are some sayâleh-trees along the road and in the lower crevices, on which at present we see nothing but thorns;—leaf, blossom, and seed are not yet. Here comes our ever-smiling sheikh with some rich prize which he has made his own, and which he means to share with us. It is a a jug-full of cold water, which he has just got from a ravine by the way. It is rather muddy, but the best desert-water we have as yet tasted. It was *mut'r*, he informed us, that is rain-water which had been detained in some hollow of the rocks. He wished us also to understand that it was *taib*, that is *good*. We had seen some half-a-dozen of our men spring away to the left at full speed, and dash into a rock-cleft; and we concluded that their eye had caught sight of some *gazellah* " leaping upon the mountains, skipping upon the hills " (Song ii. 8). We now saw the object of their pursuit ;—there was water there. It was not " living water ;" it was only a pool filled with the rain (Psa. lxxxiv. 6) ; but that was no common boon in such a valley of Baca as this. How one longs to be able, in their own tongue, to say to that kind sheikh and his willing Bedaween, " Whoso drinketh of this water shall thirst again ; but whoso drinketh of the water that I shall give him shall never thirst; but the water that I shall give him shall be in him a well of water springing up into everlasting life " (John iv. 14).

Now we come to a low ridge composed of flat stones, as if newly quarried ; then the debris of the basalt strews the ground in heaps ; then we rise to a height which overlooks a vast array of peaks and crags, black, green, red, and yellow, piled upon and heaped beside each other with giant-fragments of every shape and hue, tossed into the yawning interstices, or projected over unfathomable cavities, each one of would have swallowed up a mosque or a pyramid.

Here comes my camel-driver with a curious animal in his hand, which he has just killed as it was escaping to its hole in the sand. It is like a lizard,—about a foot long. He calls it *Thúb*, pronouncing the *th* very hard as in *this*, or rather almost as if it were written *Dzûb*. It is not unlike a crocodile in shape.

It is now a little after two, and the heat, hitherto great, becomes more moderate. A thin veil of cloud has spread itself over the sky and tempered the sunshine, " the heat is brought down with the shadow of a cloud " (Isa. xxv. 5). The road is narrow, with red cliffs on the right, and a horrid mass of charcoal-looking peaks on the left, stretching away for miles beneath us, for we are now at a considerable height. I cannot describe that billowy sea of rock that seems to heave at our left. Here rises a tall wave in mountain strength and height, there foams a mass of broken water strewed with tawny snow,—there winds the noble curve of some mighty wave just caught in the curl as it was about to break. It is awful desolation ;—the misshapen fragments all melted, torn, broken, riven, splintered, cut into slices, tossed up and down like chaff! Perhaps some of our own home-ranges would seem as hideous if they were stripped of their grassy or heathery robes ; we should then see their savage nakedness as we see here; but yet I hardly think that anything could equal this.

It is worth while correcting the false impression which possesses many as to the desert,—as if it were one vast monotony of level sand. It is not so. There is, no doubt, abundance of sand everywhere, sometimes softer, sometimes harder, sometimes larger in grain, and sometimes smaller. But the desert, and especially the Sinaitic peninsula, is quite a mountainous region; altogether a contrast to Egypt, which in general is level and tame.

We are now passing through *Wady-Budrah*, where we see a few stunted tarfas; but all else is dreariness, like "the valley of the shadow of death." We are climbing the horrid defile that leads into the lower part of the wady. It is called *Nakb-el-Budrah*, that is the pass of Budrah. A succession of precipices meets the eye on each side. Up to this time my aneroid has fallen two inches since we turned in from the sea. As we get down to the foot of the wady, five dark-red peaks, like the tombs of giants, rise to greet us, at least a thousand feet high. They overhang our path. Here there is nothing but dreariness and death, save the little lizards that are shooting from bush to bush, and the large black ants that are running about and throwing up, in a concave circle round their hole, small heaps of sand, which they have dug from beneath,—gluing the grains together by some process of their own, and then rolling up these balls of sand (which crumble at our touch) so

K

as to form concave mounds or circlets in thousands over the desert.

We enter *Wady-es-Sidreh,* which begins at the foot of these five peaks, which, my camel-driver tells me, are called *Jebel Walakhah.* In this wady all is sepulchral desolation. We see small boulders of red granite, then larger blocks of the same. But where can these have come from ? This is a hollow far from the primitive rocks,—walled in by immense cliffs of porphyry and sandstone. Our sheikh calls this *Sihah Sidreh,* which I suppose means the burnt or arid place of *Sidreh.* Were these crags but wooded, and were but a lake, however small, in this hollow, what a scene ! The Trossachs magnified sevenfold !

As it must have been somewhere in this neighbourhood that the manna was first given (Numb. xxxiii. 12 ; Exod. xvi. 1–4), it may be well to notice the theory which makes it a mere natural growth,—the produce of the tarfa-tree.

It is impossible that it could be so for such reasons as the following :—(1.) The tarfa exudes only small quantities of what is called manna. The Arabs could not exist upon it for a week. A whole wady full of tarfas would not exude enough to support half-a-dozen travellers. Will those who adopt this theory put it to the test by going to Wady Ghurandel *without provisions* and trust to the tarfa for food ? They will get water there, and if their hypothesis be the correct one, they will find enough upon the tarfas to sustain them. If these trees fed two or three millions, they will surely feed two or three individuals, especially as Ghurandel seems more productive now than in past ages. The theory is absurd ; and its absurdity is easily shewn. Suppose the desert were planted with apple-trees, would these feed two millions ? Now a good-sized apple-tree will contain a hundred times more food than the largest tarfa of the desert. (2.) The tarfa only exudes at certain seasons, March and April (Seetzen says June). When we passed through the desert there were no exudations. Every branch was bare and dry. Israel required manna constantly, in all seasons. Grant that they entered the desert just at the *proper season*, that would not supply them for the rest of the year. The manna was not confined to any month or season, but was found at all times. (3.) The tarfa does not yield its exudations regularly, even once a year. It sometimes omits four or five years, and cannot be reckoned on. But Israel was fed for *forty years* upon the manna, as it is written, " the children of Israel did eat manna forty years " (Exod. xvi. 35). Two millions of people fed for forty years upon the exudations of the tarfa ! He who believes this need stumble at no miracle. (4.) The exudations of the tarfa *come out* from the branches of the tree, they do not *come down* from the air or sky. But Israel's manna is several times over said to fall from heaven. " He commanded the clouds from above, and opened the doors of heaven, and *rained down manna upon them* to eat, and gave them of the corn of heaven." (Psa. lxxviii. 24.)

Each of the narratives implies that it was something which came down like rain. "I will rain bread from heaven for you." (Exod. xvi. 4.) Is this like an exudation? (5.) The tarfa-exudations are in composition and consistency somewhat like honey. They are quite unfit for grinding, or pounding, or baking, or boiling. Who could *grind* honey? Yet we read of the manna that the people "*ground* it in mills or beat it in a mortar, and baked it in pans, and made cakes of it" (Numb. xi. 8), nay boiled it (Exod. xvi. 23). We brought home several little pots of the tarfa-manna, and we are willing to give a handsome reward to any German or English rationalist who will undertake to *grind* it, or *beat* it in a *mortar*, or *bake* it in a *pan*. They would find it easier to believe the miracle; for certainly it is less difficult to *believe* a miracle than to *work* one. (6.) The taste of the ancient manna was "as the taste of fresh oil" (Numb. xi. 8). No one who has tasted the tarfa-manna would compare it to oil. While we are writing this a pot of it stands before us, and we have tasted it again for the twentieth time, but can find no resemblance to oil in its flavour. It is like brown sugar mixed with water. (7.) The tarfa-manna does not stink nor breed worms in a single night. Our manna which we brought from the desert is as fresh and good this day as it was ten months ago, when we bought it from the monks. There is not a worm in it. Nor has it the slightest tendency to corrupt. It is remarkable too that the ancient manna, though it would not keep over night on the week-days, yet did so on the Sabbath. This is surely something su- pernatural. (8.) The ancient manna evaporated as soon as the sun rose. (Exod. xvi. 21.) The tarfa-pro- duce does not evaporate. It gets soft in the sun, or when exposed to heat, but that is all. I am willing to let any sceptic expose my pot of manna to the sun,— the sun of Egypt or the sun of the desert,—as long as he likes, and see whether it will evaporate. (9.) The tarfa-manna does not fall in double quantity on Fridays and cease to fall entirely on Saturday. This, however, was the case with the ancient manna. (Exod. xvi. 29.) On the sixth day, God "gave them the bread of two days," and on the seventh day "there was none." (Exod. xvi. 26.) Was this natural or supernatural? Did Moses write the truth, or is his narrative a fiction? (10.) The tarfa-manna is medicine, not food. No Arab would think of feeding on it. It is moreover purgative, and it would hardly do to *feed* a man upon purgative medicine,—and nothing else,—all the days of his life. If he grew fat upon it, or even lived under it, there would be as great a miracle as any that philosophers try to escape from. Will any rationalistic believer in the fattening virtues of the tarfa-exudation, make the experiment of living upon it alone for a few weeks? It would test his credulity. (11.) The ancient manna was a thing quite unknown to the Israelites. "He fed thee with manna, which thou knewest not, neither did thy fathers know." (Deut. viii. 3.) "They wist not what it

was." (Exod. xvi. 15.) Surely they would know what
the exudation of a desert-tree was. Surely Moses
could have told them its proper name, for he had been
forty years in this very desert. Or if he did not know
it, Jethro could have told them. And besides, the mixed
multitude that came out of Egypt with them, knew the
tarfa well, for it is an Egyptian tree, and must often
have tasted its manna. Nay, every Israelite in the
camp knew the tarfa as well as he knew a palm, and
had tasted tarfa-manna as often as he had done a date.
Will any neologist say that an Israelite or an Egyptian
could possibly have been ignorant of the tarfa or its produce? Every day that we were in Egypt, we saw rows
of tarfas on every side of us, and had we been there in
March and April, should doubtless have seen them
exuding. Nothing can be more unlikely than that
Israel did not know these trees and their fruit. Both
" they and their fathers" knew them perfectly. Though
I do not believe that it was a tarfa-grove that Abraham
planted at Beersheba, as Mr Stanley thinks, yet I do
not doubt that Abraham, Isaac, and Jacob had seen
the tree and tasted its fruit, both in Egypt and in
the desert. (12.) It is an established physiological fact
that no one can feed long on one single substance
with impunity. If one had only *wheat* to eat he could
not live; for even *it* does not contain all the elements
needful for the nourishment of the body. Much more
is this true of fruit,—and especially so of fruit which
is not in itself at all nourishing, which is rather medi-

cinal than nutrimental. So that if Israel had lived
upon the manna of the tarfa-tree, two miracles would
have been necessary, one to render the tarfas about
ten thousand times more productive than they are (and
this all the year through), and then another to keep the
children of Israel in bodily health while living on that
one article. Without the first miracle they could not
have been fed at all, and without the second they would
have died in a few weeks. If Israel's manna were really
a new created thing from God, there is no difficulty
either to its amount or its quality. The God who made
it and sent it would see that it was right. Just one
miracle was needed, no more,—a great one I admit and
a continuous one ;—but what is that to the God who
made all the processes of nature, and who can work
without them as easily as with them ? Is it not better,
—nay much more philosophical and rational,—to admit
that on this occasion he took another way of producing
food than we know anything of, than to hold all the
absurdities which we have enumerated above, and to
believe that the God of truth has written a narrative for
his creatures in such treacherous language as to make
them suppose that he was working a miracle when he
was doing nothing,—that he was showering down food
from heaven in abundance (" angel's food," " the corn of
heaven," Ps. lxxviii. 24), when he was making them
feed upon worse than prison-fare, and sustaining them
on what was never intended to be the nutriment of
man or beast ? Credulity beyond all credulities ! Denial

of God's character as the God of truth and love! Malign-
ing of his Scriptures as not meaning what they seem!
Why this dread and dislike of a miracle? Why this
wish either to evade it or to reduce it to its minimum?
Is it so terrible a thing that God should come nigh to
bless us? Is the naked arm of God a thing so dreadful
to behold, that rather than admit of its having been
seen by the sons of men, God's true words must be made
void, and all manner of human fancies substituted for
the simple facts which the plainly interpreted narrative
makes known?

Mr Stanley twice alludes to the manna (pp. 22 and
28); but whether he believes in its miraculous production I am far from being sure. The note at p. 28 would
almost imply that he did, or at least that he was quite
aware of the difficulties of not believing it; but the
statement at p. 22 indicates his willingness to have
recourse to the tarfa for the supply of Israel's desert
food. "The tarfa, or tamarisk, is not mentioned by
name in the history of the Exodus; yet if the tradition
of the Greek Church and of the Arabs be adopted, it is
inseparably connected with the wanderings, by the
manna which distils from it." How much or how
little this statement implies, I do not know. The
weight of Greek tradition may be pretty accurately
ascertained by the nature and credibility of the legends which they have clustered round Mount Sinai,
such as the story of the rock indented by the body of
Moses. Arab tradition may be taken for what it is

worth ; which in matters of Scripture history is absolutely nothing.   The authority of Josephus might have
been of somewhat more value, if it at all indicated
ancient Jewish tradition ; but there is no need for
reckoning the value of his testimony, as he does not
make the statement imputed to him.   He alludes to
the manna three times (Antiq. III. 1, 6. . . III. 5, 3. . .
IV. 3, 2.), and in all these places indicates his belief of
its coming direct from heaven.   Only in the first of
these places he speaks of its still (even in his days) falling down in rain, but makes no mention of its connection with any tree, nor does he name the tamarisk.   It
does not appear that the manna he refers to was the
same as the tarfa-distillation ; at least, his allusion is so
vague that it might as well mean what is usually called
" honey-dew."   That Josephus believed this identity
is very doubtful indeed ; as any may see who will read
the passage (Antiq. III. 1–6, and not III. 2, as Mr Stanley
gives it), and it would have been better had Mr Stanley
not written so decidedly about Josephus's belief, and on
the strength of it called the non-miraculous hypothesis
the " ancient view."   Josephus is not responsible for
this view,—and as to its being *Greek* tradition,—this
would require proof, as the Greek fathers are ignorant
of it.   *Sinaitic* tradition it may be, not *Greek ;* and a
profitable tradition it has been to the convent of St
Katharin.   As to the antiquity of the tradition, that
ought not to weigh much,—still if it does, we have the
testimony of one who wrote before Josephus, *Philo*

Judæus, who, mystic as he was, understands quite literally the miracle of the manna,* narrating it at considerable length, without any hint that it was either tamarisk-exudation or Arabian honey-dew. †

The writers of the Old and New Testament evidently believed in the miraculous and celestial origin of the manna. Their words in many places are too explicit to leave any doubt as to this. Nor are we aware that any sceptic has denied that such was their belief. What weight, then, are we to attach to their belief? Ought it to influence us, or ought it not? Is it authoritative, or is it not? Is Lepsius entitled to say, such was *their* belief, but it need not be *mine?* They were deceived, they exaggerated, they indulged in orientalism. He might say so, if the Scriptures are not of God, and if "holy men of old" did not "speak as they were moved by the Holy Ghost." But if Moses and David wrote the mind of God, and expressed his meaning aright, then it is clear that their belief ought to rule ours. If *they* have said that the manna was supernatural and

* See his Life of Moses, Book I, sect. 36, 37. See also Wisdom of Solomon, supposed to be written by Philo, xvi. 20.

† Keble, referring to the manna, speaks of

> "the moist pearls now bestrowing
> Thymy slope and rushy vale."
>
> *Lyra Innocentium,* p. 222, "Song of the Manna Gatherers."

"*Thymy* slope and *rushy* vale" are greater inaccuracies than even a poet can be allowed. "Thyme" and "rushes" do not clothe the desert. If the line had run "tarfa slope and rittem vale," it would have been true, though perhaps not poetical. It would have been better had Mr Stanley not vouched so strongly for Mr Keble's accuracy.

divine, then God has said it ; and what is Greek tradition, or Arabian fables, or philosophical incredulity, in comparison with their clear words ? " What is the chaff to the wheat ?" What is man's fond invention in comparison with God's authentic record ?

But we have reached the entrance of *Wady Magharah*, or the Wady of the Cave, for here are Pharaoh's quarries and copper-mines, older than the days of Joseph. We send on our baggage-camels, and turn the heads of our dromedaries to the left. In less than a quarter of an hour we notice inscriptions on the sandstone rock. They are Egyptian hieroglyphics.

Into the history of these I need not enter. They are amongst the oldest rock-writings in the world, as old at least as the Pharaohs, if not older, yet they are wonderfully sharp in outline and perfectly readable to this day. Of them it is that Lepsius says, " We found a stately row of rock-inscriptions, close by the side of the extensive caverns, which are of greater antiquity even than those of Sar'bût el-Khadem. Some of them contain the oldest effigies of kings in existence, without excepting the whole of Egypt and the pyramids of Ghîzeh." Mr Bartlett visited the spot, and has, at great length, described the difficulty which he had in finding these inscriptions. We had no such difficulty, nor had we occasion to lose temper at our Arabs for their ignorance, as they conducted us at once to the place. Our inspection was brief ; but we felt a strange awe when standing in this lonely plain and looking

upon these most ancient of all ancient monuments,—
to think that this region once was peopled with Pharaoh's
miners, and had been the scene of busy toiling life for ages.

It is worth the reader's while to remember that this
whole region, for many a mile around, was one vast
mine, and is said to have been called in hieroglyphics,
Mafkat, "the copper land." In this district are found
large masses of copper mixed with iron-ore, and the
ruined temple of Sar'but el-Khadem is said to be built
upon vast mounds of ore. In fact here was one of the
early Egyptian colonies, which by the labour of their
hands helped to supply Egypt with its wealth.[*]

But we must not remain at the inscriptions. We
proceed to the quarries or mines themselves, following
the guidance of our Arabs; and while one of our men
remains below to watch our dromedaries, another acts
as our guide. Following him, we scramble up an immense slope of debris, some of which is natural and
some artificial. We reach the old quarry of Egypt,
after some slips and falls. It has been an immense
shelving cavity, or rather a series of cavities or cham-
bers, formed by excavating about nine-tenths of the
rock and leaving the remaining tenth as pillars to support the mountain-roof. There is nothing very striking
to the eye here, but it is a curious spot, as being the
oldest known quarry and copper-mine in the world.

---

[*] Very likely Job knew this region and referred to it, chap xxviii. 1-6.
He speaks of the vein for silver, the place for gold,—the digging out the
iron, the melting of the copper, &c.

We pick up some specimens of the copper-ore,—of which Job, who knew the wilderness, spoke when he said, "iron is taken out of the earth, and brass (copper) is molten out of the stone?" (Job xxviii. 2).

But the sun is setting, so we must not tarry. We scramble down, I with a sprained ankle, and wind our way out of this valley into *Wady Mukatteb*, the rusty peaks on every side brightening in the radiance of the descending sun. Salîm, my camel-man, is plucking a small herb, giving it carefully to his camel. He calls it *Rib'shi*. About six, as the last rays of day were dying on the cliffs, we moved into the Written Valley,—Mount Serbâl in the distance, still refusing to part with the sunlight from its towering spires. The valley at the mouth seems not above half a mile wide. On our left are peaks 1500 feet high,—red-brown in hue, and seamed from top to bottom with black stripes as if painted by the art of man. At their foot we see the smoke of a Bedaween encampment,—a poor remembrancer of the wreaths of twilight smoke ascending from the villages of our own far land. Our Arabs sing as they go. They sing to their camels to cheer them and quicken their steps. They sing to each other in responsive songs. The sun is gone from vale and mountain; but the western sky retains a silky softness of purple, which I never saw save in the desert. I cannot describe it, save by saying that it looks like a veil of shot-silk of light mild purple. It is singularly beautiful.

But the shadows are coming down, and darkness is

taking away the sharp, vivid outline of the peaks around
and before us. *Serbâl* fades at last. The moon rises
in splendour, and as we pass along, our Arabs point to
the inscriptions on our right, just visible in the moonlight. We do not stay to examine them, as we mean
to devote to-morrow to this purpose. We reach our
tents about seven. After dinner we wander over the
sands and among the rocks by moonlight; but it is too
dark to examine the inscriptions. We dare not go too
far lest we lose ourselves. The white gleam of our
tents in the moonshine is quite as sufficient a guide to
us as the Arab fires, which are now burning low. All
around is calm. " I will both lay me down in peace
and sleep, for thou, Lord, only makest me dwell in
safety." (Psa. iv. 8.)

Wady Mukatteb, Wednesday, Jan. 23.—Up before
seven. Went out to survey the valley. About sixty
yards from our tents I came upon an inscription, which
was quite within reach, and sloped so considerably that
I could rest my note-book on it. The letters at first
sight are not unlike Hebrew. A closer inspection un-
deceives you,—at least so far as to shew you that the
words do not belong to the vocabulary of that language.
The letters are about two inches and a half long, not
very deep, evidently cut by some rude instrument. The
rock itself on which this inscription is engraved is about
nine feet long by four broad, and at the foot there is
the picture of a camel. On a small piece of adjoining
rock, one foot and a half broad by three feet long, there

is a sort of Arabic inscription, quite different from the
other, in very small letters, a quarter of an inch in
breadth and half an inch in length. Immediately adjoining this another ledge projects, six feet long and
four broad, with an inscription in the usual "Mukatteb"
characters, but considerably defaced. The prevailing
characters are such as the following, ב, ר, ע, ף ; the
last of these occurring very frequently. It is very difficult to copy them, and I was so afraid of misrepresent-
ing them that I gave up the attempt. The engravings
of Pococke and of Forster are, generally speaking, faithful ; but they convey too high an idea of the inscriptions, not properly representing their rudeness and
irregularity. They are not indistinct scratches by any
means, but they are not such deep and noble chisellings
as some of Forster's engravings make them appear.

On several places at this part there are figures such
as the following, ⅄, ⌐. Still farther to the right, the
same kind of inscriptions runs on for a considerable distance ; but the rocks are not above ten feet high. Once
and again the Arabic characters occur. Perhaps, however, they may not be Arabic, but the cursive forms of
the larger letters, and in some places they certainly
look like this. A little way farther is a projecting face
of rock about twenty feet high, with a very legible inscription in the usual characters. Farther still there is
one in a more hollow rock, at the top of which is the
figure of a man with upstretched hands. The inscription
is very distinct, and is surrounded by a ring like the

hieroglyphical cartouches of Egypt. The letters are about two inches long. Next comes a mass of broken rocks, lying in all directions, and on one part of it another figure of a man with outstretched hands; camels also, and an ass with a rider. Those on this rock are larger in size. One startled me by its likeness to the Hebrew, בני ㄙ99ㄷ. The rock was about ten feet broad, by twenty long. On the high and receding front of one of the rocks a little farther along, I saw similar characters. At this point there is a break in the continuousness of the cliff, and a small ravine runs up at right angles. I traced it a considerable way, but found no inscriptions on either side. It was a striking enough ravine, and with some wood and water would have made quite "a highland glen." Just at the entrance to it, on the west side, there is an immense rock, partly written on; and still the same mysterious characters occur ፶,Ʊ,ፁ፥ Passing the ravine, there is a most vivid picture of a man leading a camel, staff in hand; then another camel at the other end of the inscription, which runs thus, ,ﻝ〇﴿ﻑﻝﻉ. The word ISI occurs more than once here. The camel is about six or eight inches in height. Farther on there is another immense block, with inscriptions; then another ravine in which I could detect nothing; but beyond this another large mass of rock quite written over. All this occurred in a space of about a hundred and ninety yards. I then turned in the opposite direction, beyond our tents to the south, and found a large rock lying on the ground, written over, like the others; then another in a slanting position, with camels and riders. These were by themselves. I then returned to our tents between eight and nine. After breakfast and prayers, we all set out together, Mr Wright with his photographic apparatus, and the rest of us to assist. We took our stand at first near the spot which I had first visited in the morning; and while preparations were making, I took Mr Wright's telescope and made a survey of the lofty hills opposite, which are about two miles across, and which send down their rough slopes quite into the valley. But I could discover nothing save curious seams and fractures running up and down the bare steeps. For the hills we saw, though nobly rugged and lofty, were wholly bare and wild. In shape and height they are not unlike some of our Highland ridges, but the green robe has been burnt off their swarthy sides. Take Glencoe as their nearest image. Strip off the heather from its slopes, burn up every blade of grass on which these goats are feeding, wash down every particle of soil from the rocks, split and seam the cliffs from head to foot, dry up the clear streamlet that washes their base and gives life to the awful grandeur;—then you may have some idea of these savage mountains.

Some excellent photographs were obtained; but it is not easy to take them of such size as clearly to bring out the inscriptions. I walked down the whole left side of the valley till the writings ceased, which they did in about a mile and a half. I then crossed over to

L

the other side, about half a mile, and came up. Found the inscriptions on both sides very much alike. In one place I saw Greek,* in another English words, and in another something that looked very like Syriac. But these are very few,—quite different in style of cutting from the others, and evidently more modern. About three o'clock we took our dromedaries and rode up the valley for a considerable way, perhaps a mile and half. We found many more inscriptions on all sides, and a good many pictures of animals, especially camels and wild goats. These were very trifling,—done for mere amusement,—representing goats in all manner of ludicrous positions. We returned to our tents about five, having spent the whole day in examining this wady, but quite unable to come to any conclusion as to the meaning or authorship of the inscriptions. Professor Beer's theory seems *untenable*, Mr Forster's *unproved*, though by no means so improbable as some would have it. It has been argued that the rocks being sandstone, and the inscriptions very shallow, three thousand years would have effaced them. This is ignorance. The rocks are certainly very friable, and in our country would soon lose their cuttings, however deep, even in a century. But the dry air of the desert preserves each

---

* It is the occurrence of these interspersed Greek words which prove the other inscriptions *not* to be of Greek origin or the work of Greek pilgrims. That Greek pilgrims wrote the Greek words is very likely. But how does this prove (as some have said) that they wrote what was not Greek?

scratch upon the softest rock. Besides, we know that these writings have at least existed since the sixth century, when Cosmas saw them and reported them as Israelitish ; and if twelve centuries have failed to erase them, three times that would be equally powerless. And then the well-known Egyptian inscription at Magharah is on the same soft sandstone, yet it has stood wellnigh four thousand years. The argument founded on the effacing power of time would be resistless in our own country, but it is good for nothing in Egypt or the desert. No frost splits the rock, no lingering damp crumbles it down. No moss nor lichen strikes its roots into these broad blocks to efface the slightest line once drawn upon them, and even those parts which the sun never reaches are as dry as the summit of the cliff. Masses may occasionally come down from the heights, but minute disintegration, such as occurs in this climate, seems unknown. The sandstone of Wady Mukatteb seems as little affected by age as the granite of Syene.

The inscriptions are not imposing in their appearance. They are shallow, irregular, and straggling. The hand of no artist is upon these rocks, nor has the tool of any expert workman in stone been lifted up upon them. They are by no means so lofty in position as we were led to believe. Indeed, except at one part, towards the south-east, where the valley widens and the cliffs rise into mountains, the ridges which wall in the wady consist of low crags, not much above a hundred or two hundred feet in height,—some sloping, others perpendicular,—some broad and flat, others round and rugged. A large number we could easily reach with the hand, and the rest with a ladder of very moderate length. Certainly no ropes nor scaffolding could be necessary in any that we saw. Their number is very great. No one who has seen them would say, as Dr Robinson has done, that they occur "at such points as would form convenient resting-places for travellers or pilgrims during the noonday sun" (*Biblical Researches*, vol. i. p. 188). From nine in the morning till three or four in the afternoon the sun never left them. They lie fully exposed to his rays. They are not hieroglyphical. They are alphabetical. The camels, goats, &c. are not meant for hieroglyphics,—nor indeed perhaps for anything save amusement.

Such were the remarks occurring at the moment, as we explored the valley. I add one or two pages more, the result of after-consideration, even at the risk of appearing to traverse the ground twice over.

These inscriptions are undoubtedly of a great age. The fact of the characters being unknown, of itself proves this; for there is no instance of a language or an alphabet being totally lost during the last eighteen hundred years. This is a serious difficulty in the way of those who ascribe them to the pilgrims of the early centuries. For as these pilgrims were, with few exceptions, *Greek*, or Egyptians speaking Greek, it seems incredible that they should have left inscriptions in a language not their own,—a language whose every trace has perished, save what is to be gleaned from these old rocks.

Any one looking at them would at once pronounce them very old. They are not merely rudely graven, but they give strong indication of their being the letters of a rude alphabet. Such is decidedly the impression which remains upon my own mind, after examining them with care, and setting them side by side with all the various alphabets that I could lay hold of.

In looking at them, one is no doubt led to ask, how it is possible that such shallow cuttings,—such mere scratches, as some of them are, could endure so well the tear and wear of centuries? There is no one that I saw cut to half the depth of the letters on our poorest tombstone, how then could they keep their edges, or indeed be preserved from total erasure, say for a thousand years, seeing three centuries suffice to obliterate the records of our churchyards?

This is, however, no difficulty at all, when the state of the case is looked into. Some of these inscriptions, for instance, are on *granite*, though most are on *sandstone*, yet the latter are in as good a state of preservation as the former, so that the hardness of the stone does not seem to be an element in the question of the antiquity of the graving; and as the granite inscriptions of Egypt, even in their minutest and most casual scratches, have stood perhaps four thousand years, no argument against the antiquity of such oriental carvings can be founded on their liability to erasure. Indeed, nothing of this kind, either in Egypt or the desert, can be erased, save by violence. It is the united action of frost and damp that crumbles our northern rocks and effaces our inscriptions. These influences do not exist in the desert, or at least to so small an extent as to be imperceptible in their results. No doubt there is occasionally, though rarely, frost during the night. But it is slight, and then it is in atmosphere thoroughly dry, and among rocks, not saturated with perpetual moisture. The winter torrents, it is true, rush down with wasting fury, but they pass off speedily, and leave the air as dry as before. Scratch your name with your penknife upon the sandstone of Wady Mukatteb, and it will remain for centuries, as perfect as on the day you carved it.

We know from the testimony of Cosmas in the sixth century, that these inscriptions have already lasted twelve centuries, which is quite a sufficient length of time to test their durability. We know, moreover, that in the adjoining wady there are Egyptian inscriptions, in hieroglyphics, on similar sandstone, which are, beyond doubt, of the age of the Pharaohs; so that if a hieroglyphical inscription in Wady Magharah has stood the waste of four thousand years, there is no physical reason why an alphabetical one in Wady Mukatteb should not be equally enduring.

These remarks, however, merely dispose of some supposed difficulties, and determine nothing as to the *age* of the inscriptions. They *may be* very ancient, but that does not prove that they actually *are so.*

The *Christian* origin of these writings seems to me very doubtful. That Christian pilgrims should write in a character known to no Christian nation from the sixth century to this, is a very improbable thing, especially when we remember that the languages which these pilgrims spoke are *known* languages. That there were pilgrims to Feirân and Sinai in these early ages is true, but those alone from Egypt would pass through Wady Mukatteb, and their time of sojourn in any spot by the way would be too short to admit of their being the authors of these inscriptions, even had their numbers made this possible. Only a body of men resident here for weeks at least, if not months, could have been the authors of these writings. And what band of pilgrims would think of settling down at Mukatteb, where there is not a drop of water? Had the inscriptions been in Ghurandel or Feirân, the pilgrim theory might have have been plausible, for in both of these places they might have remained for some time, but in Mukatteb this was impossible. That thousands of monks and hermits resided in Feirân and its neighbourhood, and that pilgrims resorted to their convents there, is admitted ; but the admission destroys the conclusion founded on it. For we naturally ask, how was it that these men confined their writing almost entirely to Wady Mukatteb? Why are there so many inscriptions in the latter valley where they could not have subsisted above a few days, and why are there none in Wady Feirân where we know that they dwelt for years,—nay ages ? And how comes it that those other spots also, where we *know* they did reside, have the fewest inscriptions, while Wady Mukatteb has the most, of which we may say this at least, that we know not whether they so much as passed through it at all.

The figure of a cross, which occurs once and again, is no proof of the inscriptions being written by Christians. For the same figure is to be found on Egyptian obelisks, and is in the form of one of the articles held in the hand of one of the gods of Egypt,—Osiris, if I remember aright; and, moreover, it is precisely the figure of the *Tau* in several ancient alphabets, such as the Phœnician, the old Hebrew, the old Greek, and the Coptic. In looking at the inscriptions themselves, it is some time before you notice that the figure is really a cross ; it looks in some cases so like a part of the word.

In one part of the wady there are some things which one does not like to associate with Christian pilgrims. The figures of goats, &c. are not merely ludicrous, but in one or two places quite obscene. This occurs near the south end of the valley, on some rocks which are particularly crowded with representations of animals, *in all manner of positions.* To say the least of these, they are absurd and laughable,—drawn evidently by some idlers for mere amusement ; and some of them not fit to be presented to the public. They are such as those with which our foolish young men disfigure the walls of some of our public buildings, and which Alexander Cruden, with his sponge, delighted to efface.

The question of their Israelitish origin is more difficult. That they might have been executed by the Hebrews while in the desert, is not by any means an unlikely thing; nay, at first mention, it seems most probable. But there are some objections to this, which appear to me very formidable.

The first objection is as to the character and the language. Ingenious as is Mr Forster's theory, it does not remove this difficulty, or at least does so by a hypothesis, of which one would like to see fuller demonstration. We should have expected the characters to approximate at least, either to the Coptic or the Hebrew, which they do not. I admit that in one or two words there is a great likeness to the Hebrew; but in all others, total unlikeness, which led me to conclude that the language must be one which, while it entirely differed from the Hebrew, had certain affinities with it in some of its letters, and possibly in some of its words.

It is very likely, nay almost certain, that Israel passed through this wady, but that they sojourned in it beyond a day or so is improbable.* From their first station

* This suggests another remark. Israel *could hardly have been both at Wady Mukatteb and at Serbál* on their way to Sinai, and it is difficult to conceive how they could have been at either of these places, *after* leaving that mountain. Yet the same inscriptions occur in both these places, so that the same people must have dwelt in both for some time. Weeks, at the least, would be required.

beyond Elim, viz., "the Red Sea," they proceeded right
on to Sinai, through Dophkah, Alush, and Rephidim.
Dophkah or Alush must have been near Wady Mukatteb;
but Rephidim must have been two or three days beyond
it. The sacred history shews us that Israel hastened on
to Rephidim and Sinai, without halting so long by the
way as to allow them time to write such multitudes of
inscriptions as we find. Besides, it is clear that they
must have pushed on without delay to their great des-
tination, for there was no water by the way, and in the
Mukatteb district, least of all, They could not have remained in the wady above a day unless they had means
of bringing it from a distance, such as Pharaoh's miners
at Magharah doubtless had. This they had not, and
hence I do not see how they could have remained at
Mukatteb any longer than was absolutely necessary for
rest. They did not get the miraculous supply of water
from the rock *for some days after*. Thus they could not
have stayed here above a day on their way to Sinai ;
and as to their revisiting this afterwards when they left
the mount, this is a very great improbability indeed, as the
geography of the region shews, besides being in no way
countenanced by the narrative of Moses. It is quite
possible that the manna and the quails may have been
given about the time when they were passing through
the Mukatteb region ; but most certainly the water was
not, till they had entirely quitted it, so that it is difficult to see how they could have tarried here at all, and
still more difficult to understand how they could draw

the figure of the rock in Horeb,—a rock which they did not know till some days after they had quitted Mukatteb.

There is a figure of a man with outstretched and uplifted hands on one of the rocks ; and when I saw it, I was struck with the resemblance to what one conceives must have been the attitude of Moses when he pleaded against Amalek ; and Mr Forster points out this. But then at this time the conflict with Amalek had not taken place, so that this peculiar figure must refer to something else. The same remark applies to the figure of the serpent ; for the attack of the fiery serpents and Israel's healing by the brazen serpent, did not occur till nearly forty years after they had left Mukatteb.

The remarks already made as to the ludicrous and improper representations on some of the rocks apply strongly in the case of Israel. I do not enjoy the thought of such pictures having been drawn by the Hebrews ; but this of course is no proof.

As I surveyed the region and marked the inscriptions, the question came up continually, who could have been the authors ? I tried to connect this wady with Magharah, and to suppose that Pharaoh's miners there had done the work. But the threefold difficulty occurred.— (1.) Why are there hieroglyphics in Magharah and not one in Mukatteb ? (2.) Why is there not one letter or word in the one place the same as those in the other. (3.) Why should the workman have taken up their abode so far from the place of their operations, and so much farther from the Red Sea and from water than they

needed to have done?   The Mukatteb inscriptions could
not be the work of the Egyptian miners of Magharah.

There is a passage, however, in Dr Wilson's work
which has struck me greatly, and which I have pon-
dered again and again, in connection with the question
before us.   He himself does not make the use of it which
I have sometimes thought might be done.   But this
does not alter the value of his statement.   He tells that
after " taking a peep through the telescope at the high
range of red granite mountains lying to the east," he
proceeded to visit them, having been struck with what
appeared to be " dark metallic veins or basaltic dykes."
In two hours he reached them after much toil, and his
description is as follows :—

" On a hill in front of them, which we had to sur-
mount before we could get to their base, we were surprised to see immense quantities of debris and slag,
with fragments of stone mortars and furnaces, which,
we doubted not, had been used in the remotest antiquity
for the pounding and smelting of ore.   When we actually
reached the mountains, we found that they had been
peeled and excavated to a great extent, where the veins
and dykes had occurred ; and that only their coarser
contents had in some places been spared.   Numerous
grooves and channels seemed to be cut in the extraction
of the ore, from the very top to the bottom of the mountains, even where they were most perpendicular, and
the mountains are completely spoiled and stripped of
their treasures.   How they were wrought, whether by

the aid of scaffoldings reaching from the bottom, or by supports let down from above by ropes or chains, it is impossible to say. Great must have been the exposure and the waste of human life in the working of them." *

Others have since visited the spot, and their statements quite confirm Dr Wilson's statements. Tools have been found, chisel-marks have been seen, tracks have been traced, routes marked from hill to hill. Inscriptions are frequent, as well as representations of animals and trees. All this shews that mining operations have been once carried on here to a very large extent, and as the Egyptian hieroglyphics are awanting, it is likely that the nation carrying them on was *not* Egypt, while the characters send us back to a period long before the Christian era.

Now, whether these vast mines were worked by some nation from the south or from the north, it matters not. Whoever wrought them would find in Wady Mukatteb the nearest and most suitable place for the residence of the workmen, or at least the most convenient depot for the proceeds of the mines, whether they were to be transported by the Red Sea into Egypt, or Abyssinia, or northward into Idumea or Phœnicia.

The absence of hieroglyphics and the nature of the character lead us to reject the supposition of the inscriptions being the work of *Egyptian* miners. But the great similarity of the Mukatteb letters to several in the Phœnician alphabet, would suggest the idea that perhaps

* Lands of the Bible, vol. i. pp. 187, 188.

the authorship of these carvings may be traced to Phœnicia. If our readers will run their eyes along any comparative table of alphabets, while he keeps the inscriptions before him, he will be surprised at the similarities which he will detect.* If he turn to pages sixth and seventh of the second of the books named below, he will see two columns containing letters similar to the inscriptions. One is the *Phœnician,* and the other is the *old Hebrew.* Mr Forster may take this latter coincidence as a confirmation of his views; and I do not deny that it is so. But one remark must be added, which is not favourable to him. While *some* of the old Hebrew letters do correspond with the Mukatteb ones, there are *more* of the Phœnician ones that do so; nay, many of the Mukatteb letters are not to be found in that column of the old Hebrew alphabet, while they are to be found in the Phœnician column. Beth, Daleth, Caph, Mem, Resh, Tau, are similar to both alphabets, and are to be read on the Mukatteb rocks; while Schin and Koph at least, if not others, occur only in the Phœnician, in the form in which they occur in the Mukatteb. There are some doubtful letters which I do not refer to, and several, in the form of which, I can trace no resemblance between the Phœnician alphabet and the Mukatteb inscriptions.

I would not have the reader suppose that there are

---

* See for instance the table at the end of Dr Wilson's volumes, or the "Alphabete Orientalischer und occidentalischer sprachen," by Ballhorn. Leipzig, 1853.

no difficulties in the way of this supposition, or that I am one of its advocates. I see objections ; but then the very strong difficulties which were in the way of former theories, do not come up here. This is all I can say. The subject asks much more investigation and less dogmatism than have hitherto been bestowed upon it. Whether it will repay the toil, one cannot say. But certainly when vast labour has not been grudged in much less promising fields, it ought not to be withheld in this. I am satisfied that the field has not yet been explored, and that it is in these mountains, which Dr Wilson so hastily surveyed, that the key to the whole puzzle will be found. I ought to add, that the above remarks are founded upon, and were suggested by, the passage quoted from this able traveller, and not from what I saw or heard upon the spot. I regret deeply that I did not penetrate into these mountain mines of which he has given us too brief a description.*

What we saw in this valley is only part of a great series of inscriptions, which the traveller lights upon in various parts of the desert. On all that may lie in our

* The fact of these inscriptions not occurring in Ghurandel or Feirân, where the Israelites and Christian pilgrims might remain for some time, and only occurring in places where they could not remain above a day, is an important one. The fact of these writings being found in Mukatteb, which could attract only miners and such like, is equally important. At the same time, I regret that Dr Robinson, in the new edition of his Researches, should treat Mr Forster's theory as so visionary as to be unworthy of notice, while, at the same time, he suggests one much more visionary and untenable.

way, we mean to keep a watchful eye, noting down
time and place.

Meanwhile we recall the words of the patriarch, whose
dwelling was not very far from these valleys :—

> Oh that my words were now written,
> Oh that they were engraven on a tablet,
> With a pen of iron and with lead,
> That for ever on the rock they might be carved !

There is perhaps no book in the Bible which better
admits of illustration from desert-scenes and desert-cus-
toms than that of Job ; and to one who has dwelt even
for a few weeks amidst these, this book acquires a double
interest and attraction. Two or three times in the
course of every chapter he lights upon words, figures,
allusions, which seem robbed of half their point and
power when interpreted in connection with European,
or even with Syrian ways, and laws, and scenery. From
the first chapter to the last the Book of Job is the
book of the desert, as truly as Ecclesiastes is the book
of the palace, Proverbs the book of the city, Canticles
the book of the garden, Romans the book of the forum,
Hebrews the book of the altar, and the Apocalypse the
book of the temple.

CHAPTER VIII.

Wady Mukatteb, Thursday, Jan. 24.—Rose before seven,—the moon still bright;—a lovely scene,—the white tents, the yellow sands, the dark cliffs,—the blue heavens! But dawn is preparing to begin, and on the western sky the glow of the east is already seen, for in the desert I have noticed that sunset throws its soft purple over the east, and sunrise gives its gay blush to the west. The peaks of Mukatteb have taken on the redness long before the rays have reached the bottom of a valley so hemmed in on every side.

Had a quiet walk ; my morning psalm was the thirty-second. I met our sheikh on his dromedary. He had set off last night and crossed the hills towards the east to visit his wife and family, who had their dwelling some ten or twelve miles off. He had travelled all night, and was now returning to his duties as our guide. Behind him rode his son, a nice little Arab boy of ten years old, by name Mûsa. Around our breakfast-table we noticed

M

some birds, slyly making advances, to pick up our crumbs. We had not indeed found the desert altogether void of life. Flocks of pigeon-looking birds, which we are told are quails, occasionally met us. A few small birds, black and white in colour, somewhat bigger than sparrows, hopped among the bushes. And everywhere we found the raven. It seems to have its haunt in every cliff and valley. We wondered how or where these birds found food for themselves in such utter wastes. Certainly here "they neither sow nor reap," they neither have "storehouse nor barn." Yet they are fed; though what they feed upon we could not say, save that they hovered round our tents of a morning, waiting our departure, to secure all that might be left of the fragments. Possibly they feed upon the ants and beetles which burrow in these sands. It was quite a bird suited to be Elijah's purveyor; and often did the story of the prophet at the brook of Cherith occur to us (1 Kings xvii. 4, 6). More than once I came between the raven and the pistol. It was once the prophet's friend, and as such I did not like seeing any one trying to compass its death.

We started at half-past eight, our way lying south-east. As we rode out of the valley we saw a good many more inscriptions, both on the face of the low cliffs, and also on some large blocks lying on the sand. Some of these were very distinct, We moved onwards, still ascending, *Serbâl* before us in his rugged grandeur. At the end of the wady we came to a narrow defile,—

rough and rocky,—through which we were to descend into *Wady Feirân*. As we wound slowly through the defile, black peaks came up on the left, and huge yellow precipices overhung our right. Farther on we were met by a long line of terraces and peaks,—white, black, red, and yellow. At half-past ten we turned to the left and entered *Wady Feirân*, which at its commencement is not unlike *Wady Mukatteb*, in its general aspect. On the left the hills were black, on the right yellow. The sun was without a cloud and the heat intense. Just at this spot our dragoman came up to us to point out the grave of "the English minister,"—Mr Ewbank of Liverpool, who had died here above a year ago. Our dragoman had met his widow at Howârah, returning homewards, leaving her husband's dust behind her in the wilderness. The grave was on the side of a mound of sand or rough soil, such as abound here. No tree, no flower! No stone nor epitaph. No mourner to sit down and weep. How solitary did it seem;—and how sad to die and be buried here! An oppressive sense of loneliness seemed to come over us as we looked at the unmarked tomb, and then turned our camels' heads to journey slowly onwards. What should hinder that our grave might be as lonely as this? The desert was all around us. Friends were three thousand miles away. Our own life was but a vapour. Yet He who is "the resurrection and the life" is in this desert as truly as in our own loved land. He has his eye upon the dust of his saints here as well as in our own churchyards, where the united in life are joined together in death. Only Arab dust may hitherto have rested here ; but the first resurrection will find its objects in many a strange spot and amid unexpected company.* Yet no ; has not *Israel* been here ? And is not the dust of many a believing Israelite sleeping beneath these sands ?

> " Thy dead ones shall live,
> My dead body shall they arise,
> Awake and sing, ye dwellers in the dust :
> For thy dew is as the dew of herbs,
> And the earth shall cast out the dead."—(Isa. xxvi. 19.)

A pleasant breeze here met us, and mists coming over the sun, the day was kept cool. In the desert we often had this slight and almost imperceptible haze ; but the genuine cloud more seldom. The enormous cumuli, which, like mountains, stand out in our northern sky, and give us such gorgeous sunsets, are not so often seen here. There seems no medium between a sky all black with clouds, " like a dark ceiling," which is rare, and a sky either wholly cloudless or lined with a thin gauze of mist, which is very common, and seems in fact the natural result of the intense heat. We praise the " cloudless clime," and speak of it as the perfection of a land. But often did I long for the clouds of the north,

---

* The first part of the following fine epitaph would not be needed here, while the latter would suit well :—

> Exutus morte,
> Hic, licet in occiduo cinere,
> Aspicit Eum,
> Cujus nomen est Oriens.

not merely because of their shade, but because of the
beauty and the grandeur which they impart to the sky.
A sky perpetually without clouds is like a country without hills.

The wady continued level and spacious, running
south-east by east, perhaps from a quarter of a mile to
half a mile wide. It is sandy and bare, though we fall
in with the tarfa and seyâleh here and there. At twelve
o'clock we still find ourselves winding along the wady,
walled in by enormous black peaks, those on the right
apparently a sort of micaceous schist. A little way on
we picked up the fruit called *Hamdhall* by the Arabs,
—or "cucumis colocynthus" by botanists. It grows
like a gourd, its slender branches running along the
sand. Its size is that of a good orange, smooth and
yellow in its rind. It is bitter and poisonous. Great
quantities are exported to England for medicinal pur-
poses. Whether this is the "wild gourd" shred into
the pot by the servant of the prophet at Jericho, is
doubtful. We shall see what the plain of Jordan contains before giving judgment.

Still the same wild hills, with strange black seams or
dykes, running down their slopes at intervals of ten
yards or so. These streaks upon the bare mountain-
flanks come out with striking effect in a land whose
rocks have not a vestige of verdure to cover their nakedness. About two o'clock saw another inscription on the
right, quite the same as the Mukatteb ones, but rather
indistinct on account of the hardness of the rock and

the consequent difficulty of carving. About three, we passed a wady which my Arab called *Wady Khesr*, to the left, where we saw some seyâlehs. A little way farther we passed another " Mukatteb " inscription, to the left, on hard rock. The wady still continued to wind round immense mountains of trap, covered with debris, and sloping right down to the sand of the valley. About four we passed more " Mukatteb " inscriptions to the left, on some large blocks of granite ; and at another turn of the wady we came to five or six, full and distinct, on granite rocks, some low down, others far up. Here *Serbâl*, with its five rugged spires, came full in view frowning down upon us. The magnificence of its peaks and crags is truly Alpine. And now the wady becomes more fruitful ; its shrubs becoming larger and finer ; some palms too beginning to shew themselves. We noticed a curious prickly tree, like a brier or thorn, which our Arabs called *Aoshadh.* Prickly shrubs are beginning to appear in greater numbers ;—but of all of them the camels greedily eat. A thorn-tree or a Scotch thistle is not half so sharp or strong in its prickles, yet the camels browse on them as if they were soft grass, nor do their mouths suffer in the least. Even with a thick glove we should rather fear to touch them,—the camel opens his mouth and crushes a whole bunch of them. It almost looked as if he were crunching nails. These prickly bushes are used by the Arabs for their fires ; and they send up a quick and lofty blaze, which sometimes threw its red gleam over a hundred rocks.

Yet they called to mind the "primal curse,"—"thorns also and thistles shall it bring forth to thee" (Gen. iii. 18) ; at the same time telling of the time when "the desert shall rejoice and blossom as the rose" (Isa. xxxv. 1) ; when "instead of the thorn shall come up the fir-tree, and instead of the brier shall come up the myrtle-tree" (Isa. lv. 13).

But the next turn to the left was certainly worth the taking. It brought us to some hundreds of noble palms, —in a lovely hollow like a garden, or as we might call it, a palm-orchard. It was

> " A palm-grove islanded amid the waste."

Inclosing it were lofty hills, at the foot of which ran mud-walls in all directions, forming the garden enclosures of the Bedaween who reside here for several months in the year. Here we first saw the *Nub'k*-tree, not unlike a damson in appearance. Its fruit was just ripening, and our Arabs plucked it eagerly both for us and for themselves, as we halted our camels for a little under its grateful shade. The nub'k in size is like a cherry, in taste like a dry sweet apple. The sound of young voices came pleasantly through the trees ; and we soon met Arab children, some gambolling, some loitering, some gazing, some driving a flock of goats with a long wand, cut probably from some neighbouring *tarfa*, and some playing upon a rustic reed, which was certainly *tenuis avena*. Not far off were their tents,— the "black tents of Kedar" (Psa. cxx. 5 ; Song i. 5),—

which seemed made of camel's hair, and also, as our dragoman informed us, of "sheep-hair." About five o'clock we passed another inscription on the left, carved on a smooth block of granite on the mountain-side.

We now reached the ruins of the convent and village. Perched upon the very top of one of the most rugged hills to the left, was an old building quite broken to pieces, and evidently commanding no common landscape of peak, rock, sand, valley, garden, streamlet, a wonderful combination in such a wilderness, — while down the sides were stones, and walls, and gateways, and caverns, and curious-looking holes in the rock, both natural and artificial. These we explored to some extent, though after all, we found nothing which we had not seen from the foot. On the right the ruins are very extensive, chiefly occupying a central hillock or off-shoot of the cliff. Here were fragments of carved stones, round tapering heads of the convent columns, relics of pottery, bricks, fragments of walls, filled-up reservoirs, pipes running under ground for conveying water. These last, Sheikh Sulimân, who guided us through the different parts, informed us were for the *Hummâm** or hot-water springs, which are found here. Our tents had gone before us, so that, when we had finished our survey, we hastened after them, and about half-past five reached them,—all ready for our reception amid a grove of palms, with the mighty *Serbâl*

---

* The editor of the Egyptian *Prefetto's Journey* asks whether it is from this word that warm baths were once called "Hummin" in England.

looking down behind the rock-wall of the wady upon our encampment. In walking about we came upon the well, where we found our Arabs, with the help of the "villagers," watering both themselves and the camels. We made them draw for us, which they did by letting down the "skin" at the end of a long rope. To our surprise the water was warm,—though fresh and sweet. The whole valley is well watered as its verdure shews,— not the verdure of *grass* as with us,—you don't see that in the desert, save round a well or a rill,—scantily either in Egypt or Palestine ;—nor the verdure of forest-trees, these are only known in the well-watered regions of Lebanon, or Tabor, or the "hill-country" of Judah ;— but the verdure of palms and tamarisks,—such vegetation as is sufficient to feed the Arab and his camel. The palm-trees here are said to amount to about a thousand, —a good many of them belonged to our sheikh, who seemed rather proud of his leafy possessions. For it is the tree and not the ground that has an owner. The latter belonged to no man in special. It was the common property of the tribe. But the former were all parcelled out among individuals, so that our sheikh was a "landed proprietor" as far as any one can have such a name in the desert, where the land belongs to all. We saluted him here accordingly as one of the lords of "the soil," or at least of the trees,—changing his name from that of "sheikh" into the Scottish one of "laird," and explaining to him the meaning of the change. He smiled not a little at being addressed in this way,—es-

pecially when in the course of the evening we invited him
to take coffee with us, and treated him as one of the "gen-
try of the land." He sat at our table for more than half
an hour, we speaking English to him and he Arabic to
us, neither of us of course understanding a word. Like
all his fellows of the desert he was skilful in *signs*, and
would have made just such a professor as James the
Sixth is said to have been at a loss for, when requested
by some foreign ambassador to produce his professor
of signs. In speaking, an Englishman uses only his
tongue and lips ; a Frenchman adds his shoulders, for
the sake of significancy ; but an Arab throws in his
hands and arms as part of the conversation ; and these
are made to move in harmony with every word he
utters, more or less rapidly and violently according to
the nature of the discourse. Even when speaking to
his neighbour, an eastern adds signs of the most expressive nature, as we saw once when our dragoman, scolding his servant for some supposed fault, which it is likely
he had not committed, sent the frying-pan at his head,
which " sign " went whizzing past our tents, making us
perfectly to understand a transaction which otherwise
would have been quite without meaning. So was it
with our sociable sheikh ;—all his words came forth with
signs, which were often very vigorous and vivid,—as
hands, limbs, face, body, all were put in motion, and,
pointed to us or to himself, to trees, tents, rocks, sky,
sand, or stars, were made to interpret the eloquence
which came forth from his swarthy but kindly lips. For

never did we see a " sign " of anger or hear a rough tone from him, either to us or to his fellows. Our drago-man, though civil enough to us, seemed always in a passion with the Arabs, and even with his own servants, and how Sheikh Sulimân kept in good terms with him was a wonder to us. The good nature of the Arab was perhaps more than a match for the hot spirit of the proud Egyptian. The half hour with the sheikh over our coffee was an interesting one to us, as he was so obliging in shewing us everything connected with him-self, his dress, his weapons, &c. Nothing stronger than coffee did he taste ;—even our tea he did not relish ;—thick black coffee was his beverage. No wine nor spirits, nor strong drink of any kind, did these sons of the desert taste. It is not only against their habits but against their religion. The law of Mahomet forbids it, and like the sons of Rechab, these followers of the prophet keep the ancient law of their faith. Our dragoman was an exception, who drank freely when he could ; but he was an Egyptian, and seemed to be as much an infidel as a Mahommedan.

I wandered out in the starlight, for the moon had not risen. Starlight among the palms of the desert ! How exquisite ! There were our tents in the bottom of the deep glen or cup of rock, perhaps a mile in diameter ; its sides shooting up a thousand feet above us, and ter-minating in fantastic spires. There were the tall palms, with stems immoveable, like an obelisk, but with gently waving branches, on whose feathery leaves the stars crowded and sparkled like dewdrops. But now the moon has risen, for it is about ten o'clock. The stars grow dim, but the bright moonshine throws itself over the scene,—gleaming through the palm-leaves, and silvering the rugged peaks, over the highest of which rests the north star, reminding us of peace and home.

Here Jethro may have fed his flock with Moses as his associate, and Israel must have rested on their way to Sinai. I do not mean that this is the "wilderness of Paran," as many have written, deceived by the sound of the name. Paran lay immediately south of Palestine, at least two hundred miles from this, and by no straining either of imagination or geography can the desert of Paran be made to extend to this spot. But this was their route to the mount of God, and lay adjacent to the region of Horeb. Over this hollow once floated the wondrous cloud,—a shelter by day and a sun by night. On these very peaks its glory rested, forming a canopy or dome of gold (brighter than that of Omar or St Sophia), which roofed in this rocky temple and lighted up the tents of Israel as they lay scattered among these palms.

Wady Feirân, Friday, Jan. 25.—Before seven found myself strolling among the palms and tarfas. The moon was above one peak, the morning-star above another, while day-spring was taking possession of a third,—Serbâl looking sternly down through a defile upon the solitude. The day came up, and I pursued my walk up the steep slopes to the north, among the broken walls,—

still-standing door-ways, and cave-like holes in which I could see nothing, but which once seemed to have been the abodes either of the dead or living, most probably of the latter, when men forgetting that God has already made peace through the cross of his Son, tried to make their peace with him, and to win a name among their fellowmen, by living the life of worms or wild-beasts in these wretched dens, neglecting every duty and breaking every tie of kindred. These ruins, which belong to the fifth or sixth century, did not awaken much interest, as the story of the misguided triflers who dwelt there was not one which told of faith, or zeal, or love, or self-denying deeds, in behalf of a needy world. Our thoughts went back to ages, long before their first stone was laid, —the ages when Amalek possessed this region, and when Israel, marching through it, met and overthrew his hosts. There is no proof indeed that this was Rephidim, —nay proof that it was not Rephidim, for there must always have been water here, so that Israel could not have lacked it, as we read that they did at Rephidim. But their next stage from this must have been Rephidim,—and to that we are now proceeding. But before doing so, let us read the holy narrative. " And all the congregation of the children journeyed from the wilderness of Sin" (which they entered when they left Elim, Exod. xiv. 1), "and pitched in Rephidim, and there was no water for the people to drink" (Exod. xvii. 1). Up till the time when they reached Rephidim they had no lack of water,—so that they must have left Wady

Feirân and been a day's march on their way to Sinai before the " chiding with Moses" took place. (Exod. xvii. 2). The region on which they entered at Rephidim is called Horeb (Exod. xvii. 6), or the wilderness of Sinai (Exod. xix. 1, 2), and appears to have been wholly destitute of water.

We started about nine, feeling sure our halting-place would be somewhat near *Rephidim*, for next day was to bring us to Sinai. The air was chill, but as the wady was rather rough, we did not walk, but kept to our camels. The road winds like a princely avenue through palms and tarfas, some of the former very tall and stately. Though the sun had been up an hour, and every ridge was flushing with his radiance, the lower part of the valley had not received a single beam, so lofty is the wall of rock with which the basin is built in. We came abruptly, at a turn, in full view of *Serbâl*, every peak quivering with the sunshine. Between it and us there seemed only a low range of hills. Here we saw some ruins on a height, no doubt part of the great monastic establishment of Feirân.

But of all the thousands of monks that once idled away their days upon these heights, not one remains. They have perished, without any monument save the crumbling stone, or the crag of the desert, or the hole of the rock. Desolation ! Yes ; but how different the picture of eastern from that of western desolation ! Few of Ossian's figures would suit here. What Arab, even

the most poetical, could understand such a scene as the
following :—

> I have seen the walls of Balclutha,
> But they were desolate!
> The voice of the people is heard no more.
> The thistle shook there its lonely head,
> The moss whistled to the wind,
> The fox looked out from the windows,
> The rank grass of the wall waved round its head.
> Desolate is the dwelling,
> Silence is in the house of her fathers.

More apt and intelligible to an eastern is Job's picture—

> Tho' his excellency mount up to the heavens,
> And his head reach unto the clouds ;
> He shall perish for ever like his dung.
> They who saw him shall say, Where is he ?
> He shall fly away as a dream.
> He shall not be found.
> Yea, he shall be chased away
> As a vision of the night.
> The eye which saw him shall see him no more.
> Never again shall his place behold him.—(Job xx. 6.)
>
> .   .   .   .   .   .
>
> His place shall deny him,
> (Saying) I have not seen him.—(Job viii. 18.)

At one part the winter-torrent had cut deep into the
soil, some three or four feet, and in doing so had laid bare
a complete side-section of the roots of a palm. We
examined these with great interest, as they are quite
unlike any other tree-roots we had seen, and peculiarly
fitted to absorb every drop of moisture that the sand
contains. In general form and structure they put us

in mind of the dahlia and ranunculus,—consisting of
long fleshy strings or ropes shooting straight down into
the soil, in numbers quite beyond reckoning, and ex-
tending over a large circle, whose width we could not
ascertain, but which, as in the case of other trees, corresponds probably to the width of the circle formed by
the branches above. What an apparatus for drawing up
the moisture of the desert, so that not a drop is allowed
to slip away ! Casting the eye up from that wondrous
network of roots to the long green tresses above, ever
fresh and verdant, the " psalm or song for the Sabbath-
day" comes to recollection,

> The Righteous One shall flourish like the palm-tree,
> He shall grow like a cedar of Lebanon.

For the time spoken of is the day when God shall raise
up to Israel " a plant of renown" (Ezek. xxxiv. 29) ;
and it is that " plant of name," that " branch of Jehovah" (Isa. iv. 2 ; xi. 1), that " righteous branch," (Jer.
xxiii. 5) that is then to flourish like the palm-tree.
Around Him are gathered the " trees of righteousness,
the planting of the Lord" (Isa. lxi. 3).

> Those that are planted in the house of Jehovah,
> In the courts of our God, shall flourish.
> They shall continue to bear fruit in old age,
> They shall be fat and green.

But how great must be the drought when that desolation
comes to pass,—" the *palm-tree* and the apple-tree, even
all the trees of the field are withered" (Joel i. 12).   Of
all eastern trees the palm is most useful.   The vine is

only for fruit, it is not "meet for any work" (Ezek. xv.
1, 5), and if it fails in its fruitfulness, it is fit only for
the fire ; a true figure of Israel and of the church, useful
only when fulfilling their office of fruit-bearing (John
xv. 6). But the uses of the palm-tree are very numerous ; not a part of it but is turned to some purpose.
Its rough trunk we used to see in Cairo cast across a
ditch for a bridge. Under its feathery foliage we had
often sat down for shade. Its fruit we were enjoying
every day, the stones of which are sent to be ground
for food to camels. Its leaves formed the baskets,
great and small, in which our oranges and fowls were
mounted for conveyance. The shavings and thin yellow
fibres formed the sponge which was laid down along
with soap in our baths at Alexandria. Its sap forms
the spirit called *arrak*, which the abstemious monks
use at Sinai. Besides all this, its branches are cut
down to be the ensigns of joy and triumph, for with
these Israel was commanded to cover their booths in
that most joyful of all their feasts, the feast of tabernacles, when they were to "rejoice before the Lord
seven days" (Lev. xxiii. 40). With the figures of these
the gold of "the holiest" was carved (1 Kings vi. 29),
and the "wall of the house round about" (2 Kings vi.
29), and "the two doors" of the temple (2 Kings vi. 32),
and "the ledges and borders of the bases" (2 Kings vii.
36), and the golden "ceiling of the greater house" (2
Chron. iii. 5). On all parts of Ezekiel's temple, which
is in reserve for the day of Israel's glory, the palm-tree

N

is seen,—on the "posts" (xl. 16), on the southern gate
(xl. 26), on the eastern gate (xl. 34), on the north gate
(xl. 37), on the doors and windows everywhere (xli. 18,
19, 20, 25, 26). For great and marvellous will be the
triumph of that day. It was "branches of palms" that
the people took, when bidding welcome to the King of
Zion (John xii. 13). And with this same emblem the
triumphant multitude appears,—"I beheld and lo, a
great multitude, which no man could number, of all
nations, and kindreds, and people, and tongues, stood
before the throne and before the Lamb, clothed with
white robes, and PALMS IN THEIR HANDS." (Rev. vii. 9.)*

As we advanced the valley widened and the palm-
trees disappeared. We have passed out of the circle of
the oasis, and the desert is now as arid and sterile as
before. The verdure has disappeared. Only the tarfas
can live here, with a few of the usual shrubs ; and these
only in the lower parts, not on the slopes. We are approaching *Horeb* or the "burnt region," and coming to
the place where Israel "found no water to drink"
(Numb. xxxiii. 14), and where Amalek came out to
fight with them. (Exod. xvii. 8). The mountains are
beginning to be less sheer in their descent, and the
peaks somewhat less abrupt. About eleven we came to
a narrow pass, at the entrance of which, on the right,

* The tabernacle had no palm-trees graven anywhere ; for it was the
figure of the Church's pilgrim-state, whereas the temple is the emblem of
the day of triumph and reigning. Neither had the veil palm-trees woven
into it, for it was the emblem of the flesh of Christ (Heb. x.), and it was
to be "rent," as the flesh of Christ was to be broken.

upon a mass of granite, is a faint "Mukatteb" inscription.

A little after eleven we entered *Wady-esh-Sheikh,* or "royal valley," as it might be rendered. The name resembles that of the valley of *Shaveh* hard by Jerusalem, which was called *Emek-Hammelek,* or "king's vale" (Gen. xiv. 18). It may get its name from its being one of the largest and most princely of all the peninsular wadys, or from its having been the abode of some great tribe, as of the Amalekites, of whom it is said, "Amalek is THE HEAD of the nations" (Numb. xxiv. 20); for the Amalekites seem to have been a mighty people, occupying a large territory in the northern as well as the southern district of the desert, and their king probably the chief of the desert-tribes. Or perhaps it might be from *Jethro,* who was pre-eminently the sheikh of this district. No doubt the tradition is, that it was so called from the Moslem Sheikh Saleh, but one is not obliged to believe all Mahommedan traditions.

Wady-esh-Sheikh opens with a pretty wide circle, covered with tarfas and shrubs of the common desert-class. On our right, shooting up over a huge mountain-wall, *Serbâl* peers down on us in majesty, like a watch-tower, commanding the whole stretch of the wilderness. Three shrubs are specially noticed here, the *Djerûm,* the *Rim'th,* and the *Ritt'm* or *Rithem,* the two former fragrant, the last a species of broom, with a small white flower, streaked with pink. It is translated "juniper" in our version, but it has no resemblance to that shrub ;

whereas the Hebrew word *Rothem,* as illustrated by
the Arabic *Ritt'm,* shews us what it is.   It was under
this tree that Elijah sat down to take shelter from the
heat (1 Kings xix. 5); and more than once did we
do the same,—for some of these shrubs are bushy and
tall, perhaps eight or ten feet high.   They formed a
shadow sometimes from the heat, sometimes from the
wind, and sometimes from the rain,—both for man and
beast.   We could not just say of these what the prophet
did of the trees of the forest, " they burn incense under
oaks, and poplars, and elms, because *the shadow thereof
is good* " (Hosea iv. 13); but still it was about the best
shadow that the desert could afford, save when we could
get under some great rock or shaggy palm.   Job speaks
of behemoth,—

> " He lieth under the shady trees,
>   In the covert of the reed and fens;
>   The shady trees cover him with their shadow,
>   The willows of the brook compass him about."—(xl. 21.)

About noon we passed some more of the black tents
of Kedar, about a quarter of a mile to the left.   We
were moving on when we saw two or three Bedaween
approaching.   They came up to us, and we halted.   Was
it in kindness, or for money, or with a hostile purpose
that they came?   They held converse with our dragoman for some time, but we understood none of it.   They
did not look ill-disposed, and their voices were friendly.
So we stood silently for a few minutes.   Their object
was soon made known.   The speaker was, we were told,

the Sheikh of Arabah, and he was inviting us to his tents to rest ourselves, and to partake of some food and milk. But as this implied considerable loss of time, as well as a *buckshish*, and as there was no object to be gained by our going, we declined, giving him our thanks for his hospitality. But it reminded us of a scene in the plains of Mamre. " Abraham sat in his tent-door in the heat of the day ; and he lifted up his eyes and looked, and lo, three men stood by him : and, when he saw them, *he ran to meet them from the tent-door*, and bowed himself toward the ground, and said, My lord, if now I have found favour in thy sight, pass not away, I pray thee, from thy servant. Let a little water, I pray you, be fetched, and wash your feet, and rest yourselves under the tree : and I will fetch a morsel of bread, and comfort ye your hearts ; after that ye shall pass on " (Gen. xviii. 1–5). It reminded us too of the scene in the vale of Siddim, when Lot went out of his house to meet the angels and said, " Behold now, my lords, turn in, I pray you, into your servant's house, and he pressed upon them greatly " (Gen. xix. 2).

Like the other sheikhs whom we had seen, this prince of the desert was humble in attire and mien, and certainly did not look "every inch a king." His small screen of black canvas was no palace, and there was no state nor authority about him. What is the exact position of those sheikhs ? What is the nature, and what the limits of their power ? How far is their authority recognised and submitted to ? These were questions

which we often asked, but to which we found no good
answer. We could hardly conceive these men exercis-
ing judicial or royal functions,—though when dressed
out in silk and gold, with sword in belt, and gay tarboosh on the head, as we sometimes saw them, they do
not look so unroyal. Yet he who would rule these deserts would require a more dignified mansion, a cleaner
turban, and a sharper sword than theirs.

The sun was cloudless in his brightness; but a fresh
breeze from the west came along to cool us. A little
after one we passed two " Mukatteb " inscriptions on the
left, cut in the hard rock, and in about ten minutes after
we passed another. We continued to wind along *Wady-
esh-Sheikh*, which was tame, the hills on each being low,
but relieved by the magnificence of Serbâl behind us.
About four we came within sight of the Sinaitic range
and got a glimpse of *Jebel Músa*, the supposed mountain of the law-giving. A little to the right we saw
distinctly through the glass the palace of *Abbas* Pasha,
on a lofty peak, which seemed almost as high as Jebel
Músa. Each pasha seems to have some special object of
passionate pursuit. One spends his life and money on
horses, another on gardens, another, like the present one,
on the army, another, like his predecessor, on building
palaces. The first object of Abbas was to find the
healthiest spot with the purest atmosphere. For this
end he took several legs of mutton and suspended them
on lofty poles in different parts of the desert. The
place where the said leg remained longest undecaying,

was fixed on as the driest and healthiest, and there a palace was built to form a summer or winter residence for his highness. The pains taken to ascertain the healthiest spot shew how much he was in love with life, and how eagerly he grasped at everything that might prolong it for a day.

One palace he had built in the desert of Suez, where the above test had been applied, and there it stands, unfinished and unoccupied, like the famous Twizel Castle at home, on the banks of the Till. This other, *Abbas* had built on the mountain adjoining Sinai; and hardly ever was human dwelling, much less the palace of a prince, perched on so wild and high a cliff,—in the centre of a region of such unmitigated bleakness and sterility. Few, save an Egyptian pasha, could have attempted such a work. But it costs him little save the lives of men and camels, and these he counts just as so many dogs, especially the former. He fixes on a peak,—he gets a plan drawn, and his officers must see it executed. A few military stations are formed in the desert to overawe the inhabitants, and then every Arab that can lift a stone, and every camel that can bear a burden, are pressed into his service. No one dare refuse. The soldiers are at hand to hunt down each recusant without mercy to himself or his family. Not that there is *serfdom* in the desert. The Bedaween are free as the wild goats of their hills. The sons of Ishmael have never worn the chain, save when caught by the pasha's soldiers and led captive to Cairo or Alexandria. All their internal feuds have never resulted in subjection to a common conqueror. He who would conquer the desert must be one who can fill its streams with water and clothe its hills with verdure.

This palace cost several thousands of camels, whose bones lie strewed throughout the desert; how many men we could not learn. The stones and other materials required to be carried from vast distances through a scorching waste and sometimes over rocks or through passes, which, even when unloaded, the camel shrinks from. On the debris of bones,—the bones of man and beast,—that palace was built ; and now it stands there incomplete and empty,—the wind of the desert sweeping over it, and the curses of the injured Bedaween rising around it every hour as it strikes their eye from afar. One might ask Ossian's question, while looking up to these half-finished walls,—

> " Why dost thou build the hall,
> Son of the winged days ?
> Thou lookest from thy towers to-day ;
> A few years and the blast of the desert comes,
> It howls in thy empty courts
> And whistles round thy half-worn shield."

Or still more truly the question of Job,—

> " Where is the house of the prince ?
> Where are the dwelling-places of the wicked ?
> Have ye not asked the traveller,
> And do ye not know their tokens ?"—(Job xxi. 28.)

We encamped about five in *Wady-esh-Sheikh*, our tents looking out upon the Sinaitic ridges in one direc-

tion, and Serbâl in another. There was nothing remarkable about our resting-place. It was under a rock,
in a quiet corner of a small plain, about half way
through Wady Sheikh. Through this valley Israel had
passed. Here they had encountered Amalek; and, on
some of these heights, Moses, with Aaron and Hur, had
watched the battle, while Joshua fought in the plain
below. Here they chode with Moses and murmured
against God. Here the water had gushed out and followed them like a river. All over this valley had once
been spread the tents of the tribes. "How goodly were
thy tents, O Jacob, and thy tabernacles, O Israel."

This wady is the most spacious in the desert, and
perhaps also the most abundant in vegetation as a
whole, though it contains no oasis to equal that of
Feirân or Ghurandel. But here, as always elsewhere,
in these wastes the shrubs are confined to the bed
of the wady, or at most to a narrow belt along
the side of the hills or slopes. Any small fragrant
shrubs, such as the *Zatûr* and *Jadheh*, that get higher
up, are quite imperceptible to the eye at any distance,
and are besides very dusky in their hue.* Towards the

---

* Mr Stanley speaks of "the thin clothing of vegetation which is
seldom withdrawn, especially the aromatic shrubs on *the high hill-sides*."
I did not see anything in the desert that I could call even a thin *clothing*
of vegetation. The widely scattered shrubs do not deserve this name.
Aromatic plants on the high hill *crevices* I did find here and there, not
certainly on their sides. When Mr S. quotes Keble's description of the
desert, with its "mountain-ledges green," (on which sheep are represented as feeding), he surely did not mean to vouch for its accuracy?

north the vegetation creeps up somewhat higher, but in the southern interior it is quite unable to ascend. Hence the mountain-slopes never look green ; and it was only when the *Lussuff* threw out its sprightly verdure from some crevice, that there was the slightest approach to this. But a green twig stuck in the bare rock once in the course of a mile, was only a signal of distress. It made the leanness look leaner. Even where the shrubs abound in the wadys there is no show of what we should call green. Vegetation is so dull in its hue that it does not look like verdure. Sometimes a streak of green runs up the sides of a hill or along its front ; but on examination you find that this is from the colour of the strata, and not from vegetation. More than once we were deceived by the appearance of both green and brown upon the hill-sides, and supposed we were approaching a stripe of vegetation or a field which the plough had just turned over, when there was nothing before us save the rock in its green or brown nakedness. Quite as effectually did this *Seráb* of the rock cheat our inexperienced eye, with its stripes of vivid green along the rugged slopes, as did the *Seráb* of the valley deceive us, with its sunny lakes and wooded isles, and noble barks moving majestically across the glassy blue.

CHAPTER IX.

Wady-esh-Sheikh, Saturday, Jan. 26.—I got up before five, as we mean to start early for Mount Sinai, taking the way through the rugged pass of *Howai* (*Nukb-el-Howai*), and sending our baggage round by *Wady Sheikh*, which winds on till within a mile of the mountain. I awoke our dragoman, who cried out " Yes, Sir," called up our two servants, *Hamân and Hummâd*, and then went to sleep again. I tried to stir the Arabs, but that was beyond my power. They would not move. There they lay in two circles round the ashes of their fires, their coarse camel-hair cloak thrown over their heads, and the sand or their wooden saddles for a pillow. It was with some difficulty that I avoided walking over them, as in the semi-darkness no one could guess that these brown-looking heaps were anything save sacks of corn or perhaps charcoal. Our two faithful servants, however, knew their duty, and set about preparing breakfast. Meanwhile, I enjoyed half an hour's walk among the rocks and over the sands in the morning moonshine.

Our dragoman certainly had a watch, but it seemed to be of little use to him, and, accordingly, when he had to get up early in the morning, for a start, it was to the skies that he looked, not to his time-piece, for the hour, or at least for an approximation to it. Whether the said watch actually measured time, I cannot say. Like other eastern watches it was peculiar in its dial-plate, for the deciphering of which some skill is needed, as not only are the numbers different from ours, but eastern hours are not the same in length at all times, for they vary with the distance between sunrise and sunset. Our Arabs had no watches,—no not our sheikh. Watches! What do these sons of the desert care for such toys? They have the sun by day and the stars by night. Their keen and practised eye reads with amazing correctness the time of day or night from these " lights of heaven" that " rule the day and night." Their mode of time-keeping carried us back to the first appointment of these " lights," when it was said, " let them be for signs, and for seasons, and for days, and for years" (Gen. i. 14).

In their cities the voice of the Muezzin announcing the hours of prayer from the minaret, divided the day for them into regular parts ; and I believe that scientific means are adopted, by astronomical observations, to keep these times exact. How often have we heard that voice at midday proclaiming these solemn words to the busy city, "God is great, God is the greatest, come to prayer, come to prayer; prayer is better than work; come to prayer." It drew in some to the mosque; it simply announced the hour to others. In the desert, of course, the hours of prayer could not be correctly observed; for no minaret rises there, and no muezzin makes the rocks echo with his message. And though occasionally we saw our men going aside to pray, or rather to repeat some verses from the Korân, and to perform a multitude of genuflections, yet in general they were not very observant of the prophet's rules and times.

We moved off at half-past six,—that is to say, we four travellers, with our camels and camel-drivers,—and our dragoman. It was cold, the thermometer at 38°. Gradually the east began to shew signs of day. At one part of our rugged road the Bedaween set fire to a bush that was growing by the way. In a moment it was consumed. I thought on Moses. He had been forty years in the desert and knew well its shrubs, and how quickly they burned to ashes. When he saw one of them on fire, and yet unconsumed, it could not but excite his wonder. As yet he had not seen the glory of Jehovah,—the Shekinah glory,—nor knew how, though it was "like devouring fire," it could dwell even in one of these bushes without consuming a leaf or twig.

As we got to the top of the first height, we had a fine view of the Sinaitic range, though not of *Jebel Mûsa*

itself; with Serbâl not far off. The rugged perpendicular cliffs and peaks, on one side lighted up with sunshine, and on the other still wrapt in deep shade, with
a few light clouds resting on their summits, presented a
view of matchless grandeur. We now descended into a
valley, where *Nukb Howai* seems to open, or rather to
close upou us; for (in correspondence with the original
Hebrew word), *Nukb*, denotes a hole bored through the
mountains; and if the name mean, as it is said to do,
"the pass of the wind," the place has every appearance of
being true to the name. It is just such a hole or fissure
as the winds of the wilderness would delight to traverse,
in their passage over the hills to *Er-Rahah*. No blast
overtook us; but we could imagine the rush and roar
of the storm through such a mountain-tunnel. Not
far from this we saw ruins,—probably some outpost of
the Sinaitic convent. Our dragoman calls all these
things *Roman;* we should prefer to call them Romish
or Greek. The desert seems, from the fourth century
and onwards, to have been the abode of monks of all
sorts, as well as the resort of pilgrims. It was not per-
secution that drove them to these solitudes, nor could it
be the desire of doing good to their fellow-men, for even
although, like St Anthony, they could preach to the
fishes, yet the desert afforded no scope for the exercise
of such gifts. It would have been the part of brave
men to have faced the evils and perils of the city, as
did the Master and his apostles. It was cowardly to
quit the shore because the storm was high, and to refuse

to man the life-boat that should have gone forth to the rescue of a shipwrecked world.

Hard by is a Bedaween burying-ground,—the first that we had come upon. No wall nor hedge surrounds it ; no cypress throws its long shadow over it. It seemed at first but a collection of stones ; but we soon saw that there was order in this collection. Stones in couplets, five or six feet from each other, and set on end, with here and there a circle of lesser stones round them, shewed us that this was a place of graves, though no name nor epitaph appeared. Perhaps it might have been originally in connection with the monastic establishment which was not far off ; but now it was but the gathering-place of Arab dust. I had seen tombs upon the lone moor, and graveyards over which the sea-spray flung itself, and plain headstones with a bare text, or a name, or even without any such mark ; but I had never seen any thing so rudely simple as these Bedaween tombs.

As we advanced the valley became gloomier, and the shadows of the awful mountains on each side threw an impressive solemnity over us. Our northern passes are are not so terribly wild ; though steep in their slopes and lofty in their peaks, they are generally wider, and their sides are not without verdure, while the stream that hurries through the rocks at the base, speaks of life and freshness. But in this "pass of the winds," on which we are just entering, all is barrenness,—brown, bare, and lifeless. To the right went off *Wady Soláf,* running westward and forming a junction with *Wady Sheikh.* As we were ascending to the pass, we saw another Arab graveyard on the right. It is rather strange to find two such places within two miles of each other, while, previous to this day's journey, we had met with none. We soon got fairly up into the pass, and came under the shadow of these mighty cliffs. Large mounds of stones appear in various places all up the ravine. About eleven the way became so steep and rough that we had to dismount. After walking, or rather climbing, up for some time along the side of the pass, we saw symptoms of verdure at the bottom, and went down to explore it. We found a bright little rocky glen, with some half-grown palms and desert shrubs. Here, no doubt, a stream runs during the wet season, or after a shower; but all that we found was a pool under the shade of a palm-tree, with masses of granite all round. It was pleasant to sit down here and read the sixty-third Psalm. After "drinking of this brook by the way" (Ps. cx. 7), we set about recovering the path we had left, sometimes climbing over, and sometimes under, the huge rocks that stopped our path, like fragments of some vast mountain-wall that had gone to pieces on the heights. Near the head of the pass, about half-past eleven, we saw a "Mukatteb" inscription of one line, surmounted with the Egyptian *Tau*, which is in the form of a cross. It was, of course, on granite, yet it was not in a better state of preservation than those on the soft sandstone of the Mukatteb rocks.

About a hundred yards farther on, we passed another, on an immense block of granite; and about sixty yards farther, another, on a similar block, in very large letters, beginning as usual with ⌂⌐   .

We now came into full view of Jebel Mûsa, and just at the spot where we did so, saw another brief inscription, and a little farther on, another. The large sandy plain of *Er-Rahah* lay in front of us, about two miles in one direction and one in another. A finer place for the encampment of a multitude can hardly be imagined. The different peaks of the great central range towered before us,—*Jebel Oreb, Jebel Kátherin, Jebel Lejá, Jebel Mûsa.* As we were leaving the pass we heard the report of a gun among the rocks, and soon after we met an Arab with a wild goat, or ibex, or *Bedan*, which he had shot. Our dragoman and he soon came to terms about it, and it was bought for our use. It was lean enough, as indeed all the animals in the desert are, for the pasture is always scanty. Jeremiah's lament over the lost "beauty of the daughter of Zion" takes up this figure, " her princes are become like harts that find no pasture, and they are gone without strength before the pursuer " (Lam. i. 6).

Some travellers have maintained that all this region was much more fruitful and more plentifully watered three or four thousand years ago than it is now. It might be so; but the evidence of this is awanting. When the assertion is made on the ground of any

o

authentic facts, it is worth notice, as every hint as to the desert's past state or history is interesting. But when it is made for the purpose of accounting for Israel's long sojourn in the wilderness, and with the design of shewing that there was no need of any continuous intervention of miracle, it cannot fail to excite misgivings in the reader's mind as to the extent to which the writer believes in the strict veracity of the Mosaic narrative.

We now descended into *Wady-Er-Rahah*, the "valley of rest." Here Israel pitched their tents before the mount in "the wilderness of *Sinai*" (Exod. xix. 1, 2), which adjoins "the wilderness of *Sin*" (Exod. xvi. 1 ; xvii. 1). The whole district is called *Horeb* in Scripture, which uniformly preserves the distinction between Sinai and Horeb, by using "*on* Sinai" (Exod. xix. 20), and "*in* Horeb" (Exod. xvii. 6) ; shewing that the former is a mountain, the latter a region.* With how many memories is this plain strewed ! Once it was covered with the "goodly tents" of Israel ; which probably spread themselves out into the neighbouring valleys, especially *Wady Sheikh ;* for by itself it could

---

* Keble inaccurately uses "*on* Horeb" instead of "*in* Horeb" (*Christian Year, Ninth Sunday after Trinity*). 1 Kings xix. 8, 11. It is remarkable that in the eleventh verse, which our translators render "upon," the Hebrew is "in ;" so that there is no authority for "on" in connection with Horeb. See p. 216. In the same hymn he speaks of "Sinai's caves." There is nothing worthy of the name of *cave* on Sinai. Indeed, being a granite mountain, it does not admit of them, as do the limestone ranges of Syria and the sandstone of the more northern parts of the desert. Elijah's cave seems to have been at some distance from Sinai.

hardly have contained an encampment of two or three millions. Once the praises of Jehovah rose from voices without number, and the smoke of the sacrifice was wafted across these peaks. Here, perhaps, in the centre of this plain, stood the golden calf, with the naked multitudes dancing and singing round it to their shame (Exod. xxxii. 6, 25). Here it was that Moses broke in pieces the stone tablets of the law,—" it came to pass, as soon as he came nigh unto the camp, that he saw the calf (which he could not see from the hill), and the dancing ; and Moses' anger waxed hot, and he cast the tables out of his hands, and brake them beneath the mount" (Exod. xxxii. 19),—just on that spot right in front of us, which the hill overhangs. But beyond these general memories or traditions we need not venture.

Take a monk with you and he will go farther ; for in the sixth century it became part of the monastic vocation to affix names and traditions to the localities of this region, for the benefit of the six thousand brethren that then occupied the desert, and of the thousands of pilgrims that in after ages flocked to this centre. You will be shewn the "Hill of Aaron," where he watched the idolatrous dance of Israel round the calf which he had made ;—the pit of Korah,—the mould of the golden calf,—the mark of the body of Moses on the mountain, —the hoof-print of the dromedary of " the camel-driver of Mecca,"* near the top of Jebel Mûsa,—the smitten rock, with its curious rents, in Wady Lejâ, which Sasâ-

* Sir Walter Scott.

feh overhangs ; you will get traditions without number,
—Christian and Mahommedan,—fastened upon every
peak, or slit, or hollow, or granite boulder.   But these
are the things which destroy the scene, disenchanting it
of the grandeur which overshadows the wondrous whole,
by the introduction of trifles, and fables, and uncertainties.   The true grandeur of this region is made up of
a few mighty events,—events which, in their awful
majesty, sit apart from every other, and are incapable
of mingling with lesser things.   They are great, and
will not mix with the little.   They are true, and will
not sort with the fabulous.   They are solemn, and certain, and real, and can have no fellowship with the
trivial, the uncertain, the unreal.   Nothing can be
more unequally yoked together than the histories and
the traditions of Mount Sinai.   Yet superstition has
woven them into one, and in so doing has robbed the
mountain of half its greatness, making us feel as if we
were in the scene of Homer's gods or Ossian's ghosts,
rather than in the spot where the prophets and priests
of the most high God had been, nay, where the living
God himself had spoken, and where he had appeared
in his glory.   It needs here an effort to conjure up the
real by itself, and to separate it wholly from the unreal ;
yet it is only when one can succeed in doing so, that the
true grandeur of the scene is realised.   What pains
these monks have been at to divest Sinai of its majesty !
They could hardly have done more in this way, had
they gone out with their paint-brushes and besmeared

the whole mountain with staring red, green, and blue. The monks of St John's, Malta, painted their silver shrines, at the approach of the French, to prevent them being stolen by the invader; and these desert monks have daubed their mountain-shrine all over with fond tales and legends, so as to hinder its true glory from being seen and appreciated. Yet thus, perhaps, God has hid the *mountain* of Moses as he hid his *body*, lest it might be worshipped. These fables and fooleries may have hindered a greater amount of superstition than they have fostered. It might have been worse for the world and worse for the church had the true cross really been found at the true Calvary, or had the broken tables of the law been actually discovered lying scattered at the base of Sasâfeh. Superstition has sometimes been a destroyer of itself as well as an injurer of the truth of God.

We need something to check our veneration for sacred spots,—and to put us on our guard lest we mistake sentimentalism for faith. The Most High dwelleth not in temples made with hands, nor upon mountains consecrated by feet of holy men. Worship does not need Sinai to excite it. If the truth concerning God, as written in "the law and the prophets," will not call forth worship, and fear, and love, nothing else will. Nowhere are we more in danger of spurious religious feelings than amid the real scenes of Sinai or Jerusalem. In so far as my being in this solemn desert makes me better understand or relish even one single verse of

Scripture, it has brought me rich blessing, well worth
all the cost, and the toil, and the weariness; in so far
as these scenes do for me what the harp of the min-
strel did for the ruffled spirit of Elisha,—soothing or
solemnising me, so that I may become more sensitive
to the "true sayings of God," concerning sin and the
sin-bearer,—concerning my desert wanderings here or
my hope of the Paradise above,—so far all is right.
But if I go beyond this, and make use of these rocks
and solitudes for working myself up into a religious
fervour, or melting my spirit down into tears, or moving
my conscience into terror,—I have gained nothing, save
perhaps a greater amount of self-delusion, by teaching
myself to confound the sensuous with the spiritual, the
human with the divine. We may not need to be very
exact in scrutinising the nature of that patriotism that
is kindled on the plain of Marathon ; but we do need
to be somewhat more particular in ascertaining the
genuineness of the piety that has caught its warmth
from the ruins of Iona.

We have often asked the question, "Was St Paul
here ?" We know that he went into Arabia (Gal. i. 17),
and his allusions to Sinai and Agar are almost those of
one who had looked upon these peaks (Gal. iv. 25).*
It is not at all unlikely that he was here, and the fact

* Mr Howson suggests Paul's visit to Sinai. (Life and Epistles of St
Paul, vol. i. p. 105.) Mr Stanley seems to adopt this ; and Mr Alford remarks, "we may well suppose St Paul to have become familiarized, during his sojourn there, with this name (Hajir) for the granite peaks of
Sinai" (vol. iii. p. 48).

is a striking one. Moses and Paul—the lawgiver and the expounder of the true meaning and use of law—meet on the same mountain. They hold fellowship across a void of fifteen hundred years, the only intermediate link being Elijah, the awful reviver of the law, and at the same time the herald of Him who is "the end of the law for righteousness to every one that believeth."

We soon traversed the plain of *Er-Rahah*, and entered *Wady-esh-Shueib*—Jethro's valley—or, as it has been subsequently called from the convent which is planted in its centre, *Wady-ed-Deir*. Here Jethro fed his flocks, and here Moses abode with him forty years. From this he came forth, like another Melchisedec, to meet with Moses "at the mount of God" (Ex. xviii. 5). He was priest of God in "Midian" (Ex. iii. 1), which appears to have been the name for some part of this region. By him was the worship of the true God kept alive in the desert, just as it was by Melchisedec in Jerusalem. Moses "did obeisance" to him, and Jethro blessed him in words which bear a remarkable resemblance to those of Melchisedec when blessing Abraham ; and it is "the less that is blessed of the greater" (Gen. xiii. 19, 20 ; Ex. xviii. 10). Jethro "took a burnt-offering and sacrifices for God,"—he provides a feast, and to it he calls Aaron and the elders of Israel (Ex. xviii. 12) —thus shewing himself greater than Aaron. Nay, he proceeds to give counsel to Moses, and he begins that counsel with the words of authority, "the thing that thou doest is not good." And it was on Jethro's counsel that Moses acted in ordering the various things pertaining to the government of Israel. The "king in Jeshurun" was counselled by one greater than himself. "So Moses hearkened to the voice of his father-in-law, and did all that he had said" (Ex. xviii. 24).

This region, then, had, long before Moses or Israel entered it, been the seat of true worship. God had here his priest and his king. And this was the reason, doubtless, why Moses, when fleeing from Egypt, betook himself to the land of Midian. He knew that a people dwelt there who feared Jehovah, and that amid the rocks of the desert he would find a friendship and a sympathy which not only Egypt but his own people had denied him. Sinai was even then known as "the mountain of God" and as being "in Horeb" (Ex. iii. 1).* Whether "the glory" had or had not then taken up its abode upon the mount we cannot say. There is nothing unlikely in the thought that this was its old abode ; not an abode to which it was just coming, but from which it was about to depart, in order to take up another dwelling ; and that just as the glory, when about to depart from Jerusalem, was displayed to Israel in Ezekiel's awful picture of it, so the glory, when about to leave Sinai, gave forth its unutterable splendour and majesty.

---

* This is the meaning of the original, which our translation injures by inserting "even." "He came to the mountain of God, Horeb-ward," is the literal rendering. The mount of God is not said to be Horeb, but in the region called Horeb.

Near the entrance to *Wady-esh-Shueib*, at the foot of the hill, there are some more rude tombs. Are these graveyards ancient or modern ? Or are they not both ? That is to say, have they not been graveyards from ages immemorial, where generation after generation have been gathered to their fathers ? For the resting-places of the dead are more fixed than the abodes of the living. They seldom change, and the child of this year is buried in the same spot as the forefathers of his tribe or race a thousand or two thousand years ago. This, then, might have been the burying-place of Jethro and his tribe. Not far off is a well. Was this the well at which Moses sat down, and to which Jethro's seven daughters came to water their flocks ? Was it here that the son of Amram found his Gentile bride (Ex. ii. 15, 21) ? Just beyond the well we saw another inscription ; and again some tombs. Then we passed the pasha's barracks, and saw a few Egyptian soldiers loitering about. At two we reached the convent, and entered by the garden gate, while our baggage, our dragoman, and our servants went up by the windlass. Our Bedaween remain outside, some preparing fire and food, others setting off for their homes ;—some to return on Monday, one or two leaving us altogether.

We found nothing of the eager welcome, and the fond embrace, and the generous hospitality, which some travellers are said to have experienced. A stout, oldish, and not over cleanly, servant shewed us to our rooms, which were on a sort of gallery which ran along the north side of the convent. There we had a comfortable divan, a rough wooden table, a floor of cement, and walls of bare plaster. The window or lattice looked out towards the garden, and beyond it to Er-Rahah. Its fit was not a very tight one, and it flapped in the desert wind, which once and again came rushing through it, and at this season was sharp and cold. The long-gowned servitor, in whose countenance sat no intelligence, brought us some arrack or date-spirit, which has an unpleasant taste, but which seemed to be in use in the convent. The monks are described as living on poor and scanty fare,—beans, bread, and water. Such is said to be the rule of the house. They did not look like half-fed men ; and we found, moreover, that very soon after our dragoman arrived, he was engaged to cook dinners for the brethren of a much superior kind.

After we had rested a little we went to survey the chapel of the convent. We had heard the bell ring, or rather the wood sound, for it is by striking a long beam of wood that they summon to service. They had three bells, of perhaps two centuries old, but they do not use these, perhaps through the force of immemorial custom. For in past ages they were not allowed to use bells. As Mahommedans do not use bells themselves, but summon to prayer by means of the human voice alone, so they seem to have prohibited the use of bells to others. Debarred the use of bells, the Christian sects had ingeniously contrived to construct and so to strike wooden bars, as to make them give out a sound not unlike a small

bell. It was this bar of timber, placed in a sort of shed
or belfry about the centre of the east wall, that had
emitted the shrill sort of sound which we had heard.
We descended to the chapel, into which light came but
scantily. It was gaudily decorated on all sides with
pictures, statues, candles, lamps, &c. There is too much
of tinsel here. A high, large, bare, rocky hall would
have satisfied our idea of a chapel for Sinai. This toy
is certainly out of place. Instrumental music is almost unknown in the churches of the east, so here it was wholly
the human voice that was employed. The chanting
saluted us as we entered, but we were only able to catch
a few words of the modern Greek in which it was read.
We heard something like a hymn to Jehovah,—Father,
Son, and Holy Ghost. The chanting was not pleasant.
It was not irreverent, yet it was not solemn. It had a
reedy sound, not unlike the drone of a bag-pipe. There
were three monks engaged in it, each with service-book
in hand and cap on head. One was standing at one
side of the chapel at a desk, another at the opposite, also
in a desk. The third wandered between the two, crossing and re-crossing the floor every two or three minutes,
chanting all the while. Two or three were loitering about
the outer aisle. We lingered perhaps half an hour, and
then left ;—but not with high emotion. This is not
worship,—at least it is not the worship of which God has
anywhere given us an example. These chanters are not
the leaders of praise to any assembly of God's saints.
From year to year they utter set sounds in which no

one is present to join. It may be song, or it may be individual service, but it is not the worship of the church. It is not even " the voice of one crying in the wilderness," for that voice drew tens of thousands together to hear the news of Messiah's speedy coming; but this voice speaks to none. A passing traveller hears it, and perhaps adds his " Amen ;" but that is all. The poor Arab understands it not : no one tries to teach him Messiah's name. He lives untaught and uncared for, and he dies unpitied, by these brethren of the convent, who are far too busy with their garden, and their almonds, and their pomegranates, and their arrack, and their chants, to have time to shew these Bedaween the difference between Christ and Mahomet, between the Bible and the Korân. It sounds well to speak of the monastic " service of song " as a " prelude of the everlasting chant before the throne ;" but what is there in this solitary repetition of words and notes, that bears the least likeness to the voice of the " great multitude which no man can number ?" (Rev. vii. 9.)

We next went down to the garden. In order to find our way and get the gate opened, we must have the servant or porter, that is, the lay-brother who acts as such. He was not at hand, so he had to be summoned by voice. " Mûsa," rung through the convent. But he was out of the way. Again, however, we heard a voice shouting " Mûsa " along the galleries, and that name thus shouted aloud at the foot of Mount Sinai, echoed strangely in our ears. At length " Mûsa " came, shabby

and dirty both in look and garb. He led us down by
several flights of wooden steps in a poor state of repair,
as indeed most things in the convent seemed to be.
Through a low narrow passage, the stone-roof of which
more than once struck unexpectedly on our heads, we
made our way to the garden. As this was the month of
January there was not much to be seen. The fruit-trees
were not in leaf; but the almond was covered with its
bright pink and white blossom, — which adorned its
naked boughs. It is the " watcher " for the spring,—
lying sleepless on its winter-couch, and then rushing
forth in naked haste to salute the sun. Hence Jeremiah
is made to use it as an emblem of the haste with which
a longsuffering God would at last perform his strange
act of judgment upon—

> the dark idolatries
> Of alienated Judah.

The fig-tree, too, was there, but with neither fruit nor
leaf. The pomegranate was not in bud; but round its
foot we picked up some of the old fruit of last year,—
hard dry pomegranates. Only the cypress had on its
dark verdure, rising in the midst of the wide-spreading
trees, like a tall minaret above the arching dome. Are
these all *exotics*,—Grecian or Persian exotics,—as some
think ? And is this garden altogether a thing of monastic art and labour ? Perhaps not. Feirân was an oasis
of palms and nubks before one stone of its convent was
laid ; and it does not seem at all unlikely that there was

some oasis here of almonds, and figs, and pomegranates in the days of Jethro. We met with several fig-trees growing wild in *Howai*, within a mile or two of this, which shew that these are not exotics. And whence came the almond-rods of Aaron and the tribal heads, if there were no such trees then in this region? Does not the selection of the pomegranate as an ornament of the high priest's robe intimate that it, too, was known in the desert?

Returning from the garden, I went to the place where the pulley and the windlass were at work fetching up our luggage. Neither Arabs nor monks were in any haste about this, acting, as all in these regions seem to do, upon the Mahommedan maxim, that "all speed is from Satan." I asked to be let down, and was proceeding to take hold of the smaller rope which is worked simply by the hands of two men, when I was stopped, and the end of the thicker rope was brought to me, which is worked by a large wooden windlass. Fastening round my body the five or six smaller ropes attached to the end of the large one, I swung myself out at the aperture, and the wooden crane soon lowered me, amid the shouts of our Arabs, who received me in their arms as I came slowly to the ground. I took the way which led circuitously up the mount, but was saluted at the outset by half a a dozen of dogs, who seem as plentiful outside as cats are within. Leaving their noise behind me, I walked slowly up the road, which is carefully kept in repair, and which conducts the ascender gradually round the hill to

the southern side. I knew that I had not time to reach
the top to-day, but I was anxious to get up as far as an
hour might allow me. In about twenty minutes I came
to snow, lying pretty deep and hard, not on the road,
but under the wall which in some places lines it. It
was the first snow I had seen since I left Europe, and it
was evidently the remains of a vast deal more. Still
ascending and winding, I came in sight of the southern
base of the mountain, with the rocks and hills that rise
right opposite. There is a narrow valley (Wady Sebaiyeh), partly sand and partly rock, into which the descent would not have been long or difficult. But I
could not spare even half an hour, as the sun was getting low, and I was alone. The wady looked dreary and
savage, bare gravel mounds and hills rising beyond it ;
nor was there any breadth of level ground for the encampment of a multitude. It was quite a contrast to
Er-Rahah. After lingering here for a little to survey
all above and below me, I returned to the convent,
getting in by the garden-door as at the first.

Having still a little time before sunset, we proceeded
to survey the convent. At its angles are crosses, and in
one of its central buildings the *crescent*, perhaps to pro-
pitiate the Arabs. We examined the three bells and
the wooden bar. We entered several of their smaller
chapels, in all of which the incense was still fragrant.
The ornaments are poor and childish. We went to the
library, but found it shut up. We looked in at the
window and saw the books in utter confusion, and evi-

dently in an imperfect state of preservation,—boards torn, leaves loose, and lettering effaced. Another room and a better bookcase were preparing, but as these were not yet fitted up, the books lay huddled together in another apartment. We would fain have got entrance to the interior to examine the volumes even as they lay, but by no persuasion could we induce the monks to give us access. So whatever of ancient lore this confusion might contain,—Greek or Latin fathers,—the gifts or purchases of twelve centuries,—remained unseen by us. The ancient Greek manuscript of the New Testament, belonging to the sixth century, named by Tischendorf the *Codex Sinaiticus*, was possibly buried among the chaos. That its custodiers knew its value, or have even attempted its collation, is very questionable. Their leisure, which is great, seems to be anything but a learned one.*

As we went round the roof, we found snow on some parts of it, and were struck with the crazy shabby look of its walls and stairs. In an open area below, we saw several bearded monks, whose vocation seemed to be that of playing with the large cropt-eared, cropt-tailed cats that swarm in the convent.

It was now near six o'clock, and Mr Wright had not returned from photographing in the plain of *Er-Rahah*. The sun had set, and if monastic rules were to be kept,

---

* Lepsius remarks, " The whole life of these four priests and twenty-one lay-brothers is the reverse of edifying. They gave us the general impression of being under a dark rain-cloud, weighed down by the continual pressure of ignorance and indolence."

he would not be admitted unless he came immediately.
We went to the "housetop" to look, but there was no
appearance of him. We hailed our sheikh, and told
him what we were looking for. In a minute he was on
his dromedary and off to Er-Rahah, along by the barracks and the tombs. Half an hour longer we waited,
and the twilight was passing into the night, but he did
not return. Often did our little servant Hamân shout
till the rocks echoed, but without an answer. Voices
are heard, and objects seen in this clear, dry, lonely
region, at twice the distance at which they are heard
and seen with us at home, so that there could be no one
within a mile, to return the hail. At last in the dim
twilight we saw a speck passing out of Er-Rahah, and
up our wady. We soon hailed it, and our little Nubian
again made the rocks ring with the name of *Sheikh
Sulimân.* The hail was now returned, and in ten
minutes the sheikh and his dromedary, with the belated
traveller, were at the convent-gate. Mr Wright had
been too much engrossed with his photography to notice
the hours ; and, besides, he had an Arab with him.
Some eight or nine fine photographs of Sinai and the
neighbouring peaks were quite a sufficient excuse for
the delay. No one save a photographer can sketch
the desert. Roberts' views are noble, and to a certain
extent true ; but they do not represent these desert cliffs
and ravines. No artist can rightly do it. Only the
photographer can portray the million of minute details
that go to make up the bleakness, the wildness, the

P

awfulness, and the dismal loneliness of these unearthly wastes.

About nine I went out and walked upon the convent-roof. The starlight over the mountain-peaks was splen-did, while the gloom that hung round these enormous precipices and impenetrable ravines, was quite oppres-sive to the spirit.

This is the scene of which David spoke—

" He looked upon the earth, and it trembled;
  He touched the mountains, and they smoked."—(Ps. civ. 32.)

This is the mountain " that was touched, and that burned with fire" (Heb. xii. 18).* We could imagine the black girdle of the thick darkness with which the mountain was surrounded, and the lightnings giving forth their quick fire through this covering, making its blackness blacker. We could imagine, too, the super-natural blaze, kindled by no earthly hand, that shot up out of the midst of this, like a living column of fire, ascending, amid the sound of angelic trumpets and superangelic thunders, to the very heart of heaven.

---

* Not the mount that " might be touched," as our translators have rendered it, but the mount " that was touched," ψηλαφωμενω,— the mount on which the finger of God rested.

CHAPTER X.

Mount Sinai, Sabbath, Jan. 27.—Rose early, and
went out to the roof to read over and examine the passages relating to Sinai. I had read them a thousand
times before; but to read them on the spot, and at the
foot of the old mountain, was new and strange. The
morning was clear, but cold. One of the monks kept
walking about also, as if anxious to give me his company. He was not very attractive in look, and could
talk nothing but Arabic. I tried him in vain with Greek
and Latin. I got this much out of him, that the peaks
which are visible from the convent are not the real peaks
of Sinai. Jebel Mûsa is " fôk, fôk,"—said he, pointing
with his finger in a way which told me that it was
beyond and above these cliffs which were overhanging
us, and on each of which we could see little crosses. It
lay a little to the south and west of us, rising like a cone
or spire out of a hollow, of which these other peaks
formed the outer edge. This was all I could get from
the monk, and as I preferred being alone, I walked to
another part of the roof.

At the angles of the convent there are pennons or flags, which, when I came upon the roof at first, had not been hoisted, but which in a short time were "run up" by the "lay brother," whose charge they were. The slender pole to which they are attached, is surmounted by a cross, and being formed apparently of some cypress stem or sapling, it has sinuosities which make it resemble the figure of a serpent. Hence some travellers have mistaken it for a representation of the brazen serpent.

It was Sabbath,—and Sabbath at the foot of Sinai. These rocks had heard the words, "Remember the Sabbath-day to keep it holy," and could testify that He who spoke these words, meant the Sabbath for a blessing, not for a curse; for rest, not for burden-bearing, for liberty, not for bondage. Yet every argument that I had read at home against the Sabbath, took for granted that the institution was evil and not good, and that Christ has brought us a happy deliverance from the Sabbath-yoke! We found how good it was to rest from our journey each seventh day, and we did not find that it made the rest less pleasant to know that it was "according to the commandment." It was pleasant to hear the Sabbath-bell, even in the midst of superstition. The frequent tolling or striking was no grating sound, either at noon or midnight.*

* "They are permitted to strike on bells, but not to suspend them." —*Laborde*, p. 315. We saw them, however, suspended, so that this law must no longer be in force.

We breakfasted at nine, and had prayers in our rooms; but at one we went out to have more regular Sabbath-worship at the foot of the hill. We preferred the free air and broad mountain-side to our narrow chamber. So we went about a mile up the hill, to the spot where it begins to look over to the other side, and there we sat down, with our bibles. We sung together one of David's psalms, and kneeling down on the rock, we joined in prayer. After reading the fourth chapter of Deuteronomy, I preached on Romans iii. 21, 22,— the sin and the righteousness,—man's sin, God's righteousness,—righteousness placed at our disposal and within our reach by that very God who on this mountain had condemned our sin,—righteousness of which we are put in immediate possession upon our reception of the divine testimony respecting it. We then sung the doxology, "To Father, Son, and Holy Ghost;" and after service we separated. I returned to the convent, and spent the afternoon in reading the passages which refer to Sinai, and in noting down texts for my class at home. Such as these came into remembrance, "Our God is a consuming fire" (Heb xii. 29); "by the law is the knowledge of sin" (Rom. iii. 20); "Christ is the end of the law for righteousness to every one that believeth" (Rom. x. 4).*

---

* The old hymn brings out the contrast between Sinai and Sion : —

Sinæ sub alto vertice
Cælo tonante, lex data;
Inter tubas et fulgura
Praesens minabatur Deus.

In the evening I enjoyed the starlight upon the roof. These blue Sabbath-heavens! How calm they looked, even when resting over a mountain so terrible as that of Sinai. It seemed as if its terrors were all confined to itself. It could not communicate these to the heavens above it, nor dim the brilliance of a single star. Orion looked brighter than ever, as he passed along the peaks, and shed down his quiet lustre upon their awful gloom.

Mount Sinai, Monday, Jan. 28.—Went to the roof about seven for a morning walk. It was just dawn. The sunshine had lighted on the topmost peaks, and was beginning slowly to descend their steep and haggard sides. I watched the descent till the sun at last reached the foot, and shot across the plain, brightening the level sands.

After breakfast met one of the monks upon the roof. He knew nothing of Latin,—a little of Italian, and as much of Greek as was needful for getting through the service of a Greek convent. He was conning an official volume, which he shewed me. It was in modern Greek, and seemed such a work as "The Whole Duty of Man" or Taylor's "Holy Living." It was a sort of directory

Nunc, temperato Numine,
Per vela carnis blandius
Amat videri, languidis
Se lumen aptans sensibus.

Insculpta saxo lex vetus
Præcepta non vires dabat;
Inscripta cordi lex nova
Quidquid jubet dat exequi.

for a "perfect life." After looking at it for a little, I drew out a copy of our Scottish "Shorter Catechism" in Greek, translated by Mr Robert Young, formerly of Edinburgh, and asked him to read it. He began at once, and read the first five or six questions to me. Though his pronunciation was different in some respects from ours, yet I could follow him entirely, as he read slowly, first the question and then the answer. He seemed pleased with what he read, and said it was good. Strangely interesting it was to hear the Catechism we had learned in childhood, and which every child in Scotland knows, read by a Greek monk at the foot of Sinai,—to listen to him as he read " Man's chief end is to glorify God and to enjoy him for ever ;" and again, " God is a spirit, infinite, eternal, and unchangeable, in his being, wisdom, power, holiness, justice, goodness, and truth." I asked him to accept the copy ;—on which he thanked me, and " bowed with his face to the earth." Soon after, he got together three or four of his brethren, and read it to them. I gave him an Italian testament and some Greek tracts. In return he presented me with some pomegranates from the garden, and some shells from the Red Sea.*

We started for the top of Jebel Mûsa about half-past ten, one of the monks accompanying us. Some of the others took the winding road to the south,—I tried the

---

* Of these shells camel-loads are brought to the convent from the Red Sea. They serve as merchandise or as gifts to pilgrims and travellers, as the occasion may require.

more direct but steeper one, just behind the convent,
guided by two Arab boys who brought me crystals from
the mountain.   Though very rugged, yet it has steps
cut or laid the most of the way.   These are said to have
been made by the Empress Helena, but are perhaps more
ancient.   Some old writers number them at 6000!   In
about twenty minutes we came to a beautiful well, quite
under some lofty rocks, called *Ma'yan-el-Jebel*, or the
spring of the mountain.   It seemed to be carefully kept,
and round it large stones were set in a wide circle, on
which might have been written "rest and be thankful."
I enjoyed the shade for a few minutes, and dipping my
guttapercha cup into it, I tasted its waters.   They were
sweet and cool.   A few small plants grew round the
inner margin, and a slight green scum covered part of
the pool; but no moss grew upon the rocks that at some
parts overshadowed it, and in others dipped into it.
Neither in Egypt nor in the desert did we find moss on
the rocks.   In the deep wells or tanks of Egypt one may
find it, but nowhere else.   It needs more moisture as
well as more shade for its growth than these lands afford.   The country of the stately palm is not the region
for the lowly moss.*

---

* Poets in their descriptions ought to be accurate.   Yet they are often
far from being so.   They write at random or draw upon fancy.   Hence
Keble speaks of the mountains of Palestine as "terrassed high with *mossy
stone*" (Christian Year, Third Sunday in Advent).   My friend, Mr Adam
White, of the British Museum, commissioned me to bring him some moss
from the East.   But though I was there at a tolerably moist season, I
could with difficulty fulfil my commission.   I could get none in Egypt.   I

I pushed upwards. One or two chapels I passed at different halting-places. They were in miserable disrepair, but scribbled over in the inside with the names of pilgrims and travellers. Then came the fine hollow or basin more than halfway up the hill, in the midst of which stands the old cypress, called Elijah's tree, hard by which there is a well or circular pond, containing a little water. The chapel of that prophet is also shewn here. It is out of this mountain-wady that the rugged top of *Jebel Mûsa* rises like a cone out of the hollow of some vast crater. Up to this Joshua and the elders of Israel ascended along with Moses. Here they halted while he went up "into the mount," and waited for his return. It was here that "the nobles of Israel did eat and drink" (Exod. xxiv. 11). It was here that "they saw the God of Israel, and under his feet, as it were, a paved work of sapphire-stone, and as it were, the body of heaven in its clearness." The multitude, who stood afar off below, only saw the "devouring fire" on the top of the mount, but the elders were allowed a nearer vision of the glory, and brought directly under it, to the foot of the great central peak which the fire was girdling round, and on which the shekinah rested. Only Moses was allowed to ascend that highest peak, and to pass into the very midst of the glory. The people thus stood in "the outer court;" the elders in the "holy place;"—

got none in the Desert. I could get none in the "terrassed" hills of Palestine. I succeeded in the valley of Hinnom, one side of which is moist and shady.

Moses in "the holy of holies." This singular valley or circular hollow, so far up the mount, explains those passages in the Scripture narrative which speak of Moses, and Joshua, and the elders, leaving the people and ascending the hill,—and again of Moses leaving the elders and going up to stand before God. So far as I am aware, the other mountains fixed on by some as the true Sinai,— Serbâl, Sasâfeh, Kâtherine, have no such resting-place. This much, at least, may be said in favour of Jebel Mûsa.

We now pressed upwards, not even staying to notice the footmarks of Mahomet's camel on the rock. There was no vegetation visible, save perhaps in a hollow or crevice here and there, a small shrub a few inches high.* The mountain was utterly bare. When actually on it, the fiery redness of its granite, which glares on the eye in the distance, softens into a dingy brown, with a slight tinge of red here and there. There were still rude steps in the rock or amidst the debris, which somewhat lessened the labour of climbing, though, after all, the ascent is very steep, and more than once we had to make our way over snow which lay nearly a foot deep in some parts. In about an hour and a half from the time we

---

* I pulled from one of these crevices the small aromatic plant called *Jadheh*, which the monks assured me was hyssop; and the *Zatûr*, also fragrant, like our *thyme*. Not that these plants are confined to this mountain. They are to be found all over the desert, as also are the *Shia*, which from the Red Sea and onwards (with some intervals) continued to refresh us all the way, and the *Ghetuff*, not so fragrant, common to most of the wadies. Also the *Ajram*.

left the convent, we reached the top,—the "grey top" of Sinai, for while the great body of the mountain is of red granite, this is of grey. Whether from decay or the peculiarity of the original formation, I do not know, the granite appeared laminated on the top, so that we were able to split off some slices with the help of our hammers, of perhaps an inch in thickness. With these exfoliated fragments we filled our bags or pockets, thinking it worth our while to carry home with us specimens of that mountain which "burned with fire," and on which Jehovah himself descended. The wind was strong and the air cold, so we took shelter under part of the low wall at the entrance to one of the chapels. While the monk who was with us was striking a light and preparing coffee, we were gazing on the scene, and writing a few short letters to friends, dated "the top of Sinai." I had taken with me "the ten commandments" in the original, on a large sheet, and, spreading it out, I read over the law, upon the summit of that mountain where it had been given three thousand five hundred years before. The cold and the driving wind were considerable hinderances, and more than once my tables of the law were on the point of being torn in pieces and carried away, but I accomplished my purpose. It was interesting at the time; nor is it less so in recollection.

The day was not clear; mists were rising in the horizon, so that we did not see afar off. But we saw the "great and terrible wilderness" around us, and it was a vision of more utter barrenness and desolation than

we had ever seen or fancied. No soft feature in the
landscape to mitigate the unbroken horror. No green
spot, no tree, no flower, no rill, no lake,—but dark
brown ridges, red peaks, like pyramids of solid fire. No
rounded hillocks or soft mountain-curves such as one sees
even in the ruggedest of home scenes,—but monstrous
and misshapen cliffs,—rising tier above tier, and surmounted here and there by some spire-like summit,—serrated for miles into ragged grandeur, and grooved from
head to foot by the winter-torrents that had swept down
like bursting water-spouts, tearing their naked loins, and
cutting into the very veins and sinews of the fiery rock.

> "How did the wide and melancholy earth
>   Gather her hills around us, grey and ghastly,
>   And stare with blank magnificence of loss
>   Right in our faces."

I need not mention the mighty *Serbâl* in the distance,
or *Jebel Kâtherin* close at hand, or the adjoining peaks
that make up the Sinaitic group. These certainly were
the spires which rose above all the rest in majestic
gloom. But all around these were masses of lower peaks,
variously coloured and as diversely shaped,—forming
one vast *forest* of hills, or rather one awful stretch of
rocky *moorland*, "a land of darkness, as darkness itself;
and of the shadow of death, without any order, and
where the light is as darkness" (Job x. 22). In ordinary circumstances this passage would hardly have
been applicable, for sunshine lights up these wilds and
mitigates their horrors. But while we were gazing, a

fierce storm drove over them ; clouds shut out the sun ; and the snow, borne upon the mountain-blast, threw a dismal shadow over what in itself was as dismal as could be conceived. It was the perfection of dreariness and horror. The snow-blast compelled us to descend sooner than we meant, having only spent about an hour upon the top. Yet during that time we saw the position of *Jebel Mûsa.** It is the pivot or centre-peak of the range, though not the highest.

Reasoning from their own ideas of grandeur, some have argued against this being the " mount of God," because it is not so noble as Serbâl or Kâtherin. This is no proof. Man's ideas of what the mount of God ought to be are not to be trusted. Others again insist on *Sasâfeh* being the mount, because it is visible from the plain of *Er-Rahah*, which Jebel Mûsa is not. Yet this amounts to nothing ; as any reader of the holy narrative will see. It is nowhere said that the people saw the mountain or its top ; it is only said that they saw the fire and the glory, which, blazing up into the heavens, would be perfectly visible from the plain. The mountain itself, whether it were Sasâfeh or Jebel Mûsa, would be quite invisible, being wrapped round with smoke and flame ; but the place where it was could not be hid, for it is written, " the mountain burned with fire unto the midst of

---

* If *Horeb* really be called the mount of God, which I doubt, and identified with *Sinai*, it may be that the former was the northern peak and the latter the southern of the same mountain, so that both might be called the mount of God, and both might give names to the deserts adjoining.

heaven, (or more literally, *up to the very heart of heaven*) with darkness, clouds, and thick darkness" (Deut. iv. 11). Perhaps the appearance presented was that of the whole mountain, up to the very top, swathed in clouds of thickest gloom (Ex. xix. 19), and then out of the midst of this girdle or mantle of awful darkness rose the supernatural flame. "A cloud covered the mount" (Exod. xxiv. 15); and then it is added, "the glory of the Lord (the shekinah) abode upon mount Sinai . . . and the light of the glory of the Lord was like devouring fire on the top of the mount in the eyes of the children of Israel." It was thus that the pillar-cloud rested on and covered Sinai, and it was thus that "the glory" (or shekinah), which had appeared to Moses in the bush, blazed up out of the cloud. Yet the mountain did not fall to pieces under the pressure of the infinite glory, just as the "bush" was not consumed when the glory rested there. Besides, had Er-Rahah been visible from the top, Moses would have seen and known what was going on behind before he descended, whereas it is evident that he only heard the shouting. but knew not what it meant till he came down and saw the calf and the dancing (Exod. xxxii. 19). Of course this is no actual proof that Jebel Mûsa is mount Sinai, but it is a strong presumption in favour of immemorial tradition, and an answer to some of the objections urged against its being so.

After gazing round on the wild scene, and securing some relics of the mountain—some memorials of our

ascent—we descended. The snow passed into rain as
we got to the foot, but all the afternoon the wind blew
sharply. In the course of the day I went into one of
the small rooms of the monks, at his own invitation.
It was dark and dingy, though not uncomfortable. He
seemed anxious to offer some kindness in return for
my small gift in the forenoon, and then shewed me
his library. It was small enough. A Greek and
Arabic Lexicon was the chief book on his shelf, and
a newspaper in the same language lay on his table.
I spied a folio, and he brought it to me. It was a
prayer-book in Greek, with the gospels and epistles ar-
ranged for the different festivals. As we did not succeed
in our attempts at conversation, I soon withdrew.

In the evening two or three of the monks visited us ;
but it was to get us to buy their pots of manna (an
exudation from the *tarfa**), at one shilling each,—and
their little skins of dates and almonds pressed together.
These dates are from the more southern point of the

---

* Lepsius, who wonders how any one can believe Israel's manna to be
anything else than the desert tree-honey, tells us that this tarfa-dew
"trickles down in incredible quantities" every morning upon the sand.
Now, we are assured on good authority, that the whole quantity collected
throughout the peninsula in the most fruitful season only amounts to
700 pounds' weight ! If the reader will divide this by 2,000,000 (the
numbers of the children of Israel), and again by the number of days in
the year, he will find what a small amount of sustenance each Israelite
must have had. There would not be so much as *one* of these "yellow
drops" of tarfa-dew to each, even had they reaped the whole produce of
the desert. Was this the meaning of the passage, "He SATISFIED them
with the BREAD OF HEAVEN ?" (Psa. cv. 40.)

peninsula, in the neighbourhood of Tor, where the
monks possess large palm-plantations, cultivated for
them by the Arabs.   This was almost the only inter-
view which we had had with them, save in a previous
part of the day, when they gathered round Mr Wright
and sat to the photograph for their pictures.   With
these they were abundantly pleased.   Their dark eyes
and faces, long beards and flowing robes, made excellent
portraits.

In the works of some travellers we have read most
exaggerated statements as to this famous convent.   Its
stateliness is praised.   I saw nothing of this.   On the
contrary, it appeared to me poor in every way, within
and without.   To be sure, no building, of whatever size,
could look stately at the base of such a mountain.
When man builds upon the top of a lofty cliff or hill
he gets the benefit of the height, and his structure is
set off by the elevation of its position ; but, when he
chooses the foot, he loses amazingly, and his palace,
however goodly, shrinks into a pasteboard-cottage, overshadowed by the enormous mountain-wall.   And so it
is with the convent.   But besides this, it is poor enough
in itself.   Its fortifications, its walls, its *cannons*, its
chapels, its buildings,—have all been made the theme
of admiration.   There must have been some spell over
the admirer's eye when he drew so fair a picture.
And as to the trees of the garden being exotics of
richer lands, and memorials brought hither by Greeks
of their native Greece,—I shall say nothing save that

there was not a tree in it for which any one needed to
go farther than Palestine,—if indeed so far. No doubt
Achaia had its cypress-bearing mountains;* but Syria
has it cypress-bearing plains.†

Mount Sinai, Tuesday, Jan. 29.—Rose at seven.
Walked out on the roof and read Psa. xl. In the distance was the plain of Er-Rahah, and almost under me
was the garden, whose trees, with the exception of the
blossoming almond and the evergreen cypress, shewed
no sign of life. No palm rises there. That tree loves
a lower region and a warmer air. Breakfasted at half-
past eight. The noise of Arab tongues outside was both
annoying and amusing. We were getting some new
Arabs and camels, and the quarrelling arose at the adjustment of the loads. It was long and most vociferous.
I watched them from the roof and saw them struggling,
one with the other, about the loads for their camels,
each one determined to take as little as possible, so that
more camels might be needed. Tents, beds, baggage,
&c. were tossed to and fro in rapid disorder, sometimes
on one camel's back, sometimes on another; and our
portmanteaus ran no small risk of being torn to pieces,
as two or three strong Bedaween rushed upon them,
each catching hold of a strap, or a handle, or a cover,
and pulling diverse ways, sought to secure the lightest

---

* Cupressifero Erymantho.—*Ovid, Epist.* Cyllenes Cupressiferæ.—
Ovid, Fast.

† Was it the tall cypress planted beside the tomb that suggested the
slender and graceful *minaret* which rises beside the *dome* of every mosque?

load for his own camel. Our dragoman had warned us of all this, and had prepared us for seeing swords and blood. Hard blows and high words, however, were all that we saw or heard. No blood was shed.

After an hour's quarrelling they were ready to move. So we prepared to start at ten, and to leave, without regret, the convent behind us. The superior, with two or three of his monks, came to bid us farewell. We had not seen him before ; but there was nothing venerable about him save his grey hairs. The monks paid him no respect or attention, such as his age, if not his office, entitled him to. He could hardly walk, and yet they did not rise from their seats to assist him, but allowed him to hobble along and nearly to fall in reaching his seat. He came, not to give his blessing, as some tourists tell us, but to receive our gold with his own hands. We offered him three sovereigns,—but he held them up in his palm, and told us it was not enough ! We told him that we meant to give no more, and bowing in eastern fashion to the group, we left our dragoman to settle with him, which he did by giving a dollar to each of the servants at his own cost. We had to pay dearly for the small amount of cleanliness and comfort which we had experienced. Of hospitality we found nothing. We had the use of two small rooms, had to furnish our own provisions, and were left to ourselves. That was all. Monastic life here is a poor shabby kind of thing ; —all out at the elbows. Sir John Maundeville, who travelled and wrote in the fourteenth century, says,

"In that abbey no flies, toads, or lizards, or such foul venomous beasts, nor lice, nor fleas, ever enter, by the miracle of God and our lady; for there were wont to be so many of such pests that the monks were resolved to leave the place, and were gone thence to the mountain above, to eschew that place; but our lady came to them and bade them return, and since that time such vermin have never entered in and had place among them, *nor never shall enter hereafter.*" Glad should we have been to find the miracle still in force; but three nights' troubled experience told us that the spell is broken and the miracle at an end;—for miracle most certainly it must have been, as every traveller in the east can testify.

As our camels paced along, we gazed up at the stupendous scene. Behind us there was the group of Sinaitic peaks, of which Jebel Mûsa is the centre, and on the right, the adjoining mountains, shooting up almost perpendicularly above us, of kindred colour and grandeur. The Cimbri, in ancient times, by way of amusement, are said to have slid down the snowy sides of their northern mountains, on their broad shields; but on what shield could either Cimbrian or Arabian have slid down mountains such as these?

Towards the left was the level plain of Er-Rahah,— where the tents of Israel once stood, and whose sands were once reddened with the double gleam of fire from the pillar-cloud and fire from the blazing mount. We soon turned to the right, and entered Wady Sheikh, whose

ridges shut out the rugged heights, at whose base we
had been sojourning.   We felt no unwillingness to turn
our back on these, and look our last on Sinai.   For in
truth that mountain is too awful, both in itself and in
its memories, to attract.   It fills the soul with awe, but
does not win the heart, nor make us wish to tarry
within sight, as if it were good to be there.   It repels,
but does not invite ; for like the law, of which it is the
memorial, it speaks of death, not of life, of judgment,
not of grace.   Its echoes waft to us no glad tidings of
the free love of God.

Wady-esh-Sheikh is a long flat valley, about a quarter of a mile in breadth, winding northwards.   When
the "wilderness becomes a pool of water, and the dry
land springs of water" (Isa. xli. 18),—this wady may
overflow the yellow sands of Er-Rahah, forming a lake
for the shadows of Sinai to rest upon,—on whose edge
shall come up "the cedar, the shittah-tree, and the
myrtle" (Isa. xli. 19),—or pouring down its waters
through Wady Feirân and Wady Mukatteb, may form
a river which will discharge its waters at Wady Markhah
into the Red Sea.   In this valley Israel would find
ample room for their encampment.   Of all the wadys
we have seen, it seems the most suitable for a pro-
longed sojourn.   The "goodly tents" of Israel could
here spread themselves out without limit.   On either
side rise up ranges of the same barren mountains and
scorched peaks,—some of them more isolated than
hitherto, as if coming up out of the sand singly, not

in clusters or ridges. The day was beautiful, and the heat would have been oppressive had it not been for a cool breeze coming quietly along the valley. In how many ways did God refresh us in the desert! Sometimes it was the " shadow of a cloud that brought down the heat;" sometimes it was "the shadow of a great rock ;" sometimes it was the foliage of the palm, or the tarfa, or the ritt'm ; and sometimes it was the genial breeze.

In a little we came to a narrow defile, with high rocks on either side, bare and rugged as usual. Then the scene changed, and we came to some curious rows of sandy hillocks. Again the scene changed, and we found ourselves in a wood of tarfa-trees, of considerable extent. Then these disappeared, and the valley became bare and tame. About three o'clock I dismounted, and enjoyed a pleasant walk. At five we encamped in the same spot from which we had started on Saturday morning. While the tents were pitching, and preparations for dinner making, I walked out alone to a short distance, enjoying the solitude and the sunset,—and remembering home-friends. The evening became rather cold. A damp mist, like that which the east wind brings up from the sea in Scotland, filled the air. Worship at ten. Went to bed at half-past ten. Heard the Arabs fighting, first with words, then with sticks and swords. This storm lasted about half an hour. I found next morning that one of our men was cut severely in the cheek, and that my camel-driver was one of the worst, for which I gave him as good a reproof as my ignorance of his language would admit. He persisted, however, in maintaining that he was *tayib* !

Wady-esh-Sheikh, Wednesday, Jan. 30.—Rose before seven. The moon and morning-star beautiful in the clear cold sky. The sky looked intensely clear and pure ; and these two lights seemed the very symbols of brightness and purity. Yet, looking up to that pure desert firmament, the patriarch said,—

> "He putteth no trust in his holy ones,
> Yea, the heavens are not clean in his sight."—(Job xv. 15.)
> Behold, even the moon,
> Yea, it shineth not !
> And the stars,—
> They are not clean in his eyes!—(Job xxv. 5.)

Even that moon of brightness, up to which I am now looking, has no splendour in comparison with His ! Even that fair star,

> Last in the train of night,
> If better it belong not to the dawn,

had not purity when placed side by side with him ! Yet still it is true—

> "Holy, holy, holy,
> Jehovah Sabaoth,
> THE FULNESS OF THE WHOLE EARTH IS HIS GLORY "—(Isa. vi. 3.)

For " God saw every thing that he had made, and behold it was VERY GOOD " (Gen. i. 31).

Slowly the east began to take on its well-known red, and the west its well-known purple of soft silk. The mighty range of mountain-peaks lay black against the brightening blue ; till one after another they caught the yet unrisen light, and crowned with the gold of day-spring, they looked like the monarchs of the waste. Walked about for an hour in the cloudless twilight. The quiet freshness was as soothing as it was bracing. At home in such a case you look down upon the still life beneath or around you, and think that in an hour all that life will be stirring. Here it is not so. You may look from dawn to midnight from these hills, but no life stirs. Life is not here, nor sound save of the wind, nor motion save of the tarfa-branch. Life is not asleep ; it is awanting. Yet this is not the place of death. Death is not here, and your feeling is not that of one gazing on church-yard stillness, where life is only in abeyance for a time. It is more akin to dreariness of spirit. You feel no link to the scene ; you enjoy it for a time ; but you are glad to quit it. The heart has no bond here either with the living or the dead ; and, like Noah's dove, finding no resting-place for the sole of its foot, it is glad to return to the homes of living men.

We started about half-past eight,—walking for a con-siderable way. In about half an hour clouds began to rise over the hills before us, till they covered the whole sky. Rain fell in large drops. We betook ourselves to a projecting rock as " a covert from storm and from rain "

(Isa. iv. 6). It was barely sufficient for shelter ;* but we were glad of it, as we were somewhat in advance of our party and had left both camels and coverings behind. The threatened rain however did not come. It proved but the skirts of a shower passing by us. On we went, with similar slight showers till noon, when the sky brightened into its usual clear and cloudless blue. About half an hour before this we had turned to the right, out of Wady Sheikh, and crossed a narrow defile over rocks like a Scottish glen, and then in about three quarters of an hour we came down upon a fine valley, where we had once more a full view of the ubiquitous mountain, which seemed to watch us at every step,—Serbâl. Crossing this wady we went up a rocky road into *Wady Berakh* or *Berah,* and suddenly came upon an Arab grave-yard, on the right.† With its simple stones, unhewn and uncarved, amid these lonely hills, it spoke most touchingly to the heart, and seemed to throw over the scene a dreary melancholy. Above ground no life appeared, beneath there was what once was life. The want of life makes the desert at all times lonely ; but the presence of death deepens the intensity of the loneliness. It seems lonely to *live* in such solitude, lonelier to die

* Job's description was illustrated in our case,—
    " They are wet with the showers of the mountains,
      And embrace the rock for want of a shelter."—(xxiv. 8.)

† One might almost have supposed that in *Berah* we have a mere abbreviation of *Taberah,* Israel's first station after leaving Sinai (Numb. xi. 3, Deut. ix. 22), were it not that the route of the Israelites would seem to have been more eastward than Wady Berah would admit of.

there,—but loneliest of all to be buried in such a place!
Who were lying there we knew not,—father, mother,
wife, and husband, brother, sister, child, such we knew
were there; and that was enough to make us feel an
interest in the spot. How many generations were there
we could not tell; they may go back to the days of
Moses, and the dust of the sons of Israel may be mingling there with the dust of the sons of Ishmael. It is
curious that so many of these graveyards should be
found in the centre of the desert, so few anywhere else.

Up *Wady Berah* we pursued our way, in a westerly
direction, for about an hour. This scene was bleak and
monotonous, and continued so all the afternoon. Here,
for the first time, we noticed some pink *crocuses* peering
out of the sand. With their tiny leaf of dark green,
and their slender flower, they formed a pleasant contrast to the usual desert-shrubs. In gathering some of
their roots, we found them several inches deep in the
sand. One species of them the Arabs eat greedily.
Its name, I think, was *Beshakh.* At their recommenda-
tion we tried them, and found them not unpleasant.
We encamped about five in this wady. While dinner
was preparing Mr Wright and I walked out, and turning to the left, soon found ourselves in a beautiful little
basin, hemmed in by a low range of steep cliffs, in
which the strata were quite perpendicular,—black and
white layers alternately, like furrows, intersecting the
ridge, and giving to it a singular appearance. It was
more fruitful than its neighbours, and there were some

flocks of white and black sheep feeding in it. As we were returning, our sheikh met us. On missing us from the encampment, he set out after us, not only to take care of us and prevent us losing our road, but also to bring us some of his best dates to eat by the way. The moist fruit stuck to his tawny hands, which were but seldom washed, and it was not quite agreeable to eat fruit off such a platter. But inconveniences such as this we had often to submit to in our wanderings. As we came slowly back our sheikh told us that the name of the valley we had visited was *Wady-El-Lajah*, and pointed out to us *Wady Geduram Selim*. The night became showery, but we were safely housed.

An old Arab, belonging to this wady, brought us his little boy for medical advice. Mr Wright prescribed for him, to the father's great joy. In the course of the evening the grateful Arab appeared with a beautiful black and white lambkin in his arms, as a present to his *Hakîm* or physician. We thanked him for the gift, but as we could not carry it with us, we declined it, with many thanks. Arabs are not ungrateful ; and they prize kindnesses shewn to their children even more than to themselves.

Wady Berah, Thursday, Jan. 31.—On going out before seven I found that there had been rain in the course of the night ; but the morning was fine, though chill. I noticed sometimes in the early dawn a few light clouds in the sky, which quickly passed away as the sun rose. This, and the very rapid disappearance of the heavy dews which we after experienced, shewed us the truth of the prophet's figure,

> Your goodness is a morning-cloud,
> And as the early dew
> It goeth away.—(Hos. vi. 4.)

Walked out into a little wady on the east, and, seated among its silent rocks, read the 103d Psalm. We started for our day's journey at half-past eight. I cheered the way by reading some old Latin hymns, and turning them into English verse. Here is a specimen—

> Alleluia, Alleluia!
>   The battle now is done,
>   The victory is won ;
>   Let us joy and sing
> Alleluia!
>
> Alleluia, Alleluia!
>   Suffering death's cruel doom,
>   Jesus hath hell o'ercome ;
>   Let us praise and shout
> Alleluia!
>
> Alleluia, Alleluia!
>   He rose the third day, bright
>   In heavenly love and light ;
>   Let us cry and chant
> Alleluia!
>
> Alleluia, Alleluia!
>   Closed are the gates below,
>   Heaven's halls are open now ;
>   Let us joy and sing
> Alleluia!

Alleluia, Alleluia!
　Jesus, by thy wounds, save
　Us from the endless grave,
　That we may live and sing
Alleluia!

We soon got into a narrow stony glen, where, after
walking for an hour, we sat down under a Seyâleh-tree.
Its thorns were plentiful, but, as usual, it was leafless.
We found the gum, for which it is famous, exuding. It
may seem strange that we should record the occurrence
of a single tree. No traveller in Europe would think
of such a thing. But in the east it is different,—especially in the desert. In lighting upon a tree or a well
you seem to be meeting with a friend. It is an event
which deserves record, for it is one which rivets you at
the moment, and fastens itself to your memory. In
the treeless waste what a prize even the most stunted of
the species seems! This is the place for teaching one
to love trees. Nor is this love without its moral lesson
and influence. It is going far to say, as some have
done, "that none but a good man can truly love a tree,
and none but a pure mind can remain open to that
peculiar class of impressions which only the presence of
a tree can make." Yet still the man who is indifferent
to a tree or a flower may be classed with the man who
"has no music in his breast."

One of our men, Selîm Atîh, outstripping the rest,
came up to us. He soon made us to understand, by
gestures and words, that he was about to leave us. He

pointed in a particular direction over the cliffs, and intimated that he was about to proceed to his home. Yes, he had a home, and his face was now towards it. He had always been kind and obliging to us, so giving him a few piastres, we bade him good-bye. He was soon away among the rocks. For upwards of an hour the valley continued stony, then it became sandy. About one we reached the mouth of a wady which turned away to the right, *Wady Kheimreigh;* but we held straight on. About two we passed another graveyard, with one or two stone-inclosures, and some small upright stones. We saw one or two new graves, with ritt'm planted upon them. Poor, yet expressive, memorial! It is all that an Arab can get. He has no myrtle, no rose, no cypress. But he has his green-leaved, white-flowering ritt'm,—the most graceful of all his desert-shrubs. And this is his remembrancer.

About three o'clock we came to *Wady-el-Khumíleh,* where, on the left, were a considerable number of "Mukatteb" inscriptions and figures on the sandstone. My camel-driver pointed in the direction of *Surâbît-el-Khâdem,* and told me how many more were there. We were not very far from it, but still too far for us to visit it. A little way on we came to a recess among the rocks on the left, where was a pool of water, at which we stopped for half an hour to give our camels drink. We sat down under a rock, as the day was hot, and watched the scene, which was thoroughly an eastern one. The group of camels,—some with their long necks thrust

down towards the water, others with their heads towering erect; then the group of men, more thirsty than
their camels, drinking eagerly alongside of them, of the
rather indifferent water,—all surrounded with a lofty
wall of rugged rock,—formed quite a picture for an
artist. We noticed tufts of grass growing here and
there, brought up by the rain which had filled the pool.
We watched the little insects creeping or hopping about
in the sun,—living and dying here, with no eye to see
them but God's.

We again moved on and continued ascending till we
came, about four, to *Wady Ramleh*, which, I suppose,
gets its name from its vast plain of sand. The plain
seemed to stretch away for miles, both eastward and
westward, with undulations and rocks here and there.
The sand was for the most part fine and small in grain,
though not so much so as in the region which stretches
between Egypt and Palestine.* There was hardly a
track or way-mark in this plain, only the cliffs of Et-
Tih in the distance to guide us. It was quite "a wilderness where there is no way" (Job xii. 24). In traversing it, we were cheered by the discovery of a few
more of the little lilac flowers, like autumn crocuses,
coming up in the bare dry sand. It put us in mind of
the "root out of the dry ground" (Isa. liii. 2). The
Arabs sometimes called it "bulb." We saw also a bulb
of a larger kind, its stalk shooting up like that of fox-

---

* "Per arenas mollissimas," says Jerome, speaking of the approach to
Egypt from Palestine.—*Epist. ad Eust.*

glove, and its flower like a cluster of antirrhinum flowers tied together on a spindle. I could not pick up the Arab name, as our Bedaween happened to be merry, and gave me what I afterwards discovered to be a mere *nickname*.

In front of us rose the precipitous range of *Et-Tih*, apparently without a break, or ravine, or pass of any kind. Yet we are told that we are to cross it to-morrow ! We encamped on a slope of the plain at half-past five. The latter part of the day was cloudless, and the sunset fine. The sun went down, like a golden ball, behind the slope of yellow sand, the vast amphitheatre of Et-Tih, with its white cliffs, lighted up by his radiance. The scene was a splendid one. I walked out along the sand to some distance before darkness came on, and enjoyed the cool breeze which was coming from the east. The only living thing around was a grey grasshopper in the sand. As I watched its motions I felt that there was not entire desolation.

Wady Ramleh, Friday, Feb. 1.—We started to-day at half-past eight. The cliffs of *Et-Tih* seem close at hand, so off Mr Wright and I set, on foot, to scale *Nakhb-er-Rakineh*, that is, the pass of *Er-Rakineh*. But the clear dry air deceived us, and we found ourselves two or three miles from the range. The *sands* of Ramleh were soon crossed, and we came upon a series of low undulations covered with small stones, beaten hard like a macadamised road. Up and down we went for two miles, outwalking the camels, till at last, losing sight of the track, we struck into the dry bed of a stream, with rocks of some height on either side. Thinking that this would soon end, and that when we emerged from the gully we should either regain our companions, or at least catch sight of them, we pushed on, climbing sometimes *over* and sometimes *under* the jagged boulders or overhanging precipices. It was hot, hard work, for hands, feet, and knees were all engaged in it,—but we thought it better to go on, as the cliffs were right above us, and we knew that somewhere or other there must be a road leading up their face. As one rock after another was surmounted, and one turn after another was accomplished, we counted on seeing some spacious exit or some guiding track. But still the mountain-gully walled us in. We now saw that we were in a bad case, for we seemed to be turning away to the right and diverging from the track altogether. Had it been afternoon, we might have been alarmed at the prospect of being benighted, but it was morning, and so we resolved to prosecute our adventure to the end. We soon came to a place where the rocks of the gully give place to steep acclivities, which we discovered to be vast mounds formed out of the debris of the cliffs, and were composed of dried clay and gravel. Leaving, then, the bed of the torrent, we commenced the ascent of one of these. It was no easy task, as the friable soil gave way under our tread, and we slipped down more than once. Having reached the top of one of these hillocks, we looked around, but camels, companions, and Arabs were nowhere to be seen. We began to fear that we had widely diverged from the track. There was, however, no remedy but getting higher, for, from the nature of the ground, we could not fail to catch sight of our caravan somewhere before it climbed the cliff and struck into the pass. Setting our faces once more to the ridge, we proceeded to scale another mound of this friable clay which lay piled up in masses before us. On reaching it we found a deep hollow between us and the range, and saw, moreover, that the slope of the cliff was broken up into ravines and enormous excavations, like quarries. Up these we must climb, and by taking a narrow shelf or ledge overhanging one of these quarries, we thought that we should reach an eminence which seemed to command a view of the whole region below. But which is the way up? We could not tell, but we must try. Mr Wright took one route, and I another. Up the steep face of another enormous mound I scrambled, sliding back at every step. Then there came a low cliff, some ten or twelve feet, which must be scaled. Selecting a recess in it where the rock is broken into steps, I ascended, and found a considerable level. But no caravan was in sight. My way now went up along the edge of a vast quarry, and was somewhat less steep.

As I was ascending slowly, two huge eagles or vultures came in sight. They then lighted down upon some straggling rocks about fifty yards off, and kept eyeing me. I sat down for a little and watched them.

I rose to go, and they also rose. Whether they counted me their prey or not, I cannot say, but they followed me,—flying in circles over my head, sometimes lower and sometimes higher, as if uncertain whether to venture on an attack or not. Afterwards I remembered Jeremiah's words, when describing the spoiler preparing to pounce on Moab :—

> " He shall fly as an eagle,
> He shall spread his wings over Moab."—(Jer. xlviii. 40.)

I recommenced my ascent and they soon left me, doubtless to find their way to their nest, in some of those grey shaggy cliffs, of which this great mountain-wall of the desert is composed.

> " Doth the eagle soar up at thy command,
> And fix her nest on high ?
> On the rock she dwelleth and abideth,
> On the peak of the rock and the strong place.
> From that she spies out her prey,
> Afar off her eyes behold it."—(Job xxxix. 27-29.) *

Often since we entered the desert we had seen the skill of the vulture in picking clean the bones of his prey ; for, several times in a day, did we come upon the skeletons of camels, which these birds had stripped of every vestige of flesh. We had no opportunity of testing

---

* See also Jer. xlix. 16, " Though thou shouldest make thy nest high as the eagles." Deut. xxviii. 29, " Swift as the eagle flieth." Being the great bird of the desert, how natural that God should speak of it as illustrating his care of Israel. Exod. xix. 4, " Ye have seen how I bare you on eagles' wings." Deut. xxxii. 11, " As an eagle stirreth up her nest, fluttereth over her young," &c.

their power of sight or scent; but all travellers concur in testimony to their mysterious power of discovering their victim from afar.

" Where the slain are there is he."—(Job xxxix. 30.)

In the course of ten minutes, by means of scrambling and walking, I reached a pretty broad ledge or shelf of the cliff, where I discovered a camel's track. I now saw far beneath me the camels toiling up the narrow mountain-path, and their drivers urging them on and watching their loads as they swayed from side to side. As soon as the Bedaween saw me they shouted, and seemed anxious to direct me. But I could not understand either their signs or their words. So I moved downward to meet them, thinking that they were turning away westward and were beckoning on me to follow. A few minutes more shewed me that I was wrong, for I saw the camels taking a turn which seemed to bring them up to the very ledge on which I was standing. I heard also the dragoman's voice calling on me to stop. I was now sure that they were advancing towards me, so, oppressed with the heat of noon, I lay down under " the shadow of a great rock." Having rested for about ten minutes, I rose and pursued the track, and, after a little more sliding and scrambling, found myself on the very top of the cliff, about half-past twelve. There I found Mr Wright, who, after he separated from me, had pursued another path, and, after surmounting similar difficulties, had reached the summit a few minutes before me. Mr Beddome was beside him, and one of our

Arabs, who had guided him up by a better path than
we had discovered. We were hot and tired; so we
lay down upon the stones and rested. The view from
the summit was splendid. To the left there was the
remaining part of the segment of the mighty cliff
stretching eastward for miles. Then came the Sinaitic
range to the south or south-east, lofty, dark, and ragged.
Right in front rose the prince of the desert, Serbâl, and
adjoining it, to the south-east, the smaller ranges along
whose bases we had passed the week before. Then the
Red Sea,—blue as the heaven which bent over it, and
as calm, with Ras Atâkah beyond, looking stedfastly
down on that spot, where Israel found deliverance, and
Pharaoh a grave. Just before me, though far beneath,
stretched the sandy plain of Ramleh, some ten or twelve
miles in length, and perhaps half that in breadth.

In a quarter of an hour our camels joined us, and after
they had rested for a short time, we all set out on our
descent on the other side of *Et-Tih*, which proved quite
as gradual as the face of the cliff had been abrupt. We
went slowly downwards over rough, rocky roads, till
about four o'clock, when we halted. This was too short
a journey, but we could not get our Arabs to move
farther. We remonstrated with our dragoman, but his
answer was, " Men and camels are weary." This might
be one reason, but the main one was that water was at
hand in an adjoining hollow. To this we hastened
down, and found several pools containing a considerable
quantity of water, with palms and tarfas on the margin,

and some wild flowers under the shade of a rock. This was *Wady Untâghah*, which I find in no maps, nor mentioned by any traveller. Indeed, our route was not the usual one. Most travellers cross *Et-Tih* by *Nakhb-el-Mureikhi*.

Our place of encampment was very stony, but the afternoon was fine, and the night cloudless and starry. We fretted a little at our short day's march,—but we made the best of it, by saying nothing more about it, after the first remonstrance.

We had frequent opportunities of observing the "zodiacal light," both in this place and others. During the absence of the moon it was visible almost every night, beginning about an hour after sunset and continuing for several hours. Resting its narrow base on the western horizon, it shot up, often nearly to the zenith, in a luminous triangle, very much elongated of course. Its track was quite distinct in the heavens, marked by a pale thin lustre, inferior in brightness to the streaks of the aurora borealis, yet steadily visible from its base upward to its very apex. We did not observe the flicker or sparkle in any part, of which Humboldt speaks. The whole of this great cone was of a faint yet fixed whiteness in every part. It was a tall pyramid of pure and tranquil light, that seemed sometimes as if it rose out of the sands, and sometimes as if it were suspended from the Pleiades, and sometimes like a rent in the blue arch, through which the light of a milder and more mellow sun beyond was finding its way down to earth, during the absence of its own.

CHAPTER XI.

WADY UNTAGHAH—WADY-EL-ARISH—WADY-EL-AUJANAH—NAKHL—
WADY HUVJAH—THE SERAB—WADY FAHADAH—WADY KHA-
RAIAH—WADY SCHERIF.

Wady Untâghah, Saturday, Feb. 2.—Walked out before dawn to enjoy the moon and morning-star. Noticed
again that though the east lightens first, it is the west
that takes on the purple radiance from the unrisen sun.
Started at half-past eight, our road lying over dreary
brown flats, with hollows, or rather pits, every two or
three hundred yards. Truly this is " the land of deserts
and of pits, a land of drought and of the shadow of
death, a land that no man passeth through (that is, no
thoroughfare), and where no man dwells " (that is,
where there is no city to dwell in), (Jer. ii. 6).

The extensive chalk-looking range of *El-Ijmeh* (or
Ajmah) stretches before us like the cliffs of Dover ; but
the blue sea is awanting. The whole region is dreary,
and with no magnificence of cliff to redeem the desolation. All along the way we see the same broken hollows
and pits, some deeper, some shallower,—the same un-

sightly mounds and emaciated rocks,—shattered, splintered, scaled, confused,—in composition more like baked earth or sun-dried clay.

We soon, however, passed into *Wady-el-Arîsh*, which is perhaps the noblest wady of the desert, if both its breadth and its extent of course are taken into reckoning. Wady-esh-Sheikh is undoubtedly prince of the southern wadys of the peninsula, and El-Arîsh as truly prince of the northern ones. Commencing at the Et-Tih range it pursues a circuitous but unbroken course through the desert to the Mediterranean Sea. It is fit to be the boundary of kingdoms, and probably was meant to be so, for may it not be to this that reference is made in God's promise to Abraham, when the whole land is given to Israel from "the river of Egypt to the Euphrates" (Gen. xv. 18). This "river of Egypt" cannot be the Nile,—because that is always called *Jôhr*, not *Nahar*, and because the boundary given by Joshua (xv. 47) seems to refer to a river not far from Gaza,—and because *no part of Egypt* was ever made over to Abraham. Egypt and the land of promise are two distinct places, which they would certainly not be, were it the Nile that was meant. Bring down Israel's border to the Nile and you rob Egypt of her richest land, whereas it was the land of the Philistines, lying north-east of Egypt, that was to be merged in Palestine, which would be the case if the river poured into Wady-el-Arîsh be the southern boundary. In this case too all that part of the desert would be included which the patriarchs occupied south of Beersheba. In that region they sat down as if by right, though in one sense strangers; whereas in Egypt they took up their abode merely for a season, and strictly as strangers, having no right at all to the land. In this way their long sojourning in these southern regions would be better accounted for. It was their own land,—given them by God as part of the land of promise. And it is yet to revert to their children in the latter day, when the original boundaries of the land are to be resumed in fulfilment of many a promise made of old.

> " The king in his beauty thine eyes shall see,
> They shall see THE LAND FAR EXTENDED."—(Isa. xxxiii. 17.)

When the wilderness receives the promised rain in the latter day, what a noble river this will form ! Indeed the whole desert seems to stand waiting, with its hundreds of wadys, for the fulfilment of the prophetic blessing,—" in the wilderness shall waters break out, and streams in the desert " (Isa. xxxv. 6). And it seems no " incredible thing " that God,—the same God who made Eden out of chaos,—should make the desert to become as the garden of the Lord. It seems no " incredible thing " that He who " made a river to go out of Eden to water the garden" (Gen. ii. 10), should, in " the times of the restitution of all things," make the wilderness a pool of water, and the dry land springs of water " (Isa. xli. 18). Göthe could say of his own fruitful well-watered land, " when I stand alone at night in open nature, I feel as though it were a spirit, and begged redemption of me ; often have I had the sensation, as if nature, in wailing sadness, entreated something of me ;"—how much more may we say of this scorched waste that it "groans and travails in pain" (Rom. viii. 22). Yes, the desert groan is the deepest and most unbroken of all. And shall it not be delivered from the bondage of corruption into the liberty of the glory of the sons of God? When earth's bright Sabbath comes, shall not the desert put off its sackcloth and put on its Sabbath-robe,—earth's Eden-verdure,—" the excellency of Carmel and Sharon?" (Isa. xxxv. 1, 2.)

Soon after we passed *Wady Barûdh-el-Ayédeh.* A large flock of camels, seventy or eighty, were feeding not far off. They belong to the Bedaween, and are here for a month or two for pasture. Our dragoman sends off one of our men for milk, but he returns without it. For several hours we have been going due-north through *El-Arîsh*, which, as it gets northward, assumes a more pleasant aspect. It is fully a quarter of a mile broad, its white gravelly channel covered, and its margin lined, with *tarfa*-trees. On each side are small brown slopes, which look like newly ploughed fields, and remind me of Teviotdale and its slopes in spring. The winter-torrents must be strong in this wady, as is indicated by the torn-up tarfas, and the large stones evidently rolled and tossed about by the force of the current. Yet all along its bed we see the black beetles running over the sand,—things of life even in this land of the lifeless.

About four o'clock the wady widened out into a large plain, some eight or ten miles in circuit, with *Jebel Sikh* on our right front, and *Jebel Badhiah* on our left front, both somewhat distant. While nearer, and towards the left, that is westward, rose *Jebel Jeremlih*. About five o'clock we encamped in the wady, down which our course had lain all the day, *El-Arîsh*.

We had occasion to notice in the evening how careful the Arabs are of their trees. Of the low shrubs they make fires, but not of tarfas and such like. Once or twice, indeed, we did see a seyaleh scorched, as if a fire had been kindled beneath it, but this was rare. Some of our party had kindled a fire within some feet of a tarfa. Scarcely, however, had we done so, than our sheikh came, and with the politest signs imaginable, accompanied of course with a flood of words which we did not understand, requested us to remove it from the tree. From the way in which he shook his head, and pointed to the different quarters, we guessed that he meant to tell us that the Bedaween of the neighbourhood would be very angry at us, if we set fire to their trees. Of course we complied with his most reasonable request.

Wady El-Arîsh, Sabbath, Feb. 3.—We rested as usual on this day, and spent it much as on former occasions. These Sabbath-rests in the desert were most grateful. The wilderness was calm as on other days, and seemed less dreary. Occasionally the ravens shyly approached our tents, in quest of food ; and we noticed on more occasions than one, that in the mornings they seemed on the watch for our departure. Hardly had our camels begun to move, when three or four of these birds would find their way to the spot to pick up our fragments. The question of the Divine speaker in the book of Job, had a meaning in these deserts which it has not at home :—

> " Who provideth for the raven its food?
> When its young ones cry to God,
> When they wander for lack of food."—(Job xxxviii. 41.)

The Arabs wandered about, and in the afternoon made charcoal out of the roots and stems of the larger desert-*shrubs;* not the *trees* such as the tarfa ; these they left untouched. The *ritt'm*, we were told, makes the best charcoal, thus illustrating the passage which mentions " coals of juniper" (Ps. cxx. 4), or more properly "coals of the rothem." I have already noticed this tree as a place of shelter from the heat, as in the case of Elijah (1 Kings xix. 4, 5). The only other place where the tree is mentioned is in Job, where it is spoken of as furnishing food for the famishing, "who cut up juniper (rothem) roots for their meat" (Job xxx. 4). This we never saw, and we could only imagine it done in the extremity of want, which indeed the passage implies,— " for want and famine they were solitary ; fleeing into the wilderness . . . They were driven forth from among men, to dwell in the cliffs of the valleys, in caves of the earth, and in the rocks" (Job xxx. 3, 6).

Wady El-Arîsh, Monday, Feb. 4.—-I rose at four,

and called Haj-Ismâel, as we were to start early, in
order to reach Nakhl at night.   Walked out about half-
past four.   The morning was cold, and there was hoar-
frost upon our tents and on several objects round us.
Between five and six the whole encampment was astir,
—fires kindling, food preparing, and goods packing.
Foremost among the packers was Sheikh-Sulimân,—ever
active, smiling, and obliging.   By the starlight, with
the help of the Arab fires, he bustled about, striking
the tents and getting the camels in readiness.   As he
was packing up our tent-gear, the old man kept singing
a lively Arab song, which seemed to consist only of a
few lines, as the same words and notes were continually
recurring.   I asked the dragoman what it meant, and
he told me that the words were, " Why is she so long in
coming?"   It sounded pleasantly in the starlight of
morning.   I wish I could have picked up the whole,
and compared its orientalisms with such a passage, as
" Make haste, my beloved, and be thou like to a roe or
to a young hart upon the mountains of spices" (Song
viii. 14).

At first when we struck our tents, there was not a
streak of dawn,—only the morning-star which seemed
ever to shine kindly upon us, reminding us of Rev.
xxii. 16, " I am the root and offspring of David, the bright
and morning star."   Then the moon came up, in her
last quarter.   Then the east began to give signs of sunrise, and the west to take on its usual purple.   Then
the sun came up without a cloud.   Our desert locomo-

tives moved off a little after seven, we walking before them.   Our route still lay down *Wady-el-Arish,* which was now of considerable breadth, and most distinctly marked as a water-course.   Our road was for a while over flat sandstone, then hard gravelly sand.   The shrubs were fewer than on the previous day, which was well for us when we mounted (which we did at half-past nine), as camels insist upon stopping at every bush to catch a mouthful, which is rather annoying, more espe- cially as the Bedaween take the part of the camels in this matter, and are not by any means pleased when you do not allow them thus to feed by the way.   Our ride was not peculiarly interesting.   The country is tame and rather flat, broken only by hillocks of chalk, like sandstone.   Before three we passed out of *Wady-el-Arish* into *Wady-el-Aujânah,* where the country seemed some- what less flat and barren, and the white cliffs of *Jebel Aujânah* rose to the eastward.   In a little we saw *Jebel Hallâl,* a range of hills far to the leftward, and nearer, in the same direction, *Jebel-el-Herem,* composed of the same white sandstone, which in the distance has the the appearance of chalk.   At five o'clock we passed out of *Wady Aujânah* into *Wady Bhuterifeh,* a wide, dreary plain, where our road lay over sand and small black debris, flattened and hardened into consistency by the rains.   The sun set about six, but we pushed on by star- light, and encamped at *Nakhl* about eight, cold and weary, having travelled without a break since seven in the morning.   It was half-past ten ere we could get

dinner, and nearly twelve ere we got to bed. A few
of the inhabitants of the *Khan* came to look at the
strangers, but we were too tired to notice them. A
guard was sent to us,—not because of danger, but as a
pretext for backshîsh. Judging, however, from the
howlings of the night, we should have said that our
guard consisted of dogs instead of the pasha's soldiers.
Again and again were we reminded of the scriptural
allusions to "dogs," to which we have already referred.
Devourers of dead camels, and disturbers of the peace,
these were their characteristics in our eyes.

Khân Nakhl, Tuesday, Feb. 5.—Morning very chill
and misty. More than once we had experienced "the
great rain of his strength" (Job xxxvii. 6); we had now
the "small rain" of which the patriarch speaks. The
thermometer in the tent was at 40°. We found this
well-known *Khân* standing in the midst of a plain. It
is a large square fort, with one or two soldiers' huts
outside, though Burckhardt speaks of its having no
habitation round it. The same traveller conjectures
that in old times the plain was covered with palm-trees,
and that from these the *Khân* took its name. This
region does not seem a likely one for a forest of such
trees. It is more probable that here there was one
solitary palm, beside the well, from which it was called
the "fort" or "inn of the palm."

At eleven we went to pay our respects to the governor of this desert fort, and to make arrangements about
guides to Petra. We found him, surrounded by about

twenty others, "sitting in the gate," the place of business
and of judgment.   Just within the main outer gate was
a large square, on two sides of which was the divan,—a
stone sofa covered with matting, and in some parts
with carpet.   We had to sit, of course, in eastern style.
Pipes and coffee were handed round ; the latter was
always most grateful, though some of us despised the
former.   The conversation at first was general, and was
carried on, of course, by means of our dragoman.   We
gave the governor many good wishes—we spoke of the
alliance between our Queen and the Sultan—we mentioned the pleasure we had received in our travels.   To
all these he gave gracious answer.   But we were intent
on business, and so I told Haj-Ismaîl to proceed to
the point.   But our dragoman was not to be moved
from eastern form.   " This is our way of doing business,"
was his answer.   After sitting thus for a quarter of an
hour, the governor proposed that we should adjourn
to his private apartments.   So, leaving the council of
twenty behind, we went off with him.   He led the way
to another open square, where a man and camel were
at work drawing water out of the deep well of the fort.
There we stood and told him our wish to visit Petra.
He told us that the sheikh was absent,—that he did
not know when he would return—it might be a week,
or it might be but two days—that he would send a man
and dromedary in search of him.   This was not pleasant
intelligence for us.   We had already been three weeks
in the desert, and were getting weary of it.   We did

not like the thought of lingering in this its tamest and most uninteresting region for even two days,—much less for a week. So, after exchanging some more civilities, we returned to our tents for consultation.

Most unwillingly, and after weighing all sides, we concluded to give up Petra and to strike straight north for Palestine, either by Gaza or Hebron. Calling in our dragoman, we told him our purpose. He was sorely out of temper at our change of plans; yet we could not understand why, for he had frequently told us that the sooner we got out of the desert the better for him, as it was only in Syria that he would make anything by us. We found, however, that he generally said anything that suited his purpose at the moment. Finding that we were determined, he told us that we must pay him for the time he had expected to be in the desert, and that, as we were thus to be seven days less, we must give him seven days' payment, that is £35. We reminded him that our contract specified nothing as to time—that he would be a gainer by our being seven days less in the desert—that we should be thus seven days longer in Palestine. But he saw none of these things. He only seemed to see an opportunity of making £35 additional out of us, and he stuck to his demand. We kept, however, to our purpose, and told him to get ready to start for Hebron, and that if there were any claims upon us for additional money, they must be adjusted on our arrival at Jerusalem. So he went off to make arrangements and to get " a man of a

good family" to be our protector in room of the absent
sheikh. In the course of the afternoon he called me
into his tent to see the new sheikh-substitute, who had
agreed to furnish camels, and to guide us to *Dhahariyah*
—nine days journey from this, and a day from Hebron.
Some five or six Arabs were in the tent, talking over
the route, among whom was the governor and his scribe
or secretary, with pen (or rather *reed*) and paper in
hand, and inkhorn in his girdle. Orientals do not write
on desks or tables. They use the palm of their left
hand instead ; and I was told by a missionary that he had
tried both ways, and found (though he could not account
for it) that he wrote Arabic much better upon his palm
than upon his desk. The contract was soon written
and duly signed, or rather sealed with the seal of the
contracting parties, and we are to start, D.V., to-morrow. The rest of the day was spent in photographing.
Mr Wright took some excellent portraits and some interesting groups—Arabs, travellers, and camels.

Our Sinaitic Arabs came in the evening to bid us
good bye and to receive *backshish*. Some were satisfied and others not. One or two did not scruple to
come back and make a double claim upon us, trusting
to our not recognising them. For though we found
them remarkably honest throughout the journey, we
saw that they did not hesitate about getting all the
money they could out of us. Afterwards, Sheikh Sulimân came to give me a complete list of the various
places through which we had passed since we left Suez.

I noted them down, but found a difficulty in catching the precise sound. He was very obliging and patient—anxious that I should get the right name—repeating it again and again. With some of the others it had not always been so. Though they were most civil in answering questions, yet they seemed to smile at our uncouth way of pronouncing their words,—more than once laughing outright, and wondering at our ignorance. Not one of them, save our two servants, Hamân and Hummâd (or rather *Mohummad*), ever sought to catch up a word or name of English. They never gave us our names, but only the general appellation of *Howadji*, that is, gentleman.

We bade these Arabs farewell with much regret. They had been faithful and kind to us ; nor did they give us any cause to say of them, what Maundeville did five hundred years ago, " they are right felonious and foul, and of a cursed nature." Yet, on the whole, they are not a noble-looking race. Some of them do look well, and move nobly—like Asahel, " light of foot as a wild roe" (2 Sam. ii. 18). But they are inferior to the Arabs of Egypt, and especially of Syria, where intermixture with other nations seems to have kept up the vigour of the race. The Bedaween, on the contrary, seem a worn out race. Intermarrying with no other nation, they have degenerated, and are in danger of becoming extinct. They do not carry the long spear of their Syrian brethren, and are in general but poorly dressed in comparison with them, though on several occasions our sheikh put

on his court-dress, and shone in silk and gold. They
have laid aside the *bow* of their ancestor ; and, though
the descendants of the desert-archer, they carry only
the matchlock and the sword. As Maundeville says—
" they wrap their heads and necks with a great quantity
of white linen cloth," which more than once we saw
unrolled and laid in the sand by our dragoman. To-
day we had an illustration of this. At Suez we had
taken another servant in room of the French Assâm,
who still followed us, and whom I have mentioned
already. His name was Haji-Mahummad—for he had
been to Mecca some years ago. He was different from
his fellow-Arabs in almost everything. Strong and well
built, he never put forth his strength, but kept it all to
himself. His face, though manly and intelligent, had
the most expressive melancholy I ever saw in an Arab.
He never smiled, yet was kind, and ever gentle. He
seldom spoke, yet was in good fellowship with all about
him. He did his work very carefully, yet with a slow-
ness and deliberation that almost betokened indolence.
He took very great pains in making our beds and putting our tents in order. He was paler than the others, and
had a squint or deficiency in one of his eyes. We liked
this silent man, who moved about so noiselessly among
us, and whose voice was never heard amid the brawling
of his fellows. He seemed poor withal—both shoes and
cloak being considerably the worse for wear. Hitherto
he had got on well with our fiery dragoman ; but to-day
a scene occurred which shewed the characters of both.

He had mistaken his orders, or neglected them, I don't
know which; but when looking out through the flaps
of the tent, I saw Haji-Ismâil suddenly spring upon
him, his eyes in a glow with passion,* and his hands
ready for blows. First, on one side of the head he struck
the quiet man, and then on the other, with all his might;
and then pushing him furiously, knocked him over among
the baggage and baskets in front of his tent. But this
did not exhaust the Egyptian's anger; so he made a
second rush upon him, and kept *cuffing* him on both
sides of the head, till he had loosened the white roll of
cloth about his turban, and knocked off the turban itself.
The Arab uttered no word of resentment, but sat down
upon a wicker-basket and commenced adjusting his
head-dress. The dragoman left off beating and commenced scolding; but no answer was made. He or-
dered him to resume his work, but the injured son of
the desert gave no heed. *Khûm*, ("get up," pronounced
goom), shouted the Egyptian, but the Arab sat still.
Khûm, roared the furious dragoman, but Haji-Mahummad moved not, spoke not, but with folded arms,
and unlifted eyes, and unmoved lips, kept gazing on
the rolls of his dishevelled tarbûsh which lay at his
feet. In despair the master turned away and let his
passion cool. In some five or ten minutes the servant,
having composed his ruffled dress (not his countenance,

---

* "Mine enemy *sharpeneth his eyes* upon me," said Job (xvi. 9). Our
dragoman's eyes helped us to the meaning of this. The wild glow of his
Egyptian eyes was like a sword springing from its sheath, sharpening itself
upon its victim before destroying it.

for on it no line had changed), rose and went about his work. The quiet man had gotten the victory. "He that is slow to anger is better than the mighty; and he that ruleth his spirit than he that taketh a city" (Prov. xvi. 32).

Khân Nakhl, Wednesday, Feb. 6.—Morning fine, but cold. Afterwards the heat increased, and at noon the thermometer in the tent stood at 80°. We are not to start till to-morrow—for what reason we know not, save that the Arabs must take their own time and way in mustering their camels. Our Sinaitic friends have not yet left us. They are not going back to Sinai, but proceed directly to Cairo to look out for another engagement. They carry letters for the post, and also our poor French cook, who has done nothing since we left Suez. Our new Bedaween have had some sad fighting about camels and camel-loads. Three or four swords were drawn; and tongues, hands, sticks, swords were all mingling and clashing. The storm blew over, very likely to rise again to-morrow. The governor invited us to his house to-night. Two of us went and were greatly interested in an eastern entertainment. I remained in my tent writing and reading. Afterwards we heard that the sheikh had arrived, and that he would go with us to Hebron. But our dragoman has already engaged the "man of good family," so that there will likely be another battle,—which may cause a little delay, but which will end, as all these Arab strifes do, in a compromise between the two parties.

Khân Nakhl, Thursday, Feb, 7.—There had been
wind and rain during the night, but the dawn was fine.
We did not like to see or hear of rain,—for we were told
that if it came, we might expect three days of it ;—and
as we were now getting pretty far north, and more into
the region of rain, we felt a little anxious about the
weather.   Tent-life in rain or wind is not very pleasant.
But the day turned out well.

As we had feared, a battle rose in the forenoon about
the sheikh.   Haji-Ismâil wanted the sheikh to come
with us, but as another was engaged, what was he to do ?
A dispute of the most fierce and animated kind ensued.
Like most Arab disputes, it did not go beyond words
and threats.   But still the uproar was appalling,—the
inhabitants of the place taking part.   The noise of some
two dozen of Arab tongues was hideous.*   There seemed
no prospect of peace.   Our dragoman came to ask what
was to be done.   We told him it was his business not
ours.   He had got himself into a scrape, and he must
get out of it as he could.   Again the uproar rose,—last-
ing, perhaps in all, two hours.   At last we agreed to
divide with him the expense of taking both, which was
not great.   So about twelve we started,—our old Bedaween running by our side to bid us farewell,—Sheikh

---

* Truly they were "masters of the tongue," as the word translated
"babbler" is literally (Eccl. x. 11.)   They were not of a "slow tongue ;"
nay, their tongue was "as an arrow shot out" (Jer. ix. 8).   We knew
enough of what they were saying to discover their profane use of the name
of God.

Sulimân as blythe and lively as ever. Most fervently did we seek blessing in their behalf. They continued looking after us, and kissing their hands to us till distance separated us. May "the dayspring from on high visit them!"

We set off, down *Wady-El-Arîsh,*—the day sunny, but with thin clouds and a strong west wind. The wind kept us cool, but then, both here and in Syria, it is the bringer of rain. How natural must the Lord's remark have seemed to those in whose ears he made it, "when ye see a cloud rise out of the *west,* straightway ye say, There cometh a shower; and so it is. And when ye see the *south* wind blow, ye say, There will be heat; and it cometh to pass" (Luke xii. 54, 55). Yet the day continued fine, though not without threats of rain. The wady is here about two miles broad; our road skirted a low sort of forest or shrubbery of *tarfas.* Our road at first was a curious one of broken sand,—that is, of hard sand cut up and seamed into long paths or ruts by the rain. We halted at *Wady-el-Hoovjah* or *Hûvjah,*—a sandy wady running up eastwards from *El-Arîsh,*—at three o'clock. A short day's journey this. But Arabs make a point of having the first day's journey short. Indeed, they would make every day's journey as short if they could, for they care nothing about time, and cannot be made to understand that others care about it. Often did we urge them to push on a little faster; but it was of no use. They loved to loiter by the way, and they thought that their camels should do the same, and expressed displeasure at us for not allowing them to stop every twenty paces for a mouthful of *tarfa*-twigs or *Akhûl* thorns. We spoke of reaching such or such a place *lîl*, that is, to-night; they shook their heads and shouted *la, la,*—no, no,—*bûkra*, to-morrow. Their standing rule is not to do to-day what can be done to-morrow. *Bûkra* is their maxim in everything save speech; for words fly out like lightning from an Arab's lips. They may be slow to work, but they are not slow to speak.

In the evening heavy showers came down; but we were snugly in our tents, reading Milton aloud, and after that the Scripture. We are now in a region apparently unknown,—at least not a trace of our route can we find in any map. Indeed, from the time we left *Wady-esh Sheikh*, we have found the maps almost a blank,—some worse than a blank. Dr Wilson's, which we found most useful and accurate between Suez and Sinai, fails us after that.* The route which we have pursued since we left Sinai is different from that of most previous travellers, and northward of Nakhl especially we find no trace of footsteps. Even the names of places are not elsewhere mentioned.

Wady-el-Hûvjah, Friday, Feb. 8.—Had a pleasant walk over the sandy mounds and among the bushes for an hour before breakfast, with my psalter in my hand. The morning was bright, but chill. We loaded a little

---

* Since writing the above I have got Dr Robinson's map in the first volume of the new edition of his work. It is the best I have seen.

after eight, and were off by nine,—walking before our caravan for an hour and a half. We crossed *Wady-el-Hûvjah*, and keeping north-east, we passed a very wide plain of sand and small stones, with hills only in the distance. About half-past ten we mounted our camels, —but found them not quite so tractable as our former ones had been. The impatience of the camel to get up, the moment he feels you touch him, is the chief difficulty. I had just got my foot across his back, when up, he started, before I had either hold or balance. The camel-driver was at hand, and he caught me; but I could neither get my feet to the ground nor my body and head upon the camel, who persisted in moving on. The Arab, however, soon succeeded in lifting me so far up that I could get firm hold of the wooden projection in front of the saddle, and I soon righted myself. The clouds in the north-west looked very dark, threatening rain. The shower, however, did not come immediately, but a cold wind from the same quarter kept blowing most of the day. About half-past twelve we saw some fine specimens of the mirage or *seráb*, as the Arabs call it,—at a short distance to the right. There were some striking though not very high hills in that direction, partly black and partly white, which, in conjunction with the mist which the noonday sun was now bringing up out of the moist ground, formed the whole scene. This mist took possession of a slight hollow, perhaps about two miles in length, and presented a most perfect resemblance to a lake shone upon by a cloudless sun.

The mist crept a little way along the base of one of the
black and white bluffs, and then there was a precipice
projecting far into this sunny lake, the darker parts of
the rock appearing exactly like trees springing out of
the crevices of the cliff. The mist then sent up some of
of its grey masses, which spread themselves along the
whole face of the hills for miles, with spaces here and
there, some large, some small, which allowed the black
patches on the hills to be seen. This produced the
scene of a lofty wooded hill, projected into the centre of
the lake, which now seemed dotted with islands, and
enlivened with ships moving across its placid waters,
while at each end two huge cliffs frowned over it.
It was fine, and continued in sight for more than half
an hour, till at a sudden turn it was shut out by a
sandy hillock. In some scientific works, we have seen
the *seráb* described at length, and accounted for on
mathematical principles, the same as regulate the appearance of distant vessels upside down at sea. The
two things are totally different, the latter being the
reflection of a real, but far off object, below the horizon ;
the other, wholly a deception, conjured up by the wondrous combination of mist and mountain. It is to this
that the prophet refers, when speaking of the renovation
of the earth in the latter day, he says, "and the parched
ground (in the Hebrew it is *sheráhv*) shall become a
pool" (Isa. xxxv. 7),—that is, the *seráb* shall really
become what it seems,—a pool,—no longer mocking the
weary traveller or thirsty Arab.

On we journeyed through a wide dreary plain, with almost no herbage of any kind. We crossed *Wady Fahâdah;* we saw in the distant west *Jebel Yelakh,* a long range; and to left front (east) *Jebel Harîm,* near which the road strikes off to Petra, and to which we seemed to be drawing nearer. The afternoon became showery, but the sky cleared again, and about four we had a splendid *serâb* on the distant right. A long semicircular range of white perpendicular cliffs was the great actor in the scene, playing chief part in conjunction with the rising mist. The whole range was taken into the magic landscape,—and all its outstanding parts or projections, which pierced through the blue haze, formed so many castles, set in the midst of a magnificent lake that swept the whole base of the cliffs. The mountain-range was *Ras-el-Fahâdah.* On *Jebel Harîm* we had no less than five rainbows in succession, each shower as it came, braiding a new iris on the rugged hill. After each shower the air seemed clearer, and the sunshine brighter. A peculiar freshness breathed up from the very sand; and we noticed in one or two places that the rains of these two days had brought up little patches of grass here and there. It was just the picture drawn by David of the reign of Messiah in the latter day,—

" There shall rule over men a Just One,
　He shall rule in the fear of God.
　And as the light of morning shall he arise,
　The sun of an unclouded morning,
　Clear-shining after rain
　Upon the tender grass of the earth."—(2 Sam. xxiii. 3, 4.)

The above passage is all the more apt and striking, because the Hebrew word for rain is almost the same as the Arabic. We had heard the Bedaween constantly speaking about *mutt'r*, and in this passage the words " after rain" are " after *mattar*." These resemblances are not without their interest.

About five we encamped in *Wady-el-Fahâdah*. As both wind and rain threatened, we took some pains with our tents, securing the pins, making the flaps tight, heaping up sand on the outside. Having dined, we had some pleasant reading, and Mr Beddome produced his flute, which soon silenced its rival, an Arab instrument of two or three reeds, which had droned and squeaked the whole day on our journey, and now threatened to inflict its sounds upon us in our resting-place. Its owner, one of our attendants, a nice Arab boy of sixteen, slipped quietly into our tent, and squatted down with a delighted face to hear our superior music. He seemed lost in wonder, both at the sweet sounds and at the instrument from which they came. He left, when we produced our Bibles, and began our evening worship. This day has been rather a dreary one,—showery and unpleasant,—yet there was no great rain, till we were fairly housed for the night. During one of the passing showers of the day, I took refuge under a ritt'm-tree; but we needed something more tight and substantial for the rain of the night.

Wady-el-Fahâdah, Saturday, Feb. 9.—Rose at seven, and walked out along the wide, gravelly plain. The

day was calm, though cloudy; and there had been some
heavy showers during night. We did not start till ten,
our Arabs being lazy, and our camels afraid of wind and
cold. Leaving the party to follow, I set off alone, skirting the base of *Jebel Harîm*, or *Hraîm* (I am not sure
which), across the breadth of *Wady-el-Fahâdah*, and
keeping nearly due north. The wind was strong, but
in our backs; still the camels shrunk from it, though
there was no rain. The sun pushed his way out from
among the clouds about half-past ten,—but this did not
hinder a smart shower from coming down on us. At
half-past twelve we saw *Jebel Hallâl*, or *Hellâl*, on the
distant left, and on the right front *Jebel Massârah*. We
next passed through a wide plain, paved with small
stones; then we crossed *Wady Meshâsh*, where we
observed a slight *serâb*,—a lake at the foot of a hill;
after which we crossed *Wady Kharaiah*, a broad plain
of gravel, with a few camel-shrubs. About two we
observed a fine *serâb* to the right. First there was a
bold headland jutting into a lake; then another headland; then a succession of islands across the whole
breadth of the lake, which was shut in by a lower promontory. The lake seemed to be miles in extent.

We now passed out of *Wady Kharaiah* into *Wady-
esh-Scherîf*,—which ought to mean " the noble valley,"—about three o'clock, going still nearly north. To
the right was *Jebel Messârah*, and in front, a little to
the left, *Jebel-esh-Scherîf*,—the long and lofty range
of *Hellâl* still running along with us in the distance.

About five we came to the foot of *Jebel-esh-Scherîf ;*
on the right (east), a little in the distance, *Jebel Bûrkha.*
About two days due east of us we observe in our maps
a place called *Ghudhaghidh,* on the way to *Petra.* We
have been inclined to ask, Is this the *Gudgodah* of
Deut. x. 7, and the *Hor-hagidgad* of Numb. xxxiii. 32 ?
The place is certainly on the route of Israel. A quarter
before six we halted in *Wady-esh-Scherîf.* The evening at first was fine,—then cloudy, then rainy. But
our tents were good, withstanding both wind and rain.

CHAPTER XII.

Wady-esh-Scherif, Sabbath, Feb. 10.—The morning was cloudy, but not rainy. Through the night the showers and wind were vehement ; and though the continued rain did force its way through our canvass in some parts, still on the whole we suffered little. After breakfast and worship, while we were reading in our tents, the sheikh came in, with several of the men. We found that not even he could read his own tongue. One of the men, who was a relation of his, could do so ; but no other. This man greatly attracted us. His name was Mustapha, and his appearance is well remembered by us all. He was above the sheikh and above all his fellows in manners and education. Not very tall, yet, beyond middle size,—slenderly but well made in his frame, with a most winning countenance, almost feminine in its features, and less tawny in complexion than his fellows, he drew us to himself in sympathy as he went out and in amongst us. He was the gentlest Arab we had seen, of a finer spirit and a lighter step,—with an eye as soft in its blue as those of the others were fiery in their blackness. Sorry that our want of Arabic prevented our free converse, we did our best to supply the defect. Ere starting, I had got a friend to write for me in English characters the Arabic of John iii. 16, from Walton's Polyglott,—" God so loved the world, that he gave his only-begotten Son ;" but somehow or other the Arabs seemed not to comprehend it, though we tried in all manner of ways to make them understand it. Haji-Ismâil said it was not good Arabic, meaning thereby, not such as he understood. Very likely it was the Arabic of literature, and so not understood by the Bedaween. Giving up this, we betook ourselves to Dr Assaad Kayat's " Eastern Traveller's Interpreter." In this we found Acts xvi. 31, " Believe in the Lord Jesus Christ, and thou shalt be saved," *Amen belmaâsseeh fatookhlâss*. We tried this sentence with the Arabs, and first of all with our intelligent friend of the blue eyes. He and they took it up at once, and with evident delight repeated the words to us again and again. They had indeed little idea of its meaning, but still it was a seed dropt into their minds, which might spring up in happier circumstances ; for it is of these that the prophetic word has spoken,—

" The dwellers in the wilderness shall bow before him."

(Psa. lxxii. 9.)

They continued in our tent for upwards of an hour. It drew nigh to the hour of our "public service," and still they remained; nor did we like to bid them go. At last we resolved to go on in their presence. We sung, and they sat listening and wondering. We read, and they continued still seated. We knelt for prayer, and, for a little, they remained looking on in silence; till at last, before the prayer was ended, they had risen from their seats and gone out of the tent.

The Korân is as great a stranger to these Bedaween, as was the Bible to the monks of Sinai. In Alexandria or Cairo one sees occasionally a Moslem reading the Korân, but even this is rare. No doubt it is read to them in their mosques, and all of them can repeat verses of it; but that is all. Of its contents they know little. There is the less excuse for this among the Arabs, because the Korân is pure Arabic, and would be perfectly intelligible to them; whereas to the Turks it must be in a great measure a sealed book, as the Arabic and Turkish are widely different, and as the Prophet's law forbids a translation of his sacred volume.

In the afternoon we sat under cover, reading. The evening was cold and cloudy,—at last rainy. Putting a few stones together, Mr Wright had made a fire for us, not of sticks like the apostle, but of charcoal from our dragoman's charcoal-bag. We sat round, reading several books aloud; and, in pleasant converse, we soon forgot the rain, which, at eight o'clock, began to batter on our tents.

T

Wady-esh-Scherîf, Monday, Feb. 11.—A cloudy dawn, though the rain had ceased. Thermometer at 58° in our tent. We started at a quarter before ten. Passed *Jebel-esh-Scherîf*, and saw *Jebel Hellâl* on the left. On the distant right *Jebel-en-Nekhah*. At twelve passed into *Wady-el-Muzeiryah*, crossing *Wady-el-Lus-sân*. The road for several hours over soft, slimy sand, in which our camels were continually slipping. One or two of them came quite down, but did no injury to themselves, or their loads, or their riders. When the surface of the sand is moist with recent rain, the way becomes unpleasant and dangerous for camel-travelling. Over rocks however rough, over stones however nume-rous, over dry sand however deep, the camel will go without fear. But the surface-softness of clayey soil brings him to a stand. He trembles when he comes to it, and a traveller's best way is at once to dismount. It was painful to see the slipping and struggling of the huge animals under their heavy loads. In the course of the afternoon we visited a small Arab encampment. The black tent or awning was set up with its back, as usual, to the wind. The owner was there smoking, and his wife was winnowing corn, tossing it up from a large sheet or blanket of camel-hair which was spread upon the ground. The wife fled at our approach, but the man bid us welcome,—handing us his pipe and offering to make ready coffee, which, however, we declined, as the day was getting down. We then passed into *Wady Suidat* about four; then into *Wady Jaifah* about five,

where we encamped. The day was rather dreary. We
went through wide and uninteresting wadys. But we
noticed that the verdure was on the increase, and we
seemed to be getting to transition-ground. We met with
many plants of the bulbous kind,—and were surprised
to hear the Arabs call them *bulbs*.

A family of vagrant Bedaween accompanied us,
whether for the sake of company, or to catch an opportunity of stealing, we could not say. Our men did not
like them. They consisted of man and wife, with three
little half-naked children. They were lean and ill-fed,
and received with great avidity any fragments of biscuit that we could spare. The offer of a piece of bread
or biscuit was the only thing that overcame the shyness
of the children and induced them to approach us. They
greedily dug up the edible roots by the way, and feasted
on them, not by way of luxuries as our Arabs did, but
of necessaries, as hungry men would do, reminding us
of Job's description of the desert vagrants in his day—

> By want and hunger they were lean ;
> Rooting up the wilderness
> In former times desolate and waste.
> They plucked up mallows by the bushes,
> And the roots of retham were their food.
> From the midst were they driven,
> (Men cried after them as a thief,)
> In the clefts of the torrents to pitch their tents,
> In the caves of the earth and the rocks.
> Among the bushes they cried ;
> Under the nettles they were gathered together.—
>
> (Job xxx. 3–7.)

Wady Jaifah, Tuesday, Feb. 12.—Walked out at seven to enjoy the cloudless morning. Started for our day's march at a quarter-past nine. In about an hour came to a part of the wady that spreads out into a plain, where there is a large number of stones, from one foot to two feet square. Some were in circles, others in long double lines like the foundations of walls. They seemed the ruins of an old town, or perhaps of terrace walls. The Arabs called them *El-Kheizeh.* One of our men brought us a little animal, which we have often seen running about and escaping into holes in the sand. It is somewhat like a large rat, but with long hind legs, short front ones, and a long tail. They call it *Jerboa.* Another of our men brought us one of the bulbous roots which grow here, wishing us to eat, and assuring us that it was *Tayib,* good. We found that it is only one or two kinds that they eat. The rest are *mûsh-tayib,* "not good." Those that we were asked to eat were the smaller kind, like a crocus or small lily. The Arabs called them *Gafor,* or *Khafur.* We saw great numbers of bulbs, like snowdrops, crocuses, &c. About half-past twelve, having passed through *Wady Retemât,* we entered *Wady Kuseimeh,* where, as in some previous wadys, there were great quantities of a plant called *Jelf,* very green, like parsley in appearance, but which the camels would not taste. Vegetation is on the increase as we move northwards, and we heard to-day the hum of the bee on the *Rittem,* which sounded pleasantly, and reminded us that we were on the borders of a more

fruitful land—" the land flowing with milk and honey."
We again came upon circles and lines of stones, like
ruins. We passed through a wady which might be
called " the stony," from its being covered with small
stones, on each side of which rose up peaked hills of
white sandstone, broken up into precipices. The *serâb*
this afternoon took the form of a distant sea, studded
over with islands, between which many a goodly vessel
went and came.

At a quarter-past two we passed some long lines of
stone, with ruins of considerable extent spreading over
a large part of *Wady-el-Ain*, on which we had entered half an hour before. Our Arabs did not know
any name for these ruins; all that our stately dragoman could tell us was that they were " Roman ;" but
to his information we could attach no value. We saw
Jebel-el-Moilah and *Jebel-el-Ain*, long low ranges of
peaks half white and half brown. This is a most spacious plain, full of vegetation, which extends for miles.
It is by far the greenest and moistest spot that we have
seen. It is said to be watered by a regular brook, but
this we did not see. But we saw snowdrops, mushrooms,
and grass in large patches. We passed a field which
had been recently ploughed, or at least *scratched* by
the oriental instrument which bears the name of plough,
but which seemed to us little more than a long and
tolerable thick branch of a tree, with a crook at one
end, and fashioned somewhat into the shape of a plough.
The ground was first broken up with an axe or hatchet,

and then furrowed with this rude plough. We dismounted here for a walk. It was quite a relief to find ourselves upon moist soil, after weeks of hard dry sand and stones. The very air seemed fresher and more genial. Our feet felt nimbler and our limbs more elastic as we moved along. We reached *Wady es-Serâm* about half-past four, and a little after this, we halted and encamped. We were to have gone forward to *Hafîr*, but we stopped short at Serâm, I suppose from the indolence of our Arabs, who disliked all haste and loved loitering, always glad to be done with travel or with work.

This is a spacious wady, well clothed with the vegetation of the desert, and with appearances of something more. Immediately on arriving, we set out for a walk, as we had then more than an hour of sunlight to make use of. We found several cultivated fields of considerable size, with corn beginning to shew itself in some of them. Right across the valley ran long lines of stones, at short intervals. They were not the foundations of houses,—but were evidently thrown across to retain the soil in its place, and prevent the rush of the occasional torrent from sweeping it away. These lines might be two or three hundred yards long,—some even longer, and were made of well-squared stones, fitting into each other, and forming a strong bulwark against the stream. On one of them we found an inscription done much in the same style as the *Mukatteb* writings. The stone was evidently not in the original site, and the inscription was a trifling one. It was as follows ⟨ ⚸ ⟩ One could not pretend to decipher it. These stones were not the work of Bedaween,—but of an older date, and raised by more skilful hands. The present inhabitants were but making use of what a more ingenious population had bequeathed to them. They were originally, perhaps, Roman, afterwards kept up by the Christian inhabitants of the locality.

It might be indeed that they were older than Roman ; —for the patriarchs occupied an undefined range of territory in this neighbourhood ; and here there seemed to meet three different races, the Egyptian from the south, the Philistine from the west, and the patriarchs from the north. Away far to the south-east of this, was *Wady Ghudhaghidh*, perhaps, as we have already suggested, the *Gudgodah* of Scripture. It is not only the similarity of names that suggests this, but the likeness of the region round about to that described by Moses. It is said that "from *Gudgodah* to *Jotbath* was a land of rivers of waters" (Deut. x. 7), and perhaps Israel sojourned in this neighbourhood many days or years. They went towards Mount Hor at first where Aaron died ; and regarding this we read that " Israel took their journey from *Beeroth* of the children of *Jaakan* to *Mosera ;* there Aaron died, and there he was buried " (Deut. x. 6). After this they proceeded westward to *Gudgodah* and after that to *Jotbath*, their route being evidently of a zig-zag kind. The narrative intimates that this region was well-watered and fruitful, which we find to be the case to this day. We had just passed through *Wady-el-Ain,* whose name implies springs or fountains. Not far off was *Wady-el-Birein,* the "valley of the two wells," which may be the place named *Bee-roth-beney-jaakan* (Deut. x. 6; Numb. xxxiii. 31), the "wells of the sons of Jaakan." It is in this region too that water is got from holes dug in the soil, named *Emshâsh,* and from pits of a deeper kind called *Themîlek.* So that the names of the places, as well as the appearance of the country, shews that it is considered a well-watered region, and might fitly be called *Jotbath* or "goodness," to signify the abundance that was there.

I pulled up some of the green stalks, which were not above an inch or two above ground. They seemed to be a kind of wheat. On several patches of the fields the rain and the torrent had made considerable inroads, sweeping away the soil in some parts, and overlaying the crop in others with sand. It seemed to have been what Solomon calls " a sweeping rain that leaveth no food " (Prov. xxviii. 3) ;* and shewed the necessity for these terrace-

---

* This sweeping flood is quite different from the overflowing Nile. The former carries away the soil, the latter deposits it. Still the latter is an inundation which for the time *overwhelms* the land, though it does not sweep it away. It is this that the prophet Amos refers to twice over when speaking of the flood of desolation that was to overwhelm (though not to destroy) the land of Israel,—

> "It shall rise up all of it, as a flood,
> It shall be driven out and inundated,
> As by the river of Egypt."—(Amos viii. 8.)

> "It shall melt;
> And all that dwell in it shall mourn;
> It shall rise up, all of it, like a flood,
> And shall be inundated,
> As by the river of Egypt."—(Amos ix. 5.)

walls which we had been examining, and which seemed
to be laid in regular intervals across the whole valley.
A great deal of vegetation was apparent everywhere,
save on the steep gray slopes of the hills. We returned
to our tents as darkness was settling down on them, and
were met by our sheikh with a grave face, so that we
felt as culprits waiting for a reproof. He had missed us
from the encampment, and fearing that we might lose
ourselves, or meet with evil at the hands of the natives,
he had gone in search of us, but had come back unable
to find us. He shook his head, looked grave and dis-
pleased,—and both with words and signs gave us to
understand how wrongly we had acted in straying out
alone, as the Bedaween here are not to be trusted. We
were obliged to him for his care of us, but as we had
seen no danger, I dare say we were not sufficiently
grateful.

In the course of the afternoon we had rather an unpleasant scene. The actors in it were the sheikh and
one of our chief men,—a man of two camels, whose
name was *Aaudheh.* The former,—said to be the owner
of a thousand camels,—is a young man,—soft and indo-
lent,—given more to smoking than to useful deeds,—
but good-natured and most obliging to us. The latter
was a middle-aged and middle-sized man, but fierce in
temper and rough in manners,—rather thin in face and
body, but tough and wiry in his frame-work. He was by
no means obliging, and sometimes he was rude in words,
both to us and to his fellows. Often did he complain

about the overwork which he said that his two camels were undergoing, though they were neither overloaded nor overwrought, and one of them was as ill-tempered as its owner. He tried once and again to get us to stop short at three or four o'clock, threatening to go back, and letting it be known that he did not care for dragoman or gentleman, as all that he wanted was to get his camels fed. Between this man and the young prince of the desert a discussion arose by the way. The latter was anxious to take us all the way to Hebron, the former was determined not to move an inch beyond the contract, or rather, if possible, to avoid coming up to it. The road to *Medeenat* (or "the city," as they called Hebron),—the dangers of it, the troubles of it, and the like, were all discussed, but in language which left us for the present in total ignorance of the meaning of the conversation. By degrees the parties grew hot, at least the *serf* did; but his chief kept cool, though speaking sharply, as we could discover by his accents. The dragoman and some of the Arabs were trying to cool the rising wrath, and to soften the hard words. But in vain. The conversation grew hotter and hotter,—till at last, at some fierce word uttered by Aaudheh, and enforced by the flash of his fierce Arab eye, and the significant flourish of his disencumbered arms, the sheikh slid down from his dromedary and drew his sword. Aaudheh, who was walking by my side, was unarmed, at least he had no jambeh, or scimitar, although his baroudeh or matchlock was slung over his shoulders.

But he saw the other's movement, and instantly seized two or three stones which, in his angry hands, would have been dangerous missiles. I seized one arm, and an Arab seized another, whilst two others did the same to the sheikh. The sheikh yielded at once; but the serf struggled to get free. Seeing, however, that the feeling was against him, he consented to be pacified at last, and threw aside his stones as the sheikh sheathed his scimitar. Peace was restored, and we proceeded. Aaudheh scowled and seemed dissatisfied, because he had been compelled "to keep the peace." The sheikh looked troubled; and said a few words mildly to the other,—to the effect that he was ashamed of having exhibited such a spectacle before the *howadji* (gentlemen),—and that if Aaudheh insisted on renewing the strife, he must do so in some private place. This, however, was not a satisfactory adjustment of the matter,— but we could do nothing by the way. In the evening, however, we went out, after dinner, and took our seat among the Arabs, round one of their blazing fires,— those of us who smoked, sharing their pipes, and those who did not, their coffee. We spoke with the dragoman about the occurrence of the day, and he, along with Mustapha, undertook to effect the reconciliation. Accordingly we sent for Aaudheh, who was seated round the other fire. He came, and we found that he had cooled. He was willing to "be friends," as also was the sheikh to "be friends" with him. So he stepped across to the place where the latter was, and they took each other's hands at once. Having done this, they threw their arms round each other's neck, and kissed on both sides of the face several times. They then sat down side by side like brothers ; and so the last trace of the cloud passed away. The scene was like that of Esau and Jacob embracing each other (Gen. xxxiii. 4).

Afterwards, the sheikh, Aaudheh, and some of the Arabs came into our tent, where we had a good charcoal fire, as the night was cold. Mr Beddome produced his flute, and the children of the desert listened with delight to his music. It sounded most sweetly in the solitude,—only the notes of such an instrument seem almost too soft and refined for such a place and such an audience.

Wady Serâm, Wednesday, Feb. 13.—Rose before seven, and walked out. Climbed a rocky hill, where I had a fine view of sunrise, and watched the light gradually stealing down the sides of the hills. To the west there appeared a beautiful serâb,—a small wild lake, with a girdle of lovely hills, such as one meets with so often in our quiet glens at home. During breakfast, we were cheered by the lark, as he soared and sung in the flushing daylight. Walked on before our camels, and examined the terraces more fully. Near the northern extremity of the wady, we saw several inscriptions in a character very like those at Wady Mukatteb. There was the same frequently recurring ⊔, with goats and camels. Near these there was a cave, into which we looked, but found nothing. On

both sides of the wady we saw ruins to a large extent,
indicating the sites of some considerable villages or
towns, and on these ruins there were inscriptions like
those already noticed. The buildings in some cases had
been large in size, more like villas than common houses.*
They were not in the low ground, but all on the elevated
parts, to be beyond the rush of the winter-torrent. Their
foundations were on the rocky flats and slopes, with
which the low hills that hem in the valley abound.
The Lord's parable of the wise and foolish builders
occurred to me as I looked at the ruins. A house built
on the sandy or lower parts of the wady would be immediately assailed by the rising stream as soon as the
rains commenced. Against it " the stream would beat
vehemently," because it would be in its very channel.
Of course it would fall, and the " ruin would be great,"
because the rush of the torrent, undermining its very
foundations, as well as beating against its walls, would
sweep every stone away. A house built upon the rocky
slopes of the wady, would be in a measure beyond the
reach of the flood at first. And when the flood did
arise, and the stream beat vehemently upon the house,
no injury would be done, for the rocky foundation would
hinder the undermining process, and thus the walls could
withstand the violence of the flood. (Luke vi. 48, 49).

It is curious to observe how carefully the towns of

---

* They are called Khurbet es-Seram, the ruins of Seram. Our Arabs
seemed to call them *serab*, but I must have been deceived by the likeness
of sound.

the East have avoided the lower grounds, and always chosen the heights. In some cases this has, no doubt, been simply for protection against the assault of an enemy; but in general it is because of the invasions of the floods. With us a lower site is of less consequence. We can safely build upon the very margin of the stream, because we know that it has its regular channel, by which it will pursue its wonted way and leave our homes untouched. But in these eastern regions, where the rains are not spread over the year, but come down at certain seasons like waterspouts or cataracts, there is no channel for the stream; or rather the whole breadth of the wady is the channel for the time, and no building is safe in any part of it. Nay, the *soil* is not safe, but is swept off by the current, and hence the terraces of these wadys are not so much intended as the means of creating an artificial soil, as of retaining the natural soil of the valley in its place, and preventing the cultivated fields from being converted into a bare rock.

It may be to these alternate scenes of drought and flood that Job alludes:—

> " Behold !
> He withholdeth the waters, and they dry up;
> He sendeth them out, and they overturn the earth."—
> (Job xii. 15.)

Our Bedaween here pointed out to us *El-Aujeh*, at a considerable distance to the left or north-west; and spoke of *El-Ab'd*, or *Abdeh*, as being to the right, or east, and a day's journey from us. I note this because others hold that these two are the same.

Having crossed a small height, we came into *Wady El-Hufîr* or *Hafîr*, where we found extensive ruins and terrace-walls as in the preceding valley, with like traces of cultivation and like spots of verdure. These stretch for miles along the wady, as if there had been an unbroken continuity of dwellings or villages in this region. How changed from the fruitfulness and populous life of other days!

> " He turneth rivers into a wilderness,
>   And the water-springs into dry ground ;
>   A fruitful land into barrenness,
>   For the wickedness of them that dwell therein."—
>
> (Psa. cvii. 33.)

About twelve o'clock, we came nearer El-Aujeh, and got a good view of it, though we did not go out of our way to examine it. The telescope did us sufficient service. There are two sorts of peaks ; the higher looks like a castle, but turns out to be only the peculiar castellated formation of the rock. The lower is an old fortification, and both in situation and appearance was not unlike Home Castle in Berwickshire.

We now came to immense beds of lilies and hyacinths, of various kinds, tall and broad-leaved ; one species only was in bloom, thrusting up its lilac flower amid a profusion of leaves, upon a tall stalk, some two feet long. The plants grew thickly together and covered miles of the sand. No grass was visible between.

The road here winds along the slope of the low hill on which these lilies were growing; and here one of our camels, who had always shewn his unwillingness to be loaded, now gave proof of his willingness to be relieved of his load. He commenced prancing furiously, apparently with the intention of disburdening himself. Nor did he fail; for in a minute barrels of water and cages of fowls came to the ground. No one, however, was injured; the casks stood the shock, nor did the fowls take any harm. The animal was soon seized and reloaded, in spite of all his objections and expostulations. We had an opportunity of seeing the awkwardness of the camel's movements, of which Jerome speaks, and which he tells us had made "a camel's dance" a proverb in old times.*

We next passed into a stony waste, with poor vegetation, and entered *Wady Senieh.* No mountains appeared in any direction, nothing but the wide waste around, in cultivation scarcely better than the desert through which we had passed. A cool breeze came from the north-east, and slight clouds throwing themselves between us and the sun, took off the scorching heat. The zenith, as usual, appeared low and the horizon wide. The day was fine.

Between one and two we came into *Wady-el-Ab'deh,* where doubtless stood *Eboda,* mentioned by Ptolemy as a Roman city, and which either took its name from or

---

* "Risimus in te proverbium, camelum vidimus saltitantem."—*Epist. Adv. Helvidium.*

gave it to the wady. It would appear that in this region the Romans had established themselves in great strength, their footsteps being visible everywhere. It is not unlikely that the "wilderness of Beersheba" (Gen. xxi. 14) extended itself in this direction, and the cultivation, of which we see traces, was begun in the days of Abraham and Isaac. As the region formed a sort of neutral ground or common, between Egypt and Palestine, it was a likely spot for the patriarchs to fix upon, where, undisturbed, they might obtain sufficient pasture for their flocks. Though occasionally molested by the Philistines, they yet, in general, seemed to have had this semi-desert in peaceful occupation ; and through them these plains were brought under a partial tillage, which went on for ages, reaching its height under the Roman conquest, and after that, gradually sinking back into a sterility probably greater than that from which it was at first reclaimed.

The wady was sandy, but still marked by a considerable amount of vegetation. It was studded everywhere with the liliacious plants, which I have already noticed, as well as with crocuses and similar small bulbs. Nor were these stunted and meagre ; they were tall and bushy, as if the soil were quite congenial. It was pleasant to hear the hum of the bee, and to mark it as it went singing along through the air or stooping among the camel shrubs, which were growing plentifully, and claiming this territory as the desert. We felt that this was border-land. The intermixture of the lily with the

tarfa and the ritt'm, seemed to imply the contention for
the mastery, between the sand of the desert and the soil
of the land flowing with milk and honey.

All suddenly, at this spot our men, leaving the
camels, made a rush towards a huge mound or cairn of
stones on our right. Their manner was so furious that
I thought there was something wrong, and that possibly
they might have seen some serpent or wild beast lurk-
ing among the debris. They cast stones, they lashed the
mound with sticks, they spat, they cursed, they yelled.
Then, in a few minutes, they returned peaceably and
pursued their way. Having asked an explanation of
the scene, I was told that this was the tomb of *Sheikh
Amri*, a cruel chief of other days, whose memory is so
hateful to the Bedaween, that they cannot pass the
cairn which covers his bones without this frantic ex-
plosion of abhorrence.

The frequent allusions to the oppression and doom of
the wicked man in the Book of Job are worth noticing,
as shewing a similar state of things to what is exhibited
still in the East. In some of these references we seem
to see the desert-tent and the desert-lamp, the desert-
fire and the desert-cairn :—

> " The light of the wicked shall be put out,
>   And the spark of his fire shall shine no more.
>   Light shall be darkness in his tent,
>   And his lamp shall be put out with him.
>   His confidence shall be rooted out from his tent,
>   It shall bring him to the king of terrors,
>   It shall dwell in his tent, which is none of his.

> Brimstone shall be scattered over his habitation.
> Beneath, his root shall be dried up,
> Above, his branch shall be cut off.
> He shall be driven from light into darkness,
> And chased out of the world.
> They that come after him shall be astonished at his day,
> As they that went before were affrighted.
> Surely such are the dwellings of the wicked,
> And this is the place of him that knew not God."—
>
> (Job xviii. 5–21.)

In a subsequent chapter the speaker takes up the subject, and after asking, Where is the dwelling of the wicked? he points forward to their day of doom, intimating his belief in the resurrection of the "unjust," as clearly as he had elsewhere intimated his belief of "the resurrection of the just":—

> " The wicked one is reserved to the day of destruction;
> They shall be brought forth to the day of wrath.

Yet, meanwhile, his body rests in his silent heap or cairn, such as this which is now before us, of this wicked sheikh :—

> " He shall be brought to the grave,
> The watch shall be set over his cairn.
> The clods of the valley shall be sweet to him,
> Men will draw after him,
> As those before him are without number."—(Job xxi. 30–33.)

After passing some more terrace-walls we came to the dry bed of a river. The channel was not very broad but tolerably deep,—much deeper than we had been accustomed to see in the desert. Its bed was beauti-

fully pebbled, and its banks fringed with various shrubs,
that shook their green leaves over its white stones.
Had there been but the pleasant flow of water, however
small, there would have been as picturesque a glen as
our own island could furnish. Even as it was, the
scene was most attractive, forming such a contrast to
the wastes which we had traversed ; and we could almost supply its one defect by fancying

> "The burn stealing lone thro' the lang yellow broom."

We now passed up a sandy eminence and came into
Wady-en-Nehiyeh at a quarter before three. On all
sides were hillocks of bright yellow sand, of a softer
and moister kind than any which we had hitherto seen.
The shrubs were finer and more plentiful, indicating a
moister if not a better soil. The ritt'm especially shot
up in beauty, and liliacious plants were scattered pro-
fusely around. Several small flowers also were making
their appearance here and there. But who had sowed
them ? It seemed as if the soil of the desert were filled
with innumerable seeds which need but the rain to call
them up. We observed grass upon the more sheltered
and better watered places, while large flocks of sheep,
with thick tails, were feeding in all directions. We
were evidently passing out of the desert into a region
which, perhaps, had once been more fully cultivated,
and which was quite capable of yielding something to
the hand of the tiller. But though the lower parts were
thus somewhat greener, the hill-slopes were as bare and
stony as ever.

A little before four I left the party and ascended the ridge to the right, to examine what appeared in the distance like ruins on the long, level top, which was perhaps about three hundred feet in height, and to which there was a gradual slope over rough, loose stones, which covered the whole slope. Here I observed such letters or figures as the following :—

There were, perhaps, some fifteen inscriptions in all of the above kind. They bore very considerable resemblance to the Mukatteb ones, though they were not exactly the same. They looked sharper and more recent. I walked along this flat ridge for about a mile, and came upon several circular mounds which had the appearance of ruins. One of these was of considerable size. The inscriptions were on flat pieces of horizontal rock, not on the side of any eminence. The ridge was above *Wady-en-Nehiyeh.*

Descending, I rejoined the party, of whom I had not allowed myself to lose slight ; and, as we moved northwards, we came upon some ploughed fields to the left, where there was a man with an axe cleaving the baked soil,—" breaking up his fallow-ground," or rather cutting up the ground when brought by rain and sun into that state described in the Book of Job :—

> " When the dust groweth into hardness,
> And the clods cleave fast together."—(Job xxxviii. 38.)

The birds were singing blythely and hopping from
shrub to shrub.   About five o'clock we passed into
Wady-er-Ruhaibeh, and encamped.   The evening was
fine, and the sky without a cloud, yet the heat was
moderate.   The air seemed to breathe of spring.   All
was freshness and balm.   I walked out, and took my
seat upon a sandy hillock, with the ritt'm and shia
pressed down under me for my carpet, till the darkness
came down.

We have traversed this day a region of much beauty.
We are still indeed moving through border-land, for
fruitfulness and barrenness are fighting hard for victory
over each other.   There is as yet more of the latter
than the former, but the progress is visible.   We have
got real verdure at last, though it is but scanty.   We
miss the unbroken plains of grassy pasture, for which
no mere patches of green can make up.   We miss the
green knolls and the glad river-sides of the north.   We
miss, too, the daisy and the primrose.   But, notwith-
standing, the scene has been brighter to-day than any
through which we have come for many weeks, and we
feel as if we were really " coming up out of the wilderness " by a gradual but cheering ascent of road, which
is, mile after mile, throwing off the lean and scorched
nakedness of the desert, and putting on the rich clothing of Syria's happier soil.

CHAPTER XIII.

Wady-er-Ruhaibeh, Feb. 14.——Rose before seven. The morning was sunny, but there was the appearance of frost on our tents, and a heavy dew lay around. Had a pleasant walk among the shrubby knolls of sand, where I found, at intervals, a considerable amount of genuine *grass.* The lark singing, almost out of sight, in the sunshine, made most cheering music,——quite like a morning psalm. The warble is the same as in our cloudier skies ; nor could any one mistake it. It was a pleasant thought that there was such a song, coming up each day, in such a solitude, where there is no ear but that of God to hear the melody. It sung to the silent sands and the unwaving shrubs, as pleasantly as to the greener fields of other climes. Nay, its song seemed to have fuller compass, and its wing more unfettered range in such a waste. How well the song and the solitude seemed to suit each other !

We moved off at nine, through a broad, undulating region, stretching eastward and northward, forming a sort of semicircular sweep on our right and in front. In the distance spread the low hills of Palestine, ranging nearly east and west. This was our first glimpse of "Immanuel's land;" as indeed the hills are the first objects which you greet in any land, save Egypt; for *there* only is there no outstanding object visible afar off to bid you welcome. A welcome from the hills of Palestine was one worth having.

The whole valley was covered with lilies, among which the small land-tortoises were creeping about. We took possession of some of these, in order to bring home a specimen of the more respectable live-stock of the desert. At a quarter past ten we came to some ruins, in which we found stones of many sizes and shapes, round, square, and oblong. There were several fragments of pillars, which, from their exact resemblance to those which we had seen at Sinai and Feirân, were evidently the remains of ecclesiastical buildings. On one of these pillar-fragments there was an inscription. It was considerably defaced, but looked very like those of Wady Mukatteb. On a small eminence we came upon the ruin of a large building, 45 ft. by 52 ft., containing six equal compartments. The stones were massive and well-hewn,—some of them round,—the remains of pillars or corner-ornaments, such as the convent of Sinai shews on the roof at several of its angles. Farther down, we came to another well-defined ruin, 33 ft. by 40 ft., divided into four compartments. Farther on we came to larger buildings of a similar kind, with terrace-walls and massive stones in all directions. Fragments also of pottery were scattered about. Not ten minutes further on we came to a large tomb-like building, which, though partly ruined, is still in tolerable preservation. It seemed in some respects like a *wely*, or tomb of a moslem saint, in others like a small chapel, such as might have formed an appendage, to the convent not far off. Its exterior (such as the *dome*) was more like the former, its interior more like the latter.

Above this tomb, on a height of perhaps thirty feet, there is a large well or cistern. It might be some forty or fifty feet in diameter, well-built on all sides, and with steps leading down to the bottom. This last feature in a well occurs but seldom in the desert. There the wells are deep and narrow,—that is to say, not wider than six feet in diameter. But in Syria, where they are often not so much wells as cisterns or tanks, these steps down to them are often seen, as in the case of the pool at Hebron and Solomon's pools. The well at which Eliezer found Rebekah, when he went to seek her as a wife to Isaac, was of this kind, for we read that " she went down to the well and filled her pitcher and came up " (Gen. xxiv. 16). The wells of Mesopotamia, no doubt, resembled those of Syria more than those of the desert. The well before us was very old, though perhaps the present cistern was merely the successor of one much older. For these wells seem not to have altered their site from the earliest days in which they were built. Frequent repairs and changes they have undergone, but the well itself remains much as it was. The question occurs then, was this the well which Isaac's servants dug, after their conflicts with the Philistines? The name *Ruhaibeh* looks very like *Rehoboth* (Gen. xxvi. 22), and the objection urged by Dr Robinson that Scripture only mentions a well, not a city (whereas there has been a city here), is of no weight, seeing a city might rise up in after ages, though not a stone of it was laid in Isaac's day. Indeed, the whole of this region is strewed with ruins of cities built in subsequent times. This may be the site of Isaac's well, nay, it may be the site of Hagar's well,—*Beer-lahai-roi* (Gen. xvi. 14), which was " in the way to Shur," and " between Kadesh and Bered;" or it may be Hagar's other well in the wilderness of Beersheba (Gen. xxi. 14, 19). Certainly it must have been somewhere in this region that all these scenes took place, and these wells were found.

Any one acquainted with the geography of the region, will see that Ruhaibeh quite suits the scene of the sacred narrative. Isaac went to Gerar (Gen. xxvi. 1), which was, most probably, a little south-east of *Gaza*. Having become rapidly prosperous while there, he was driven by the envy of the Philistines from Gerar itself to " the valley of Gerar" (ver. 17), which was probably one of the wadys which abound in that district. There he " pitched his tent," a little way south of Gerar itself. As Abraham had formerly sojourned here, there were wells still to be found, though "stopped" by the Philistines after Abraham's death (ver. 18). Besides reopening these, Isaac's servants "digged in the valley and found there a well of living water" (ver. 19). As the Philistines strove for this, and for another well, which they digged, Isaac and his household were gradually driven southward beyond the reach of the Philistines, till at Rehoboth they found rest (ver. 22). All this quite corresponds with Ruhaibeh, and the probability is completed when we read again, "he went up from thence to Beersheba" (ver. 23), which was less than a day's march distant.

We now ascended the low hill above the well, attracted by the appearance of ruins. We were not disappointed. These ruins cover a very large space of ground, and are evidently the remains of one of the many ancient towns scattered over this neighbourhood. Foundations, walls, and even streets are visible in all directions. We wandered amongst them for some time, surveying their different parts with no small interest,— entering houses, climbing walls, and marking the different compartments. The city is said by some travellers to be called *Ruhaibeh;* but the only name by which our sheikh knew the place was *Khurbit-el-Beer,* "the ruins of the well." All is utter ruin and solitude. The sound of the millstone is gone, the voice of man is not heard; no trace of the living is to be found, and no monument of the dead is there. Was that old well the beginning, and that moslem *wely* the end, of the city's history?

The district is not a very safe one to travel in. There are some lawless prowlers here whom our Arabs did not seem fond of meeting. We could imagine, in this region of ruined cities, the scene described by Job, in the career of the outlawed robber :—

> " He pitches his tent in desolate cities,
> In houses which no man inhabiteth,
> Which are ready to become heaps."—(Job xv. 28.)

As we did not take up our night-quarters here, we did not hear the " complainings" of " the moping owl," as did the American traveller ; but the quick-darting lizards among the stones we saw, as in other places.

Our sheikh kept close by us the whole time ; but evidently was impatient and uneasy at our lingering so far behind the caravan. Pointing sometimes in one direction, and sometimes in another, he shook his head, looked grave, and spoke of " bad Bedaween." But we saw none of "the tents of the robbers" (Job xii. 6), which seem to be even more plentiful in some parts of the desert now, than in the age of the patriarch. Urged, however, by our sheikh, we hastened down into the valley, and, walking briskly, we soon overtook our camels.

We passed large fields on our right under cultivation, while on our left rose a range of low sandy slopes or hills. In this neighbourhood Abraham and his son had been, tilling these very acres. " Then Isaac sowed in that land, and received in the same year an hundredfold ; and the Lord blessed him" (Gen. xxvi. 12). The Arab husbandmen were busy with the plough,—an instrument as poor and inefficient for the purpose of turning up the earth as can be conceived. Here it was drawn, not as usual by oxen, but by camels. Some ten or twelve of these we saw at work in various directions, in the course of our forenoon's ride. They look very ungainly in the field, and do not seem at all suited to this kind of work. It is for bearing burdens, not for drawing either ploughs or carriages that the camel is fitted. In the field it seems quite out of its element. It is in the desert that it shews to advantage,—especially when moving on over sand under the pressure of some heavy load, under which any other animal would have broken down. The cultivation continued for two or three miles along the valley of Ruhaibeh; and then about half-past eleven, we passed into sand again. The way was very circuitous and rather hilly, but beset on both sides with the same lilies as before, in great abundance, along with some of the usual desert shrubs.

About twelve we came to *Wady-el-Khulasah*, with mountains on the right, which our Arabs called *Makhrah*. Here we found another detachment of ruins, shewing how continuous had once been the course of population in this district,—city after city having been planted within a mile or two of each other. All this of course infers a very much higher state of cultivation than at present shews itself, or even seems possible from the appearance of the country. The infidel has sometimes pointed the finger to Palestine, and asked how was it possible that it could have maintained such a population as Scripture assigns to it? We take him to Ruhaibeh and its neighbourhood, and bid him look at these ruins. What do they mean? Are we to judge of past fruitfulness by present barrenness,—of past numbers by present desolation? Or we ask him to turn his argument against the Roman historians of the latter, and question their veracity, seeing they tell us of the cities which once flourished here, and of the population which covered those now empty wastes,—wastes over which the patriarchs wandered, through which the great Roman road once passed, and in which Christian churches once flourished.

The whole region now begins to brighten up. It is no longer "a land that is not sown" (Jer. ii. 2), such as we have hitherto been passing through. It is a land " made soft with showers" (Ps. lxv. 10). It is not indeed the goodly land of vines and olives, of streams and fountains (Deut. viii. 7, 8); but it is at least not a waste. The "pastures of the wilderness" (Ps. lxv. 12) are here. The sternness of the desert features is now relaxing into a smile. Not only is the valley becoming green, but the slopes are beginning to be clothed with the same hue; nay, "the little hills rejoice on every side;" for though their verdure is still poor and unable to reach their summits, yet it is sufficient to take off that aspect of dreary nakedness which the desert presents, and which, by its long continuance, has grown quite oppressive to us. The green of the scattered shrubs, which we met with almost every day, was but a scanty relief. Cheering as were the palms of Wady Ghurandel and the tarfas of Wady Sheikh, they only partially mitigated the sear and lonely lifelessness of hill and vale. For they rise out of the bare sand ; and the want of the green sward beneath takes away more than half the gladness of their verdure. I had no idea previously that so much of earth's beauty depended on the *green* of its *floor*. Nothing can be a compensation for the want of this.

> " . . . gay green,
> Thou smiling nature's universal robe !
> United light and shade ; where the sight dwells
> With growing strength and ever new delight."

But we had now come to a region where nature seemed putting off her sackcloth, and exchanging the grim frown for the happy smile. The change was welcome. And though there was no palm, no olive, nor tree of any kind around, yet even without these, the landscape seemed gay and goodly. It was *unadorned,* but still it was *clothed.* In Feirân it was *adorned,* but not *clothed ;* and we found that no amount of the former could be an equivalent for the want of the latter.

Had there been here some lofty mountain, from which we might have viewed the far-off region on either side of us, we should have seen, to the east, Mount Hor rising up in its bare, rocky grandeur, with Petra in majestic ruin not far off, while, in the north-west, we should have caught a glimpse of the " great sea." Or had we struck again into Wady-el-Arish, we might, without

difficulty, have taken our course down its well-marked
channel, till we reached its mouth at Rhinocorura,
where the torrent that had its birthplace in the ravines
and fissures of Et-Tih, pours its flood, after many a
bend, over the sands of the Mediterranean. It was
always interesting to us as we passed along, not only to
see what could be seen on right and left, but to imagine
what could not be seen, as we marked it upon our maps
and reckoned up the distance between it and us.

About half-past one we came to *Khurbit-el-Khu-
lasah*, the ruins of *Khulasah*. In this name seems to
be preserved the Roman *Elusa*, mentioned by Ptolemy
in the second century. The remains are very extensive ; and the stones are of all sizes and shapes,—shewing even in their fragments the carefulness with which
they had been hewn and prepared. There is a large
quantity of broken pottery scattered about in all directions,—indicating how much earthenware had been in
use in these cities. The " potter's vessel" lay in fragments (Psa. ii. 9) ; and we could understand the meaning of the figure used by the prophet to set forth Israel's
desolation :—

> " He shall shiver it as the shivering of a potter's vessel,
>   Breaking it, he spareth it not.
>   And there shall not be found among its fragments a shred
>   To take up fire from the hearth
>   Or to skim up water from the pool."—(Isa. xxx. 14.)

Many fragments we did find, but all thoroughly useless
for any purpose,—not one above two inches square at

the most. When these are of any size they are most
useful for lifting the glowing embers, either to kindle
another fire, or lighting the pipes of such of our Bedaween as smoked,—for they did not all do so. But the
pieces under our feet were so small, that they could be
no preservative to the fingers. Still more useful would
they be to "skim up" (as the word is) water from the
pool;—for though the idea of "scooping the brimming
stream" comes from a land of broader rivers than the
desert knows, yet often did we see the Arab, in his
thirst, making use of various appliances to quench his
thirst at the pools by the way. Sometimes they "bowed
down upon their knees to drink" (Judges vii. 5).
Sometimes they "lapped of the water with their tongue
as a dog lappeth" (Judges vii. 8). But a fragment of
earthenware with a slight hollow would have been quite
a prize. I found my gutta-percha cup of great use, and
by means of it I tasted of every well, or pool, or stream
that we might light upon; but even a piece of pottery
is not in such circumstances to be despised. In all this
region, however, we came upon nothing save mere fragments,—though certainly these fragments were in great
abundance. They were of various sizes and colours,—
some red, some bluish, some dun, some whitish. Here
we picked up a broken handle of a pitcher; there an
ornamented piece of the rim; then a solid piece of the
base. But still they had all been thoroughly broken,
as if pounded to pieces under the heel of the spoiler.

Not far from this was a beautiful bed of a stream,

x

which we should much have liked to see in its fulness.
But it was dry. Yet even these dry channels here are
much more pleasant to the eye than the sandy depres-
sions to which we had become familiar under the name
of *wadys*. To these wadys your fancy had not only
to bring water, in order to give them beauty, but to
plant their banks with trees and clothe them with grass.
But here you had just to supply the stream, and immediately all was beautiful.

Hard by were the ruins of large buildings, some
square, others circular, the stones not rude but well-
hewn. Here we found a regularly-built well, upwards
of twenty feet deep and twelve in diameter, with some
troughs beside it. Troughs beside wells, needful in all
countries, are quite indispensable in the East. Hence
the frequent references to them in Scripture. " She
hasted, and emptied her pitcher into the *trough* (we
should just have poured the water on the ground, but
it is too valuable in the East to be thrown away), and
ran again unto the well to draw water" (Gen. xxiv. 20).
" The priest of Midian had seven daughters : and they
came and drew water, and filled the *troughs* to water
their father's flock" (Exod. ii. 16). Finely-carved stones
were scattered about, of various sizes. A little further
on we came to another well, whose arch-formed mouth
rises above ground. Then we reached another, considerably larger, called *Beer-Khalasah*, partly arched at
the top, and rising up conically a few feet, with an aperture in the centre, large enough to admit of a bucket or

skin-vessel being let down through it, yet sufficiently small to make it capable of being covered with a stone or rock. With us it is a matter of smaller moment that the well should be carefully covered over,—for water is not so precious in our moister climate, and our wells are not in danger of being filled up with the sand-drift. It is otherwise in the East, both in Syria and in the desert. Hence the care with which the wells or springs are " shut up " and " sealed " (Song of Sol. iv. 12). The mention of this in Jacob's history shews us that the stone was as necessary in Syria as in the desert. " He looked, and behold a well in the field ... and *a great stone* was upon the well's mouth ; and thither were all the flocks gathered, and they *rolled the stone* from the well's mouth and watered the sheep, and *put the stone again* upon the well's mouth in its place " (Gen. xxix. 2, 3, 8).

After leaving this, the lilies disappear for a little. The stones of *Elusa* lie scattered over the valley, with great quantities of pottery of all colours,—white, black, and red. In a little, the lilies recommenced, covering vast tracts of ground as before. Here too the *ritt'm* abounds ;—for this is the desert of Beersheba, through which Elijah passed on his way to the Mount of God (1 Kings xix. 1-4). Here it was that " he came and sat down under a *ritt'm*-tree ;" for we read that, having left his servant at Beersheba, " he himself went a day's journey into the wilderness," which would bring him to this very spot. Here it was that he requested for him-

self that he might die, and said, " Enough now, O Jehovah, take away my life ; for I am not better than my
fathers."*   Here it was that " he lay and slept under a
ritt'm-tree ;" and here it was that the angel touched
him and said, Arise and eat.   Here it was that " he
saw the cake baken on the coals, and a cruise of water
at his head," of which he partook, and then laid him
down once more beneath the shadow of the shrub.
Here it was that the angel came the second time and
gave him food,—food prepared by no human hand,—
food upon the strength of which he went forty days
(ver. 8).   It was the bread of the mighty ; and in this
desert, as in the days of Israel, " man did eat angels'
food."   Why the journey occupied forty days is not said.
It need not have taken half that time.   But God had
lessons to teach him by the way.

Nearly two miles from the ruins already described
we came upon others, at half-past two o'clock.   There
was a small eminence covered with fragments of hewn
stone.   In the centre was a well,—perhaps originally
one of those dug by the patriarchs, for wells here do not

---

* Some of the old commentators have discovered a tradition respecting
the tree under which the prophet lay and slept, which makes us smile.
It is said that the shade of the ritt'm is noxious, and that he sat down
under it as one courting death !   Any one who has seen the Arabs enjoying the shade of that tree, or has enjoyed it himself in a sunny noon, will
have no great difficulty in defending Elijah from the charge of meditated
suicide.   Whence the commentators took this tradition I do not know.
The reader will find the tradition itself and a defence of the prophet, in
Paxton's " Illustrations of Scripture."

easily change,—and if filled up they are dug again, as we see in the case of Isaac. It had been carefully built, and was upwards of four feet in diameter. Around were many fragments of pottery,—ancient of course,— for who has been here for many a century to leave his fragments on these fields ?

We ascended gently for an hour, and then came down into *Wady-el-Khuzay,*—a fine valley covered with vegetation,—chiefly consisting of shrubs, though interspersed with grass. A flock of sheep, black and white, was feeding on the pasture. Advancing half an hour further, we found the shrubs decreasing, and the grassy herbage becoming more plentiful. As we move northwards the wilderness gradually dissolves into the fruitful field. Yet not without some such retrogression, as makes one at times think that it was quite resuming dominion. For it was not so much the wilderness that was encroaching on the tillage, as the tillage that was pushing its way into the wilderness. In truth, it seemed as if there were a tide of vegetation setting in from the north, and making its way south over the desert sands. Sometimes a vast wave rushed forward, over the plains, and occupied large space. Then it returned and left the interval bare, so that the verdure seemed sometimes gaining and sometimes losing ground,—just as in the case of an advancing tide. Such was the aspect which this border-land presented to us.

About four, we passed into *Wady Murtubeh,*—a grassy vale, according to desert-reckoning, but bare enough when compared with Strathmore or Teviotdale. The usual shrubs scattered their dusky vegetation over the wady, though less thickly than before. We examined some ruins on a mound, consisting of well-hewn stones. Hard by was the bed of a stream, which after rains must contain a considerable quantity of water. It was now dry. The white pebbles, as well as larger stones with which the channel was strewn, formed quite a contrast to the wadys of the desert. Along its margin some grassy slopes spread themselves out, and gave a softer beauty to the spot than any which we had hitherto seen.

We are now on the parallel of the Dead Sea. It is no doubt several days' journey distant from us; but had we been able to mount high enough, we might perhaps have seen the southern margin of these solemn waters, where four cities lie entombed. We certainly should not have grudged trouble or toil to get a glimpse of *Bahr Lût*, and of *Usdum*,—the names still retained by the natives, shewing how tenaciously the story of Lot has clung to that sea, and how well even Arab tradition has remembered the doom of *Sodom*.

About five o'clock we ascended the gentle ridge above *Wady-es-Seba*,—and there we found as sweet and green a vale as we could wish to see. It was not a large hollow, but it was pleasant, and sheltered on all sides. The undulating slopes and rounded hillocks, half in light and half in shade, yet bathed in as bright a sunset as an eastern sky can furnish, and all this mingled with the memories of patriarchal suns and sunsets,—of the times when, perhaps, on this very spot, " Isaac went out to mediate in the field at the even-tide" (Gen. xxiv. 63),* presented a scene as exquisite to the eye as it was soothing to the spirit. It was something too to be in a region hitherto but little traversed by travellers. Few eyes of strangers rest on these hills, and few feet of strangers pass through them. Egypt and Sinai have been visited by thousands, and described till they have become familiar to those who have never left their own shores; but this district is almost unexplored.

It reminded us of some of the downs of our own island. We seemed to breathe more freely when coming to the green earth again ; for though we had, during the last three or four days, been cheered by verdant spots, we had not yet lighted on a region so thoroughly green. Home, with its fresh fields, seemed nearer, and the link more visible between it and us. In the soft grass there seemed something kindred and companionable. It seemed to know us, and we it, as friends. What a power this verdure seemed to possess of bringing up thoughts, and scenes, and faces, which the desert sands had banished !

The way from *Wady-el-Martubah* to *Wady-es-Seba* winds most tortuously, yet most gently, through a pass between the various undulations which divide the two wadys. We took nearly an hour to traverse it ; and at

---

* " And Isaac came from the way of the well Lahai-roi : for he dwelt in the south country" (Gen. xxiv. 62).

six o'clock we halted in a hollow upon the ridge which overlooks Wady-es-Seba. We should greatly have preferred moving forward and pitching our tents beside Abraham's wells; but it was late, and we were content to remain on the heights above Beersheba,—the more so because the hills of Judah were full in view.

Heights above Beersheba, Feb. 15.—Rose a little after six, and wandered out on the heights which surrounded our tents. The sun was still unrisen, and the morning was slightly cold. There was no frost so far as I could judge; but the thin and almost invisible vapour, as it rose from the moist ground into the chill, wan air, suggested that possibly there might have been some during the night. But every sign indicated a day of heat and sunshine. The alternation alluded to by Jacob I could easily understand : " in the day *the drought* consumed me, and *the frost* by night " (Gen. xxxi. 40).

Our camels were scattered on the numerous slopes in search of food. On these heights the lilies abounded, with grass and low shrubs between. I noticed that the camels did not touch the lilies at all ; but cropped what lay between. It reminded me of the words, "he feedeth *among* the lilies" (Cant. ii. 16). We did not here see any flocks feeding, or any " young harts " leaping ; but in other places we had frequent occasion to notice the sheep and lambs browsing on the like pastures,—*among* but not *on* the lilies, for while the lily furnishes no acceptable food for flocks and herds, it seems by the shade of its high broad leaves, to retain the moisture,

and so to nourish herbage wherever it grows. The place
of lilies would thus be the place of the richest pasture,
as Solomon evidently indicates, when again using the
figure, he speaks of the "young roes which feed *among*
the *lilies*" (Cant. iv. 5, and again vi. 3). They grew in
almost incredible numbers and luxuriance ;—often where
nothing else flourished, corroborating the prophet's allusion, "he shall grow *as the lily*." (Hosea xiv. 5). Their
tapering leaf is richly green, and hence the "heap of
wheat set about with lilies" (Cant. vii. 2), would form,
by the contrast, an object of no common beauty, the
pale yellow and the vivid green setting off each other,
as the leaf of the primrose does its own yellow blossom.
Close by these lilies there grew several of the thorn-
shrubs of the desert ; but above them rose the lily,
spreading out its fresh leaf of green as a contrast to the
dingy verdure of these prickly shrubs. "As the lily
among thorns, so is my love among the daughters"
(Cant. ii. 2). Whether this be the lily of the valley, I
do not know. It grows on hill and valley, all over this
region. Nor is it of one species only, but of several, as
we could easily see, though only one species was in
flower. That which was in flower the Arabs called
usweih. It was larger than the others, and shot up its
lilac, hyacinth-looking flowers from a tapering stalk,
sometimes two feet long.*

---

* These long lily-stalks were used by several of our party as a sort of
whip for the camels. They answered the purpose tolerably well, being
rather tough and strong.

The sun came up, as I was wandering among these
grassy knolls, and threw his light upon the distant hills
of Judah, covering them with a veil of mellow purple.
The larks were singing overhead, the camels were feeding around, the Arabs were moving about beneath, and
the tents were brightening in the sunlight, as I moved
slowly down, recalling patriarchal memories, and thinking how often Abraham and Isaac had trodden this
ground, had fed their flocks among these lilies, and had
enjoyed the morning sunshine as I was now doing.

We started about eight, the travellers preferring to
walk, leaving the camels to follow. A morning walk
to Beersheba! We needed no adventitious circumstances to add to the interest of the route ; yet the clear
sky above us, and the fresh grass beneath our feet,
were most exhilarating. The descent is a very gradual
one, the path winding through the same kind of gentle
undulations as on the preceding day. We passed several
beautiful hollows, rich in pasture, just such as we could
suppose the patriarchs to have known, as places for their
flocks to feed ;—not, perhaps, to "rest at noon" (Cant.
i. 7), for this requires more shade than these hollows
could afford,—some rock, or cave, or group of trees,—
yet to feed at morn or even, or it might be in the
watches of the night (Luke ii. 8). The birds still cheered
us with song as we passed, and the moles were busily at
work under our feet, casting up the brown soil, just as
in our fields at home. The knolls were of all variety of
height and figure, varying the scene at every turn. We

wandered slowly on, cheered by the fresh grassy fragrance which was rising about us, as the heat drew up the moisture from the soil. As we walked together, we read aloud the various passages in Genesis connected with this locality. They came to us with new interest and meaning.

As we got down to *Wady-es-Seba*, about half-an-hour from our time of starting, we observed a hollow of considerable size, in which there were ruins. The terrace-walls and foundations of houses were quite visible; and on all the small knolls there were great quantities of stones, many of which had evidently been used in building. Yet we do not know of any city here; though it is not unlikely that the whole of this wady was once well-peopled. Its fruitful and well-watered soil would draw population to it in all ages. By the way we noticed quantities of the *coloquintida*, formerly seen in several places of the desert. To the west for a short space we marked some low white cliffs. In one or two places the ground was quite broken and cut up by torrents; but no water was to be seen in their sandy beds. Broken pottery was strewed in all directions, both on the level track and on the mounds. Flocks of sheep and camels were feeding here and there.

A little after nine we came upon an extensive plain, whose level breadth was relieved by numerous undulations and beautified with green. Again we saw ruins, similar to the former and not a mile distant from them. We noticed also a long strip of green table-land, with

fragments of pottery in considerable quantities. At
half-past nine we reached the water-course, on whose
banks,—upon the level ledge which ran along for some
distance,—were ruins like those we had already seen. In
the greener parts camels were feeding. The channel of
the river was thickly paved with pebbles, and with white
stones of some size, and was about one hundred and fifty
feet broad. Immediately on reaching the other side you
come upon the wells, from which it took, and still takes,
its name, *Beer-es-Seba,* the "well of the seven," or the
" well of the oath."

But this river-bed is the boundary of Palestine. We
shall not at present step across it. We leave the entire
land for another journey and another volume. The
tribes of Simeon and Judah lie before us, but we do
not, in the mean time, enter on their territories.

For some days past we have been traversing the land
of the patriarchs,—for the border-land that lies between
the desert and Palestine may well be honoured with
that name. It is the region which they specially occupied when they were "strangers and pilgrims on the
earth" (Heb. xi. 13). No doubt they did sojourn, at
times, in the land itself ; but this southern territory, less
preoccupied and less exposed to hostile assaults, they
seem to have preferred. Of Jacob this may not appear
altogether true, but of Abraham and Isaac we may say
that this was the country which they knew best and in
which they dwelt longest.

The home of the patriarchs was here—of Isaac especially, who took up his dwelling by the well *Lahai-roi* (Gen. xxiv. 62); and the history of this region is a history of the patriarchs. Just as the desert has only a history of forty years, the time when Israel was there; so this " south country" has a history of little more than a century, the time when the two elder patriarchs had their sojourn in it.

They builded no cities in it, for their dwelling was in tents, and with these they were content. Their faith rested on the city which hath foundations, and until it should arrive they were satisfied with the tent alone. Here Abraham and Sarah, Isaac and Rebekah, Ishmael and Hagar lived. From this it was that Isaac was led up to Moriah, like a lamb for sacrifice; for, as Jerome notices, Abraham must have been living here and not in Hebron at that time, else he would not have taken three days to reach Jerusalem.* In after ages the Romans came and occupied the country, making roads through its whole length, and building cities on the slopes of its valleys. But of their doings here we know little. Cities and temples, and in later ages churches, rose where the tents of the patriarchs had been pitched, —but these have passed away. Not a stone is left upon another.

The patriarchs, though they chose it for their residence while living, did not take it as their abode when

---

* He speaks of him as being in Gerar, not nearer, for from the oak of Mamre to Moriah is only hardly one day's journey, " vix unius diei iter plenum."

dead. They built no tombs, they hewed out no sepulchres for themselves or their children. Their dust was
to be conveyed to Canaan, and rest in the cave of Mach-
pelah. They might live and they might die in the
land of strangers, but not in it would they be buried.
Their bones must be gathered to their fathers, and their
dust sleep in a soil which they could call their own. A
resting-place in death was more to them than a dwelling-
place in life. The latter was of little moment, seeing
they were strangers here; but the former was of much,
seeing it bore upon their resurrection-hope, and of that
hope they desired to testify by their guarded dust and
rock-hewn sepulchres.*

There were no goodly mountains here, like Carmel,
or like Lebanon; nor any streams such as Jordan or
Kishon; nor any lake such as that of Galilee. There
was nothing to mark the country in any special way.
There were no great features to form a fatherland round
which their affections or their patriotism might entwine
themselves. Nor was it a land flowing with milk or
honey. It was a fruitful land no doubt, but a plain and
unambitious territory, very much like the lowly men
who occupied it. It was less likely to be coveted than

---

* In the desert we saw frequent graveyards, and also in Palestine, but
none in this middle district. Not only have the patriarchs no such monu-
mental memorials, great or small, but Roman, Christian, and Mahommedan
have none. The patriarchs have left the well, the Moslems the wely, the
Christians the dismantled convent, and the Romans the ruined city. That
is all.

most lands, by the stranger, so that here they might sit down in peace, and pass the few days of their pilgrimage in unmolested calm,—walking with God, while they walked with each other, in these quiet vales.

It was not the land of the palm or the olive ; the vine, the fig, the pomegranate preferred the warmer air or the richer soil. It was a land of pasture, nothing more, —a land where, like Abel, they might feed their flocks without toil or care,—with less of the ancient curse,— the "sweat of the face" (Gen. iii. 19), than they might have had on more fruitful plains. It was a land suited for nothing but the unbustling life of shepherds,—the life that leaves most leisure, and affords most opportunity, for fellowship with God. Egypt was the land of those who had their portion here, and with it they had nought to do. The desert was the region of the wanderer, living on miraculous manna from heaven, and water from the rock, but neither the wandering nor the miracle was to be their portion. Canaan was the place of the settled habitation, where in the well-built cities their children were one day to rest ; but that rest was not to be their lot. Here, however, was a land unlike all of these, just as their mode of life was to be unlike all that went before or should follow after. It was just such a land as suited them, the land of the stranger and the pilgrim. How well did the country and the dwellers suit each other ! How beautifully does this nice, this gracious adaptation shew forth the wise and watchful tenderness, with which the God of Abraham and Isaac and Jacob provided for his chosen family during that time when, in his unexplained purpose and providence, he left them still outside the goodly land. Nor is the simplicity with which they trusted his faithfulness and followed his guidance less to be noted. It is worthy of our imitation; and, remembering this, we gaze and gaze again upon that narrow strip of land, where the footsteps of faith have left so visibly their ineffaceable imprint. For these things were "written for our learning that we, through the patience and comfort of the Scriptures, might HOLD FAST THE HOPE" (Rom. xv. 4), even as did these patriarchs in the midst of far thicker clouds, and keener trials of faith than we have known.

This home of the patriarchs was not within sight of Jerusalem; but it was far removed from Ur of the Chaldees, out of whose idolatry they had been rescued. It was not within sight of Lebanon, but it was beyond the vision of Sinai and its awful fellows. Yet though Jerusalem and Lebanon were far out of sight, still the promised land was near. Its hills were always within view. So that, while waiting here for the time when God was to lead them in, they could keep their eye upon its heights, or sometimes pass across the boundary to wander over, or for a season to pitch their tents upon its sunnier plains. Surrounded by deserts on every side they would be cheered by the perpetual vision of a land flowing with milk and honey, clothed with the olive and the vine,—a land in which their children, and their children's children, if not themselves, were in coming days to dwell.

Since Abraham first left his home on the banks of the Euphrates, he had known no certain dwelling-place. Sure of a resting-place somewhere, because God was beckoning him on, yet not sure of it anywhere, till he should sit down in Canaan, he was content to move or to rest as God should bid him. And though it was on Canaan that his heart was set, yet, next to Canaan, he seems to have preferred this region above all others. More truly still did it suit Isaac's gentle spirit. It was fitted to be the home of quiet faith, such as his, and of family tendernesses such as he delighted in. He chose it, therefore, for his place of sojourn, and most truly might it be named the land of Isaac. Once and again the world broke in upon him, and would have striven and quarrelled with him; but he resisted not. He retired before the quarrellers; he departed from the scene of strife, content to be wronged for the sake of peace and love. Yet in retiring before the injurers, he marks his sense of the evil and the wrong, by the names he gives to the scenes of the strife, calling the one *Esek* (strife), and the other *Sitnah* (hatred). And then, when he gets beyond the region of contention, he gives vent to his satisfied feelings by the name *Rehoboth* (room), which he affixes to the undisturbed resting-place in which he is now permitted to sit down.*

It was not the land of miracles. God did no mighty

---

* Gen. xxvi. 22. Had David Isaac in his view when he said, "Thou hast not shut me up into the hand of the enemy; thou hast set my feet in *a large room*" (Psa. xxxi. 8)? The original words are the same.

Y

work here ; nor did great events occur, save that once
or twice an angel passed across its fields in his ministry
of love. It was the land for the unfolding of simple
faith,—faith that grows out of no sign nor wonder, but
roots itself in the sure promise of the *El-Shaddai*,
" fear not, I am thy shield and thy exceeding great
reward ;" and, so rooting itself, anticipates the fuller
grace of after days, " blessed are they that have not seen,
and yet have believed " (John xx. 29).

They who delight in monkish traditions or miracles of
spurious saintship, will be disappointed here. No great
deeds were done nor great words spoken here. There are
no outstanding points on which Greek fables or Latin lies
can fasten themselves. If it is a region not made illustri-
ous by true miracles, it is one not disfigured and debased
by false ones. In this respect, there is a peculiar satis-
faction in passing through it, and surveying its tranquil
fields. The spirit is relieved from that fretting sense of
mockery which mars such scenes as Sinai or Bethlehem,
or even the Mount of Olives. In these places superstition has done its worst, to desecrate spots which otherwise would have been viewed with unmingled interest
or awe. There is no such defilement here. *This* region
at least has been spared the mockery. You have not
here to separate the true from the false ; all here is TRUE.
There may not be much, but what there is is real.
These plains, and hills, and slopes are just what they
were, when Isaac wandered over them ; and the eye is
not distracted with uncertainties, nor offended with

fooleries, such as elsewhere vex the spirit in tnese eastern
lands. More than once in the Desert, we found the lone
acacia covered with the rags which Moslem devotees had
hung upon its branches;—and just with such rags of Greek
tradition, we might say that we found Sinai covered.
But here neither Moslem nor Greek had intruded their
mockeries. The land lay quiet before us, in the pure
happy twilight of the patriarchal morning. What an
infliction upon a spot or region are these anilities which
travellers love to record, and even philosophers to adorn.
The Egyptian plague of frogs was not more loathsome
than these swarms of monkish lies. Happy the scene
that escapes their polluting touch. Yet we find men
who stand aloof from the mention of true miracles di-
lating fondly on the false. We find men who take no
interest in a spot, from its being the undoubted scene of
authentic miracles, expressing great interest in another
spot which has only been the scene of monastic fraud.
The true wonder forms no additional attraction to the
place ; the false wonder actually *creates* an attraction
and gives world-wide name to an obscure locality. Such
has been the unreasoning perversity, not merely of
mediæval superstition, but of modern philosophy. Not
that rationalism actually loves the falsehood or gives
heed to the fable ; but it so dislikes the true that it is
glad to seize the occasion of setting the two side by side,
that the one may cast discredit on the other, and the
reader be led to the conclusion that he cannot believe one
without believing both. The rationalist and the tradi-

tionist shake hands with each other across a narrow
stream. The former says that Bible miracles are not
true, and thereby brings them down to the level of the
monkish lie; the latter says they are true, but so are
the miracles of St Anthony and St Katherine, thereby
so encumbering the true with the load of the false as to
sink them both together.

If, then, in looking at these patriarchal hills and
vales, one feels disappointed that he can find no Scripture miracle to attach to them; he is comforted with
the thought that here is a territory undisfigured by
fable or forgery. No sixth-century saint has hung his
rags upon these shrubs; no idle pilgrim has carved his
name upon these rocks; no monk has bedaubed these
slopes with his paint-brush. They are all just what
they were, four thousand years ago. It is not, indeed,
now the *living* land. It is dead; and it is the face of
the dead that we look upon. But it is a face un-
marred and unaltered. " Decay's effacing fingers "
have not swept away one line of beauty. The countenance is as placid in its loveliness as when the sleep
of death first stole over it, and fixed its features. Ages
have not altered it; and nothing has passed away
save that which could not be retained,—the life and the
youth, the health, the freshness, and the joy.

It is only during the history of the patriarchs that
this region is brought into view. After that, it is almost lost sight of, save when a single verse informs us
that Elijah passed through it on his way to the Mount

of God. For even Israel did not enter it in their march
to Canaan. At their first approach, when the spies
were sent out, they were in the wilderness of Paran,
which, though in one sense it formed part of this territory, yet more truly belonged to the country lying east
of it. At their second approach, when their forty years'
wanderings were ended, they still took an eastward
route, keeping by the Gulf of Akabah and Mount Seir,
in order to turn the flank of the mountains of Moab
and enter Palestine by Jordan. And as it is a region
almost unknown in the later ages of Bible history, so
is it one which, in subsequent times, has been left un-
visited by the traveller. Hence it looks more fresh,
because hitherto undescribed ; it takes firmer hold of
your mind, because it carries you back at once to the
times of old, and makes you feel that, in your survey of
it, you are indebted to no one, but are looking at it with
your own eyes, not with those of travellers who have gone
before you. Nothing seems to come between you and the
patriarchs themselves, save time, which has only served
to make the spot more venerable. The crowd of *events*
which in other places comes between you and the men
of old, distracting your eye and taking off the impres-
siveness of the view, is here unknown. Your thoughts
are not divided among a multitude of conflicting me-

---

* We turned to the left at the point where Israel must have turned to
the right. Thus we missed *Wady-el-Hadharah,* which seems really to be
Hazeroth (Numb. xi. 35) ; at least the likeness of the name, and the suit-
ableness of the place, form strong presumptions in favour of this.

mories, each effacing the other ; they settle down upon
one single object, and are absorbed in one unhindered,
unbroken vision.   It is not like looking across plains,
or streams, or hills, to some wondrous land beyond,
where the intervening objects break up the oneness of
the prospect and perpetually suggest the idea of the
distance and the obstacles between.   It is like looking
up to the heavens through the invisible and silent air,
in the whole stretch of which there is not one object on
which the eye can rest, short of the stars.   The thought
of distance passes away, the intervening air seems more
to unite than to divide, till there seems, for the time, to
be but two objects in creation, yourself and that heaven
of stars, into which you seem unconsciously to have
passed, almost without an effort or a volition.

We were glad that we had been led through this
unknown region, and that we had thus seen the home
of the patriarchs, the cradle of faith, ere the bondage
was endured or " the law added because of transgres-
sion." We had not meant to pass that way.   Our plan
was to visit Petra, and from Petra to turn straight
to Hebron, crossing Wady Arabah by the supposed
Kadesh Barnea,—striking north-westward by *Arara* or
Aroer, and thence, perhaps, through Wady-el-Khulil to
El-Khulil (Hebron) itself.   Had this been carried out
we should have missed the whole of this most interesting region,—a region, I confess, fuller to me of deeper
and more sacred interest than the marvellous ruins of
Edom's wondrous capital.   Reluctantly had we given

up our original plan, and we now found that though we had been made losers in some respects, we had been gainers in others. The country we had traversed is but little known—in some parts not known at all, for the route we had taken had been pursued by no traveller before us. Dr Robinson supposes that he was the first who passed through the territory from Rubaibeh to Beersheba,—yet even he did not traverse the whole of it, as he struck in upon our route only at El-Abdeh, a little south of Ruhaibeh. This fact of itself added something to our zest and interest. In Egypt and the Desert we had, for the most part, pursued a beaten track, and found almost every spot noted by former travellers. Here we had lighted on an undiscovered mine. We had come upon an almost unknown territory, seen by hardly any, described by none. It was the land of Abraham and Isaac—the land of the tent and the flock—a land to which our only guide-book was the Bible.

Not for many Petras would we have missed this region. It has nothing striking : it is homely all over. It has nothing marvellous like the great city of the rock ; but it has something more congenial, more heart-thrilling than the ruins of amphitheatres, or temples, or arches, or tombs. It has the memories of more ancient days, and the visions of a truer life floating above its fields. It has the happy, yet solemn, associations of patriarchal faith and love linked with all its scenes.

THE END.

APPENDIX.

ROUTE FROM SUEZ TO NAKHL.

I add the places on our route, as given me by Sheikh Sulimân at Nakhl. I am not sure that in all cases I have caught
the exact word, as it is exceedingly difficult to get hold of
words and names from the lips of the Bedaween. They cannot understand why there should be any difficulty in picking
up their words; and even when they repeat them to you,
they do so in a way which shews that they do not at all see
where your difficulty of apprehension lies. I set down here
what I learned from the sheikh, because he mentioned several names which I do not find elsewhere :—

Suez.
Ayûn Musa.
Mafargûterukh.
Wady-el-Adtha (pronounced
    Ahadthah).
El-Wady.
Wady Sâdr, or Sudr.
Wady Wardân.
Wady-el-Amarah.
Ain-el-Howârah.
Nukeia-el-Fûl.
Wady Ghurandel.
Wady Salmîn.
Wady Useit.
Wady Thâl.

Wady Shubeikah.
Wady Tayibeh.
Abu-Sanemah.
Wady-el-Mahavah.
Wady Nakhl.
Wady Malachah.
Wady Shellal, or Shellah.
Nakb-el-Bûdrah.
Sihah-Sidreh.
Ti-bag-el-Ranmen.
Wady-el-Mararah-Tiguneh.
Wady Mukatteb.
Wady Nesserîn.
Wady Romanah.
Wady Nidieh.

Wady-en-Nefûs.
Hajir Hallatîn.
Wady-el Hessueh.
Wady Moharab.
Wady Alyat.
Wady Feirân.
Wady-el-Khahazzeh.
Ger Abûnohammar.
Wady Sahab.
Gerasafah.
Wady Arbah.
En-Nakb (Howai).
Hajir-el-Gerîsh.
Thelmah-el-Rahah.
Wady-er-Rahah.
Nahamah.
Sheikh Herorun.
Deir (the Convent).
Jebel Katarîn.
Jebel Mûsa.
Jebel Sufsafah.
Jebel Orib.
Jebel Arabah.
Wady Arabah.
Wady Sheikh.
Wady Waswerah.
Al-Aghabah.
El-Wady.
Si-ez-Zulakah.
Wady Tarfa.
Wady Bûkhseh.
Wady-el-Mohr.
Wady Selîf-Saleh.

Wady-el-Lakhafer (?)
Wady Monamen.
Wady-et-Tamah.
Wady-el-Berah.
Wady-Busr-el-Lîl.
Wady Geneh.
Wady-Shegheh-el-Ajûs.
Wady-el-Estaneh.
Wady-el-Hajir.
Wady Barakh.
Wady Theibeh.
Wady Khehasikh.
Wady Mareyiukh.
Wady-el-Khumîleh.
Wady-el-Marerah.
Surabit-el-Khadim.
Raml-el-Marakh.
Wady Jerf.
Hamuleh-Nadheh.
Nakb-el-Rakineh.
Nuteighineh.
Banat-el-Ajideh.
Wady-el-Arish.
Wady Jeremlih.
Sabiyam Badhiah.
Wady-el-Magharah.
Mahdat-el-Melekh.
Ruiz.
Madhah-el-Aujan.
Wady-el-Aujan.
Abu-trefih.
Derb-el-Haj.
Kalât-Nakhl.

Here the sheikh's enumeration stopped, for he left us at Nakhl. He gave several names which were not mentioned to us at the time we passed the place, and which I do not find elsewhere. I may have mistaken them, but I thought it better to set them down, as a good Arabic scholar could at once detect the word, and know its meaning. He omitted one or two places which were mentioned at the time.

I add the names of some of our men, as I took them down at the time.

Sheikh Sulimân, Ujabhar-Ben-Mûsa.
Hussan Amer.
Ali Kleah.
Salim Teher.
Salim Alaj (my own attendant).
Dahel Kherih.
Atih Gormon.
Hamed Nassah.
Salim Sherareh.
Ali Shaheen (a man with a long beard).

The names of the different pieces of dress, &c. are as follows :—

Jambeh, the sword or scimitar.
Barûdat, the gun.
Tabunheh, the pistol.
Hattem, the ring-seal.
Markûb, shoes.
Abiah, loose upper cloak.
Khûftan, under-cloak, a vest.
Sûfan, cartouche-box.
Sivitah, belt.

Jambah, pouch.
Shâl, shawl,
Tagreh, skull-cap.
Tarboosh, fez-cap, &c.
Thabh, under-shirt with long tails.
Enahl, skin sandals.

INDEX.

INDEX.

This is a mistake. The cultivation was poor enough,—still the fields were under the plough, as we saw. The name of the wady may refer to its springs, or generally to its well-watered fields.

AKHUL, 182.—The *Akhûl* is the prickly shrub which is so very common all over the desert and in some parts of Syria. The camels are fond of it, in spite of its sharp prickles. It burns freely, and gives out a very bright blaze, with a crackling noise. Often did we hear the "crackling of thorns under the pot."

ALEXANDRIA, 18...Bazaars, 25...Cæsar's Camp, 20...Convents, 29 ...Library, 20...Tract Depot, 27.—On what authority I know not, Jerome identifies No with Alexandria,—" et urbem No quæ postea versa est in Alexandriam" (*Ep. ad Eust.*). Yet he refers to the Seventy as translating it by Diospolis (*On Ezek.* ch. xxx.) ; see farther his Commentary on Hosea, ch. ix., and on Nahum, ch. iii., in which latter place he dwells at some length on the point. Alexandria must have been a noble city,—the noblest city of its day,—rising as it did, just before Rome reached its height. When Amrou took it in 640, he could say, "I have taken the great city of the west, which contains 4000 palaces, 4000 baths, 400 theatres, 12,000 shops, and 40,000 tributary Jews." Alas for the mighty city of other days " Son of man, wail for the multitude of Egypt, and cast them down, even her, and the daughters of the famous nations, unto the nether parts of the earth, with them that go down into the pit. Whom dost thou pass in beauty? go down, and be thou laid with the uncircumcised " (Ezek. xxxii. 18, 19). In walking through the streets, I was attracted by some Greek *signs* above the doors of tradesmen, such as the following:—Καφφενειον και ξενοδοχειον, over a sort of tavern Ραπτης γυναικων, over a milliner's shop. Δημητριαδης Μουμου, ωρολογοποιος, over a watchmaker's. Over an apothecary's I read, φαρμακοπωλειον ; and a confectioner had hung out a board on which was painted, Ζαχαροπλαστειον και κατασκευη γλυκου απο νεα.

ALMOND, The, 221.—The Hebrew word is שָׁקֵד, *Shâkad* or *Shaked*, the awaker or watcher, from the verb to be sleepless, or to watch, because the almond seems to watch for the first breath of spring. The blossom is not *white* as some make it, applying Eccles. xii. 5 to the old man's white head. It is pink, or rather partly pink and partly white. Pliny speaks of its "flore rosaceo," and says, floret prima omnium amygdala, mense Januario." It occurs about ten times in Scripture (Exod. xxv. 33, 34, &c.) The word *Lûz* is also used in

Hebrew for almond. At least the Rabbinical writers use it ;—and to this the Arabic and Syriac names correspond. Hence the word, which our translators have rendered *hazel* (Gen. xxx. 37), is supposed to be the almond.

ALPHABETE ORIENTALISCHER, &c., 174.—*Note.*

AMALEKITES, 195.—Philo gives λαος εκλειχων as the meaning of Amalek, *i.e.* "the people licking up," which, by a mistake of the printer I suppose, is given in Yonge's translation "the people looking up" (Bohn's Ed. vol. ii., p. 168). Jerome gives "terram lingentes" in one place, and in another "populus brutus, sive populus lingens" (De nom. Hebr.). "A people that licks up" is generally accepted as the meaning of the word; but Gesenius and Stockius are silent. The Amalekites were a very ancient and powerful people. From Gen. xiv. 7 it is plain that they were in power before Abraham's time, and, in part at least, dwelt south of Mount Seir. Num. xxiv. 20 evidently means that they were really "first of the nations," both as to antiquity and power (for it is a poor gloss that makes this to mean "the first that attacked Israel"). They dwelt towards Shur (1 Sam. xxvii. 8), which brings them down beyond Wady Ghurandel, just about the place where they fell upon Israel's rear. They were no mere nomadic tribe, but seem to have had a permanent settlement in the Desert long before the days of Israel. Gesenius says that Arabian genealogists mention them among the original inhabitants of the Desert. Philo calls them Phœnicians (Life of Moses), and Herodotus says that the Phœnicians affirm that they (the Phœnicians) came from the Red Sea, and that, spreading northward, they occupied the Syrian coast (Book vii. ch. 89). From 1 Chron. iv. 42, 43, it is clear that they inhabited Idumea, so that there is thus a curious link between Phœnicians, Idumeans, and Nabathæans; the Amalekites being the root of these. It was not Phœnicia that sent down its colonies to the Desert; it was the Desert that sent up its colony to Phœnicia. It was probably the Amalekites who worked the mines adjoining Mukatteb, and the rock-writings there may be Amalekite inscriptions. This would account for the unknown nature of the character, and also for its resemblance to the Phœnician and Nabathæan. In saying so, I do not mean that the mysterious word עם with which most of the inscriptions begin is "Amalek." I found solely on the fact of that nation being possessors of that part of the Desert from the first. I do not know what authority Heber had for enrolling them among "the hireling guards of Mirzaim's throne," as they mustered to pursue Israel,—

"The parched and sinewy sons of Amalek."—(*Passage of the Red Sea.*)

There is no proof that the Amalekites had anything to do with Egypt.

AMARAH, Wady-el-, 117.—Though this is near *Marah*, yet the radical *Ain* at its commencement shews us that the two words are quite different. *Amárah*, or more more properly *Ghamára*, may be from the Arabic word which corresponds with the Hebrew עָמַר, to depress.

AOSHADH, a prickly shrub, 182.—Of these were several kinds in the desert. (See Akhûl.)

ARAB Cruelty, 49...Funerals, 24...Villages, 33.

ARRACK, 193, 220.

ATAKAH, 86..."Deliverance," Ras-Atâkah, the head of Atakah.

AUJEH, El-, 302, 303.

AYUN-MUSA, 107...Water of, 118.—Ayûn is the plural of the Arabic word which corresponds to the Hebrew עַיִן, eye or fountain, because of its likeness to the eye. In Scotland a bubbling spring coming up out of the ground is called a "well-ee," or "wall-ee," *i. e.* the eye of the well; though this may be from "wall" which Gawin Douglas, in his translation of Virgil, uses for a wave, or whirlpool, or bubbling water. "The wally sea" is his expression. The Hebrew בּוֹר *bohr*, or בְּאֵר *beer*, corresponding to the Arabic word, comes from the word to dig; thus expressing the idea of man's finding his way *down to* the water, as Ain gives the idea of the water *coming up* to man and gushing out.

BAZAARS, Eastern, 25...their confusion, 39.

BEAUMONT, Quotation from, 77.

BEDAWEEN, Meeting with, 196...Resemblance to Abraham, 197... vagrant, 291...quarrel and reconciliation, 297.—Bedaween, or Bedawin, is the plural of Beddwy, or Bedawi, which signifies a man of the desert. *Bedu* means a desert. Our men used to prefer being called Arabs, as if Bedaween were a name of reproach. It is, however, merely the distinctive name of the dwellers in the desert, just as *Jebeliyeh* is the name for mountaineers.

BEER-LAHAI-ROI, Hagar's Well, 314.

BEEROTH, 281, 296.—Beeroth bene-Jaakan, (Deut. x. 6)—the wells of the sons of Jaakan, or as we find the name in its abbreviated form,—Bene-Jaakan (Numb. xxxiii. 31).

BEERSHEBA, 305, 328, 330.—Jerome speaks of Beersheba as being "in regione Geraritica," and mentions it as known in his day to be in that region. He mentions that the town was called Berdan, quod Latine dicitur puteus judicii. *De Locis Heber.*

Sir John Maundeville (A.D. 1322) speaks of Beersheba as "a very fair and pleasant town of the Christians," and adds, that "some of their churches still remain" (chap. vi.) Certainly there is no trace of these now. How far this author is trustworthy, may be learned from his telling us that from Beersheba to Hebron is "two good miles:" but perhaps he meant "two good days' journey." His knowledge of Scripture history could not be very accurate, for he informs his reader that Beersheba "was founded by Beersheba, the wife of Sir Uriah, the knight, on whom King David begat Solomon the wise" —(*Ibid*).

In Gen. xxi. 33, we read that Abraham planted here "a grove." or more literally אֵשֶׁל. Gesenius and others render this word by "tamarisk,"* meaning the tree which the Arabs call *tarfa*. Certainly we never heard the name *Ehshel* applied to the tamarisk-tree in the desert or in Palestine. The tarfa-tree is not a likely tree to be planted for its shade. Its leaves are so thin and wiry, that they give no shelter either from heat or rain. In the desert it is a small tree, and even in Egypt and at Sidon, where it is seen to best advantage, it is not a large one. The word occurs but three times in Scripture, the first is the place just referred to. The second is 1 Sam. xxii. 6, "Saul abode in Gibeah, under a tree (ehshel), having his spear in his hand, and all his servants were standing about him." No tarfa-tree that we saw or heard of, would admit of this. Even those we saw in Egypt and round Sidon would not. Besides, the tarfa is, from its peculiar structure, quite unfitted for such a purpose. It does not rise in one stem, and after attaining some height throw out spreading branches. It seems to be all made of stems springing from one root, which is the worst kind of tree for shelter. The third place where the word occurs is 1 Sam. xxxi. 13, "they took their bones and buried them under a tree (ehshel) at Jabesh." This passage in itself proves nothing; but it has a parallel one in 1 Chron. x. 12, where the same event is recorded.

* Robertson suggests a different Arabic root from that which Gesenius adopts. —*Clavis*, p. 151.

and it is said they " buried their bones under *the oak* (ehlah) in
Jabesh." Now the *ehlah* does not mean the tamarisk, whatever it
may mean. Hence Gesenius agrees with our translators in rendering Gen. xxi. 33, "trees" a "grove." Yet Mr Stanley says, "it
can hardly be doubted that the tamarisk is intended in Gen. xxi.
33," (p. 22). We should rather have said, "it can hardly be
believed." There is no reason given save that Abraham was now
"exchanging the vegetation of Palestine for the wild and scanty
shrubs of the desert frontier" (*ib*.) But Beersheba has no lack of
vegetation, and long before we came to it, we found abundance of
this; nay, more, Dr Robinson remarks, "the shrubs (of the desert)
ceased, or nearly so, green grass was seen along the lesser water-
courses," &c. (vol. i. p. 300).

BELLS at the Convent of Sinai, 218, 219.

BERAH, Wady, 249.

BESHAKH, a plant, 249.

BIREIN, Wady, 296.

BOTTLES, 60, 320.—The Hebrew words are as follow:—(1.) נאד,
Nohd; which occurs six times in the Old Testament, and seems to
have been of *skin* (Joshua ix. 4; Judg. iv. 19; Ps. cxix. 83). (2).
נבל, *Nehvel*, which occurs nine times, and was evidently of earthenware (Isa. xxx. 14, "bottle of the potters;" Lam. iv. 2, "earthen
pitchers.") There is no proof of its meaning a *skin-bottle*, as
Gesenius says it does, deriving it from the verb of the same radicals,
to be withered or flaccid. It would seem rather to have for its
root the same verb, in the sense of being vile and common; for
that earthen pitchers were so reckoned is plain from Lam. iv. 2,
" the precious sons of Zion comparable to fine gold, how are they
esteemed as earthen pitchers, the work of the hands of the potter." (3.)
בקבק, *Bakbuk*. This occurs only three times, and means a bottle
of earthenware (Jer. xix. 1, 10). It is derived from the sound which a
narrow-necked bottle makes when emptying. (3.) חמת, *Haymeth*,
which occurs four times, and also indicates an earthen vessel. It was
this that Abraham is said to have given to Hagar (Gen. xxi. 14); such
things doubtless being quite common at Beersheba. It was at this
place, and in the desert around it, that we found such quantities of
pottery. These earthen bottles we generally saw on the *heads*, not
on the *shoulders* of the Syrian women. We often wondered how they
balanced them, as they seemed often off the perpendicular. When

carried on the head, they require no aid of the hands; but when carried on the shoulders they do. Dr Robinson speaks of the *water-skins* as illustrating Gen. xxi. 14, in the case of Hagar. But it was not a *water-skin* that Abraham gave to her; it was a *haymeth* or earthen vessel.· (4.) אוֹב, *ob* or *ohv*. This word occurs sixteen times, but is with one exception translated *wizards* or *familiar spirits*. The exception is Job xxxii. 19, and were it not for the difficulty of understanding the epithet *new* in its connection with wizards, the word *bottle* would not have been thought of. Elihu compares himself to a pythoness or necromancer, whose breast heaved with the fury within.

BRICK Cylinders of Egypt, 21.

BUDRAH, Wady, 145...Nakb-el-Bûdrah, 145.

BUILDING, Eastern Method of, 199, 200.

BUSH, Burning, 205.—The allusions to the scene of the burning bush, and to the bush itself, are numerous in the old hymns. It is called in one place,

> " Rubus incombustus
> Moysen qui terruit."—*Mone's Hymni Latini*, vol. ii. p. 9.

Again it is called,

> " Rubus urens
> Non comburens."—*Ib*. *ib*. p. 58.

Elsewhere it is named, " rubus flammans mire."—*Ib*. p. 277. And again, " rubus visionis."—*Ib*. p. 289.

CAIRO, 35...American Mission, 45...citadel of, 64...English Church, 45...mosques of, 62...petrified forest, 66...streets of, 39...Shubra gardens, 64.—Its proper name is Musr-el-Kahirah, which means *Musr* the grand or victorious. *Musr* is the name by which the Arabs know it, and save when speaking to us, they never called it *Cairo*. They used also to call Egypt by the name of *Musr*, a manifest relic of the original name *Mizraim*,—from the son of Ham (Gen. x. 6). Europeans have thrown off the *real* name of the city *Musr*, and kept the mere epithet *Kahirah* or *Cairo*; nay, by a singular perversion, they have called it " *Grand* Cairo," supposing that *Musr*, not *Kahirah*, meant grand or victorious. The following is *said to be* a correct summary of the statistics of the city:—" The city of Cairo, the capital of Egypt, and one of the richest cities of the East, contains 400 mosques, 140 schools, 11 lazarettes, 300 public cisterns, 46 squares, 240 streets, from 500 to 600 alleys, as camel is said to take its name (which in Hebrew and Arabic is nearly the same) from its revengeful propensities. Certainly we saw nothing of this. Other things about it we had often occasion to notice ; its broad spongy foot—its curiously jointed limbs—its hard protuberances on knees and thighs, to enable it to kneel down upon the roughest ground—its long neck, by means of which it can crop its food by the way without stopping—its sharp-pointed back and hump, which keep fast its saddle and load without much fastening—its prominent eye-bones—its small nostrils, capable of being closed at once, and lined with fine hair, through which it sifts the air, so as to enable it to breathe freely even when clouds of sand are covering it—its sagacity in choosing and rejecting certain shrubs—its patient docility—its harsh, though sometimes melancholy utterance—its endurance of thirst and toil—all these characteristics we had occasion frequently to notice. We observed also how gaily our Arabs decked its head and neck. Our dromedaries had fine leather collars, all ornamented with small shells from the Red Sea, carefully sowed on in fancy patterns by Arab industry and taste. We observed, too, how our men used to sing to them—especially in the afternoon and towards evening—apparently to cheer them and quicken their pace. It was a monotonous hum certainly—but the camels doubtless enjoyed it. In a curious old book, called " Polyhistor Symbolicus," by Nicolaus Caussinus, there is the following reference to this :—" Camelus musica ac modulatione plurimum capitur. Itaque si, fessus longo itinere, subsistat, ductor, non flagris aut verberibus ad progrediendum eum stimulat, sed sonitu cantuque demulcet. Alioqui ageret frustra." His application of this is that " pueri bonæ indolis non verberibus cogendi," &c. p. 314. The thigh-joint of the camel is noticed by Horus Apollo in his Hieroglyphics of the Nile, μονη των ζωων τον μηρον καμπτει, διο και καμηρος λεγεται. *Hierogl.* 95. The difference between a camel and dromedary seems to be just the difference between a cart-horse and a riding-horse. They are the same as to the "hump." The two kinds are mentioned by Jerome in his life of Hilarion, " locatis camelis et dromedis, ob aquae in eremo penuriam." (Works, vol. i. p. 113) In the same life he gives the story of a huge Bactrian camel that was exorcised by the saint! It took thirty men to hold it with the strongest ropes!

CAROB-TREE, or Karub, 8.—The pods of this tree are supposed to be the *κερατία* of Luke xv. 16—the "husks that the swine did eat." Kharoob is the Arabic name of the tree, and is adopted as the rendering of "husks" in the Arabic version. These are like a large bean-pod, but brown and flat,—common in Malta and Egypt. The name "locust-tree," given sometimes to the Kharoob, seems to come from the idea that these husks are the "locusts" on which John the Baptist fed. Jerome's figurative interpretation of husks is curious. After giving one founded on Ezek. xvi, and referring to Israel's sin, he adds another. He calls them the "food of demons" and goes on thus—"dæmonum cibus est carmina poetarum, sæcularis sapientia rhetoricorum pompa verborum; hæc sua omnes suavitate delectans," &c. See his Exposition of the Parable of the Prodigal Son in his Epistle to Damasus, vol. i. p. 408.

CLEOPATRA'S NEEDLE, 20.—For information as to this ancient obelisk, the reader may consult Wilkinson, or any of the works on Egyptian antiquities. The name, Cleopatra's Needle, must be a a very modern one, for in George Sandys' time it was known as *Pharaoh's* needle. It was erected sixteen hundred years before Christ, by Tuthmosis second. See *Lepsius' Letters*, p. 11.

CONVENT (of Sinai), 217–240.—In the journal of the Egyptian Prefetto there is the following notice as to this Convent. "There is no record when this Convent was built, except what remains on a stone over the great door, the inscription on which is in Arabic characters so ancient that none of us could read them, except the year *Οημ*, which denotes 526. This stone, according to the tradition of the fathers of the Convent, first stood over the Chapel of the Bush, and was placed there by St Helena; but after the great church and the walls of the Convent were built, this stone was moved out of its ancient place and fixed in the wall where it now stands. But in my opinion this history is without foundation, because St Helena lived in the fourth century, whereas the aforementioned inscription belongs to the sixth century. I rather think, therefore, that this stone was engraved and fixed up by the order of Justinian, who was the founder of the Convent," (p. 23). This author speaks of *six* chapels within the great church, and *seventeen* others in different parts of the Convent. He does not seem to have been impressed with the stateliness or grandeur of the Convent; for he thus writes,—" There is nothing of curiosity to be seen, all the buildings, &c. being built of rough bricks, in great confusion and irregularity, without either symmetry or order, making here and there crooked and dark passages, with several ascents and descents" (p. 20). He tells us, however, that the Archbishop and Superior *Jaanikius* gave him " a very elegant supper," which quite corresponds with what we saw and heard, viz., that the hard fare of the Sinaitic monks is only a report of credulous travellers ; not of George Sandys certainly, who visiting them in 1610, observed "their gulling in of wine with a dear felicity" (p. 96). The Prefetto enumerates "almonds, apples, peaches, olives, figs, pomegranates, pears, and grapes," as the produce of the garden, adding, " as this month happened to be the season for ripe grapes, as well as many other fruits, we gave a loose to our appetites " (p. 24). He states the number of steps up to Sinai as 15,000, (Sandys gives them at 14,000, p. 97), and mentions that, at the gateway through which you pass when about an hour up the hill, confessionary priests used to sit to hear confessions and grant absolutions to the ascending pilgrims, acting upon Psalm xxiv, 3, "Who shall ascend into the hill of the Lord . . he that hath clean hands,' &c. Though he was himself a Greek Prefetto, he is evidently ashamed of the Greek traditions, most of which have not even grace of conception to recommend them. "I think it more advisable," he says, " not to repeat them " (25). The Bishop of Clogher, who edits the work, calls them " those cursed and hellish frauds practised by the Grecian monks of Mount Sinai" (p. 35), which is rather stronger language than one is inclined to use in such a case.

COPTS, The, or Kopts, or Gypts, 37, are the only real representatives of the ancient *Egyptian* race. Their name (as well as their history) shews this, though perhaps the name may be from *Caphtorim* (Gen. x. 13). There are said to be 10,000 in Cairo. Their language preserves to us the ancient Egyptian in the same way as the Italian preserves the Latin. They stand aloof from all other Christian sects, and seem to be the descendants of the ancient Christians of Egypt. In former ages they were very numerous ; at present they number only 150,000, or about the fourteenth of the population of the country. In Upper Egypt there are whole villages of Copts. They are considered the best tradesmen and secretaries, as well as the most skilful artificers. See *Lane's Manners and Customs of the Modern Egyptians.* The population of ancient Egypt was scattered all over the world, to India on the one side, and to Britain on the other, as had been prophesied (Ezek. xxix. 12), and for a while the scattered race preserved the name of Egyptians, wherever they went. Hence a statute in our own country in the reign of Henry Seventh concerning strangers coming to the land, who called themselves Egyptians. The old French traveller Beaugrand calls them *Gophtes*, and speaks of them as occupying the house which Joseph and Mary did "for seven years" when flying from Herod, which he says was at the place called Memphis, about a league from "Grand Cairo."—*Relation Nouvelle et tres-fidele du voyage de la terre Sainte, &c.* Par F. Felix Beaugrand. Paris, 1700.

CORSICA, 4.

CROCUS, 249, 254.

CROSS, 168. Crosses in the east are not always the symbol of Christianity. Dr Robinson mentions the fact of the Arabs marking their camels with this figure,—dipping their fingers in the blood of a sheep (vol. i. p. 182, 2d edit.) Gesenius, under the word תָו, says, "a sign in the form of a cross branded on the thigh or neck of horses or camels; whence the name of the letter Tau, which in Phœnician, and on the coins of the Maccabees, has the form of a cross." The old editor of the hieroglyphics of Horus Apollo, refers us to several early writers as mentioning that when some Egyptian temples were destroyed, in the reign of Theodosius, hieroglyphics were found in the shrine of Serapis, in the form of a cross. (*Caussinus, e Societate Jesu; Symbola Ægyptorum*, A.D. 1694, p. 191.)

CULTIVATION, 293, 305, 309, 317, 325, 330.

CUSTOMS in the East—grief, 42...The head, 40—The hands, 42... The Shoe, 40...Visitors, 43.

CYPRESS, 221.

DESERT—Appearance of Birds, 178...Districts of, 139...Echoes of, 115...Encampment in, 74...False impression of, 145...Moonlight in, 95...Ravens, 178...Scene in the, 129.—The general Arabic word for the Desert is *Shâwl*. There are several words for it in the Hebrew, each one with a meaning of its own. (1.) חָרְבָּה, *Ghorbah*, from the verb to be dried up or made desolate (occurs upwards of forty times). Though sometimes translated by the general word desert, or rather in the plural "deserts" (Isa. xlviii. 21), it means more properly desolations, ruins, cities that have once been inhabited, but are now dried up or deserted. Lev. xxvi. 31, "I will make your

cities *Ghorbah*." Job iii. 14, " who built *Ghoraboth* for themselves,"
i. e. places that are now desolate, like the Pyramids or the Pasha's
palaces in the Desert. Psa. ix. 6, " destructions (Ghoraboth) are
come to a perpetual end," *i. e.* the desolations of the land are now
at an end for ever. Psa. cii. 6, " an owl of the desert," literally
" an owl of the ruins," such as Dr Robinson heard at Ruhaibeh. It
is the word used in Ezek. xxv. 13, with reference to the desolation
of Edom and Teman (Petra ?). The Arabic word for ruins is
Khuraib, and is the common word applied to the ruins of the desert
places, as *Khurbet-es-Seram* (p. 301). The radical letters of this
word correspond to those of *Horeb*, which means *dry* (Judg. vi. 39),
but is also used in the same sense as *Ghorbah.* Jer. xlix. 13,
" Bozrah shall become a desolation, ' Horeb.' " (2.) יְשִׁימוֹן, *Yeshî*
môn. This is the word frequently translated as a proper name
Jeshimon (Numb. xxi. 20). It is from the verb to be laid waste, but
refers not so much to cities as to places. It occurs only about thirteen
times. Psa. lxviii. 7; Isa. xliii. 19. (3.) מִדְבָּר, *Midbár*. This
occurs about two hundred and seventy times. Lexicographers
make it to be properly a " desert *pasture* country," though certainly
in by far the greater number of instances it means the pastureless
wilderness. Jer. ii. 2, 6. Yet it is the word used in Joel i. 19 ; ii.
22, " the pastures of the wilderness." (4.) עֲרָבָה, *Haravah*, which
occurs about seventy times, and is from the verb to be dry and
barren. It is the same word as is translated so often " plains."
Numb. xxii. 1; Josh. iv. 13. See Isa. xxxv. 1, 6. (5.) צִיָּה,
Tseeyah, a land of drought, from the verb to be dry or parched. It
occurs about sixteen times. Psa. lxiii. 1; Jer. ii. 6. (6.) תֹּהוּ,
Tohu, the word used in Gen. i. 2,—empty waste. Job xii. 24 ; Ps.
cvii. 40.

DOGS, Eastern, 25...at Sinai, 222.—We recognised in the Arabic
Kelb the Hebrew of similar sound, from which *Caleb* took his name.
A small dog which our dragoman purchased at Nakhl, was named
Hapseh. It was a sort of pointer, only of smaller limb, not unlike
a young greyhound.

DRAGOMAN, 46, &c.—The word is properly *Targuman*, or as our
Arabs used to pronounce it, *Túrgoman*, which means a translator
or interpreter. The Hebrew word is to interpret or comment.
Hence the *Targum* or Rabbinical interpretation of Scripture.

DROMEDARY, 70.—Jemel is the burden-bearing camel, and *Hajin* is the riding-camel, so called from the Mecca pilgrims using it. Dromedary is *camelus dromas* (καμηλος δρομας), a light-running camel.

DTHUB, 144.—Burckhardt speaks of having seen this species of lizard, and says it is eighteen inches long. See Thub.

EASTERN CUSTOMS. See Customs.

EAST WIND, 107.—Is it not the east wind to which Job refers (xxvii. 21; xxxviii. 24, קָדִים) the same as the khampsîn winds of Egypt and the *scirocco* of Malta? The other references to it in Scripture confirms this. (1.) It blasts (Gen. xli. 6). (2.) It brings locusts (Exod. x. 13). (3.) It is tempestuous (Job xxvii. 21; Ps. xlviii. 7; Jer. xviii. 17). (4.) It is accompanied with great heat (Jonah iv. 8). Scirocco is the word Shari, or Sharik, east, from which comes the word Saracens, men of the east.

ECHOES of the Desert, 115.

EGYPT, compared with Rome, 16...Description of, 19...Dust of, 44... Fulfilment of Prophecy, 23–32...Old, 59.

EGYPTIAN, Hieroglyphics, 155...Pilots, 15. George Sandys thus describes the "Egyptian Moors," as he calls the fellahs or peasants of Egypt:—"They are men of a mean stature, tawny of complexion, and spare of body, *shrill-tongued*, and nimble-footed. . . They are not long in dressing themselves, being only wrapt in a russet mantle; nor have the women any better coverture, hiding their faces with beastly clouts, having holes for their eyes, which little is too much to see and abstain from loathing. . . A people breathes not, more savage and nasty, crusted with dirt and stinking of smoke. Some of them dwell under beggarly tents, and those esteemed of the old inhabitants."—*Travels*, p. 85.

ELIJAH'S Cave and Tree, 215, 233, 323, 340.—One does not need to say that there is no proof of this being Elijah's cave, and the tree of course could not be his. Yet Greek, or rather Sinaitic tradition, affirms both. It would seem that no sooner did the monks settle themselves down here, than they commenced a regular series of inventions, without any regard to previous tradition or the truth of Scripture history. They wanted something to shew to pilgrims, in order to get money from them; and they have invented *facts* as well as scenes, without number. When the Egyptian prefetto visited Sinai, he passed a night in this hollow or "vale," as he calls it, for the time required to ascend, by those who have to pay their devotions and burn incense at all the holy spots, is ten times that of an ordinary traveller. He mentions *two* cypresses here, and two olives, whereas we saw but one cypress and no olive.

ELIM, 123–125.—See Ghurandel.

EMEK, Hammelek, 195.

EMSHASH, 296.—There is more than one wady of this name, which is natural enough, for wherever the emshâsh or water-pits occur, they were likely to give name to the place. For information as to the digging of these in modern times, see " Account of operations to find water in the desert between Cairo and Suez," in the *Journal of the Royal Geographical Society,* vol. i. p. 252.

ENCAMPMENTS, Marks of, 115…Marks of Israel's, 116.

ER-RAHAH, Plain of, 209, 210.

EXAGGERATIONS of Travellers, 240.

FEIRAN, Wady, 132, 179.—That Wady Feirân cannot indicate the site of the *wilderness* of Paran, is evident from the passages which speak of that wilderness in connection with the immediate south of Judea. Gen. xxi. 21 shews that it lay not far from where Abraham was dwelling. Numb. x. 12 does not imply that Paran was close to Sinai, but that the cloud, after rising from the wilderness of Sinai, pointed to the wilderness of Paran, and did not rest till it rested there. Numb. xii. 16 adds nothing to our information, save that the wilderness of Paran stretched considerably to the south, so that soon after leaving Hazeroth, Israel found themselves in Paran. Numb. xiii. 3 shews us that Paran and Palestine adjoined each other. Numb. xiii. 26 identifies Kadesh and Paran, thereby fixing Paran immediately to the south or south-east of Judea. Deut. i. 1 shews that Paran was not far from the gulf of Akabah. Deut. xxxiii. 2 speaks of *Mount* Paran, which is not necessarily in the desert of that name, but which, from being named next Mount Seir, would seem to be in that neighbourhood. 1 Sam. xxv. 1 is explicit proof that Paran and Palestine adjoined. 1 Kings xi. 18 proves the proximity of Paran and Idumea. Hab. iii. 3 seems clearly to place Paran and Feiran together, which is confirmed by the reference to Midian in the seventh verse, for a comparison of this with Numb. xxii. 4 shews that the land of Midian, referred to by the prophet, is not that near Sinai where Moses dwelt, but that near Moab. It is possible so to understand Deut. xxxiii. 2, as that Sinai and Paran should be linked together; but granting this, still it remains clear that even were *Mount* Paran in the neighbourhood of Feirân, the *wilderness* of Paran had nothing to do with that wady. Of Paran, Gesenius says it means "abounding in foliage ;"—and adds, "it is an uncultivated and mountainous region between Arabia Petræa, Palestine, and Idumea; altogether different from this is the region and valley of Feirân near Mount Sinai, as was long ago observed by Makrizi. These were confounded even by Niebuhr." Though Gesenius in one place gives Paran as meaning beautiful or abounding with foliage, from פָּאַר to adorn, yet elsewhere he makes it "abounding in caverns," from the verb to bore or dig, which would correspond with the statement of Josephus respecting that part of Idumæa,—"at the valley called Pharan he (Simon of Gerasa) enlarged many of the caves, and many others he found ready for his purpose" (*Jewish War*, b. iv. ch. ix. sect. 4).

There may have been two *Parans*, one in the north and the other in the south of the desert. For certainly the "wilderness of Paran" could not be far south of Palestine, and yet Wady Feirân seems to point to the southern region as also acquainted with the name; and Jerome speaks of Raphidim as being "juxta montem Horeb . . prope Pharan." *De locis Hebr.*—Josephus speaks of Paran as abounding with caverns, in which case it would take its origin from the word to dig or bore in the earth. Feirân may be from the Hebrew and Arabic verb to boil up, to be hot, because of the hot springs here. It is singular that the word also signifies beautiful, abounding with foliage. See *Gesenius.* If *Serbâl* mean "the palm-grove of Bâl," then the connection between Feirân and Serbâl is clear. The old town of Pharan probably lay in Wady Feirân, and existed long before the Christian era. It is possible that *Serbâl* might be called *Paran*, from its proximity to and connection with the wady and town of that name.

FELLAH, 33, 316.—Fellah means a peasant. Its plural is *Fellahîn*, cultivators of the soil, in opposition to *Bedawîn*, wanderers of the desert.

FILFLA, island off Malta, 12.

GEDURAM SELIM, Wady, 250.

GERAR, town and valley, 314.

GHUDHAGHIDH, 286, 295.—Dr Robinson mentions this as a broad sandy wady, on the way between Petra and Hebron. He gives "diminutions" as its meaning, but without any attempt to explain why it got this name.

GHURANDEL, Wady, 121...Palms, 122.—Dr Olin depreciates this

wady, and goes so far as to say " the palm-groves amount to only eight or ten neglected stunted trees, which are scattered along the road for a mile or more " (*Travels in Egypt, &c.* vol. i. 362). Of course, he could not have seen the wady, else he would not have made a statement so totally incorrect. Within half a mile of our tents there were some forty or fifty palms,—hundreds more farther down. In regard to names as well as places, Dr Olin is very incorrect. His spelling of Arabic words is the worst which we have seen. *Gesenius,* under the word *Elim* in his Lexicon, mentions that a German traveller had found, in the neighbourhood of Ghurandel, a place still retaining the name,—" Ehrenberg informed me that he had found a valley called *Yalim* in that neighbourhood, in which word it is very probable that there is a trace of the ancient name." —(*Lex.* p. 38). *Lepsius,* though he thinks *Ghurandel* to be *Marah,* not Elim, yet mentions that in this neighbourhood on the coast there is a harbour called *Abu Zelîme,* and adds, " the very name, *Elim,* had reference probably to the harbour of *Abu Zelîme.*"—(*A Tour from Thebes, &c.* p. 57). Lepsius is minute and accurate so far as localities and names are concerned ; but in his attempts to fit these into their places in Scripture history, he is not anywhere to be trusted. He assumes that there is no miracle in Israel's deliverance and wanderings. The water of Marah was sweetened by the infusion of a desert herb ! The manna is merely the exudation of the tarfa ! The quails are to be found at any time in the desert ! There was no miraculous gushing forth of water from the rock ! Moses, who knew the desert led Israel to *Wady Ferân,* where there was water ! The whole geography of the Peninsula must be accommodated to this rationalistic theory. Hence *Serbâl* must be Sinai, &c. because Israel could only journey where there was water and pasturage, and *Serbâl* is hard by *Ferân,* the garden of the desert. In speaking of Ghurandel, Constantine Tischendorf tells us that " the trees swarmed with turtles."—(*Travels in the East, translated by Shukard,* p. 102). This is great exaggeration.

Horeb is the name of a region, not of a mountain, is evident from the fact that the preposition עַל, *upon*, (which is frequently used in connection with Sinai), is never used in connection with Horeb. The occurrences are as follow:—Exod. iii. 1, "he came to the mountain of God, to Horeb." Our translators insert "even," but without a cause. The passage does not mean to say that Horeb and the mountain of God are one, but the opposite,—"he came to the mount of God (Sinai), in the direction of Horeb," or literally "Horeb-ward" חֹרֵבָה. Exod. xvii. 6, "I will stand before thee there upon the rock *in Horeb*" בְּ, from which passage it appears that Horeb must have been a *region*, for *Rephidim*, where they pitched (ver. 1) was evidently *in* it. Exod. xxxiii. 6, "by the mount Horeb," or by the mount which was in Horeb, *i. e.* Sinai. The preposition here is מ. Deut. i. 2, "from Horeb," same preposition. Verse 6, "spake unto us in Horeb" בְּ, where it may mean the region; as also in the nineteenth verse, "we departed from Horeb." Chap. iv. 10, "thou stoodest before the Lord in Horeb" בְּ, which must refer to the *region*, for all Israel did not stand in the mountain. The fifteenth verse has the same preposition, and may mean the same thing. So also ver. 2, where Horeb seems to be different from "the mount" in ver. 4. In chap. ix. 8, it is the *region* that is referred to, "in Horeb ye provoked the Lord;" and also in xviii. 16, and xxix. 1, where the prepositions are all the same. 1 Kings viii. 9, "the two tables of stone which Moses put there *at* Horeb," or "in Horeb" בְּ; and it was not in the *mount* that Moses did this, but in the plain below. Chap. xix. 8, "went unto Horeb, the mount of God." There is no preposition here, but עַד, and the meaning is, "he went as far as the mount of God, which was in Horeb." For the narrative shews us that, on arriving at Horeb, he lodged in a cave (ver. 9), and that when he was staying there, in Horeb, God called him to come forth and stand upon the mount (ver. 11),—shewing the distinction between "Horeb" and "the mount." 2 Chr. v. 10, is "at Horeb," or "in" בְּ. Psa. cvi. 19, "they made a calf *in* Horeb" בְּ, which we know they did not do *in the mountain*. Mal. iv. 4, "which I commanded him *in* Horeb" בְּ, which of course does not necessarily mean the hill. These are all the places in which Horeb occurs. None of them *must* mean the hill,—most of them *cannot* mean it, but refer to a region of that name, in which Sinai was situated. Lepsius makes Rephidim, Horeb, and the mount of God, to be the same; and makes the scene between Jethro and Moses, with the subsequent organisation of the people, to have taken place in Rephidim, referring to the eighteenth of Exodus, and speaking of Moses' camp being *on* the mount of God. Besides the inaccuracy of putting *on* for *at*, there seems to be a mistake as to the scene itself, which is quite an *episode*, standing alone, and connecting itself with the second verse of the nineteenth, "they were departed from Rephidim, and were come to the desert of Sinai." It is evident that this great organisation took place during the long period during which they were encamped before Sinai, and not on their road to it. Was *Horeb* the name of the region before Israel came to it? Very likely it was the name by which Jethro knew it. Some have called it the old Amalekite name.

HOR-ES-SUDHR, 117.—This was a hollow to which our Arabs gave the above name.

HOWARAH, Well of, 118.

HOWAI, Pass of, 203.

HUFIR, or HAFIR, Wady, 303.

HUMMAM, 184.—"Hot spring," the Arabic and the Hebrew corresponding in meaning, "to be warm." Parkhurst gives as cognate words the Latin caminus and the English chimney. He might rather have put the Greek χαμινος and the French cheminée. He adds, "Hummums (hot baths), an Arabic word, brought from Turkey." The name of Ham, the son of Noah, is from the same root. In giving the meaning of Ham, a recent lexicographer has gone out of his way to say things of this patriarch which Scripture does not warrant. There is no proof that *Ham* was a wicked man. It seems to have been Canaan that mocked Noah, not Ham; and it was on Canaan that the curse was pronounced. Ham saw his father's state, and went to tell his brothers. That is all that is said of him. The "younger son," mentioned in the 24th verse, is evidently Canaan (Gen. ix. 22–25). "The Proper Names of the Old Testament Scriptures Expounded and Illustrated," by the Rev. A. Jones. A most useful work, though in this and other instances he follows too much the general run of commentators.

HYMN, Latin, 229, 251.

HYSSOP-PLANT, 134, 140, 202.

INSCRIPTIONS, 130, 155, 158–176, 178, 181, 182, 208, 209, 217, 253.

INSPIRATION of Scripture, 104, 105, 106.

INTERPRETATION of Scripture, 105, 126, 127,

ISAAC, 327, 332, 333, 337.

mirabiliter collocatum est." Her story is also related in the Latin hymn, given at length by Mr Neale in his *Hymni Ecclesiæ*, p. 210, 211. Daniel gives one or two fragments of hymns in her praise. Thes. Hymnol. vol. i. p. 313 ; vol. ii. p. 119. They are not worth quoting.

KHAFOR, (Plant,) 292.

KHALASAH, Beer, 322.

KHEIM, Jebel, 11.—This name, meaning the old hill, suggests its Arabic origin. *Jebel* is hill, and *Kheim* is the same as *Khadem*, the old, as Surâbît-el-Khâdem, Surabit the old,—the mountain in the Sinaitic desert. The Hebrew word is similar.

KHEIMREIGH, 253.

KHEIZEH, 292.

KHESR, Wady, 182.

KHULASAH, Wady-el-, 317...The ancient Elusa, Ελουσα, ruins, 320...Pottery, 320.

KHUMILEH, Wady-el-, 253...Inscriptions, 253.

KHURBIT, Ruins, 315, 322, 331. (See Desert.)

KHUZAY, Wady, 325.

KURDHIYEH, 113.

LAJAH, Wady-el-, 249, 250...flocks there, 250.

LATIN—Inscription in St Paul's Bay, 6.

LEPSIUS, his account of the Tarfa exudation, 239.

LIBRARY at Sinai, 224.

LILIES, 303, 305, 329.

LITERAL, and Figurative, 127.

LUSSUFF-PLANT, 134-140.—Old travellers call this Lassaf. Perhaps this is *El-Ussuff*. If so, it corresponds to the Hebrew אֵזוֹב, and the Greek υσσωπος, and the English hyssop. (See Hyssop.)

LYONS, 3.

MACLUBA, or Mukallibe, 9—is the name given by the natives to one of the large mounds of ruins near Birs-Nimrûa. See *Sir R. K. Porter's Travels*. The Arabs called the River Orontes, El-Nahr—*el-Maklûb*, because it has its course from south to north, contrary to the general run of Syrian rivers. *Rosenmuller's Bibl. Geogr.* In Abulfeda the region of the Dead Sea gets the same name.

MAFKAT, the copper land, 156.

MAGHARAH, Wady, 155...Inscriptions, 155...Lepsius' description of, 155.—The Arabic word signifies a cave, and corresponds to the Hebrew *Mearah*. (Gen. xix. 30; xxiii. 9.) Mearah is mentioned as a place in Phœnicia, not far from Sidon. (Josh. xiii. 4.) This is another of these desert places which correspond in name to the Phœnician.

MALTA, 4...Library of, 10...Phœnician Temple, 10.

MAKRAH, Mountains of, 317.

MAMLOUK-TOMBS, 64.

MANNA, Rationalist theory of, 131...Miracle of, 146...Not the produce of the tarfa, 146...Allusion to, by Mr Stanley, 152, by Mr Keble, 154.—To shew the determination of some not to believe in the miracle of the manna, I quote the following passage from the *Penny Cyclopædia* under the article Arabia, p. 210, "The farinaceous deposit called manna, familiar to all readers from the use made of it by the Israelites during their wanderings in the desert, is now, according to Niebuhr, chiefly, if not exclusively, found on the leaves of a species of oak called *Ballût*, or *Afs* according to others. It is a pellucid substance exuded by the leaves of different kinds of trees, chiefly the *Hedysarum alhagi* of Linnæus." The *Ballût* or *Bellût* does *not* grow in the desert at all. North of Beersheba it begins to shew itself, and about Hebron it is plentiful. But the desert contains none of it. How Niebuhr could have made such a statement I do not understand.

MARAH of Scripture, 119...Lepsius' theory of the miracle, 119... Placed at Elim, 124...Placed at Ghurandel, 119.

MARAZAH, Wady, 112.—I give this name because our Arabs gave it to me. I do not find it mentioned by others.

MAREOTIS LAKE, 31.

MARK (ST), 23, 30. Jerome seems to have no doubt that it was Mark who first preached the gospel in Alexandria, and was minister there. He thus writes in his Epistle to Evagrius, "Lest any one should contentiously maintain the plurality of Bishops in one congregation, hear another testimony in which it most manifestly proved that Bishop and Presbyter are the same, Tit. i. ; 1 Tim. iv. ; 1 Pet. v. 1. . . . When one was afterwards elected to be set over the others, it was done as a remedy against division (in schismatis remedium). . . . For even at Alexandria, from Mark the Evangelist to Heracles and Dionysius, bishops, the Presbyters always named as Bishop one chosen from themselves and placed on a higher rank. . . . For what can a Bishop do, except ordination, which a Presbyter cannot?"

MARKHAH, Wady-el-, 136.—"Refreshment." Dr Wilson translates this "the valley of ease," (vol. i. p. 180). Dr Robinson, who calls it Murkhâh, gives it simply "relaxed,"—both translations being substantially the same.

MUKATTEB (Wady), p. 157–176.—The word Mukatteb means *written* both in Arabic and Hebrew. It is the word used for the writing on the stone-tables of the law (Exod. xxxi. 18; xxxiv. 1, 28; Deut. iv. 13.) As the inscriptions are the most notable things in this wady, we give their history, with some remarks, in addition to those made in the text. They were first discovered in the beginning of the sixth century, though Niebuhr, as we shall see, says they were known in the third. *Cosmas*, an Alexandrian merchant, called Indicopleustes from his voyages to India, traversed on foot the Sinaitic peninsula. From a bustling traveller he became a quiet monk, and in the leisure of monastic solitude wrote his *Christian Topography*,—a book, absurd enough in its astronomical speculations, but faithful in its details of fact. " Cosmas," says Dr Robertson, " seems to relate what he himself had observed in his travels, or what he had learned from others, with great simplicity and regard for truth."—(Robertson's Hist. of India, Sect. 2.) In that work is contained his narrative respecting these inscriptions. To his eye they appeared of great antiquity and of an unknown character. Many of them were on fragments of rocks which had rolled down from the cliffs, and these fragments were evidently old, one after another having in the lapse of ages found its way into the valley. From the fact that on some of these pieces the inscriptions were found *inverted*, he thinks that they must have been executed while the rocks were in their original position on the cliff. To myself this appears doubtful.

It would seem that there were some Jews with Cosmas, whom he had fallen in with on his journey, or who had accompanied him in his tour. They read the inscriptions to him, and gave him the traditional account of the way in which they were executed. They told him that the authors of the inscriptions were their forefathers, when sojourning in the Desert. Cosmas evidently had no doubt that the account thus given was the true one. He relates it as such; and certainly the appearance of the writings corroborated the statements of these Jews. Yet I suspect they must have imposed somewhat on Cosmas, for there is no evidence of there being any Jewish tradition on the subject, and when I questioned one of the Jewish Rabbis in Jerusalem as to these inscriptions, I found he knew nothing of the matter. He had not so much as heard of the inscriptions. He was eager to hear what I had to say about Sinai, but he took no interest in Wady Mukatteb.

From the sixth to the sixteenth century, we hear nothing of these inscriptions. About the middle of the sixteenth century, Peter

Belon, or Bellonius, as he latinizes his name, a Paris physician, seems to have visited Arabia, and, in the year 1554, published a quarto volume in French, in which he mentions the inscriptions. About a century after, Athanasius Kircher, a German antiquary, wrote his work *Œdipus Ægyptiacus*, in which he notices the inscriptions. His work was published at Rome in 1652. A few years after, Balthaser Monconys, a French traveller, visited Arabia, and published his remarks on the inscriptions in 1665.

In 1706, Montfaucon published the work of Cosmas, with a Latin version and notes. Montfaucon's work was entitled, *Collectio Nova Patrum Græcorum, Eusebii Cæsariensis, Athanasii et Cosmæ Ægyptii. Gr. et Lat. cum notis. Paris,* 1706. *2 vols. folio.* Mr Forster gives 1707 as the year when Montfaucon published Cosmas. But if the *Dictionnaire Bibliographique* be correct, it was a year earlier. See vol. i. p. 67, under *Athanasius.* In editing this, he bears high testimony to the trustworthiness of Cosmas, giving implicit credit to the facts, and pronouncing him *fide dignus ac sincerus scriptor si quis alius.* At the same time, though without any reason given, he sneers at the idea of the Hebrew origin of the writings, giving it as his opinion that Cosmas was deceived by the lies of the Jews,— *Hebræorum mendacio deceptum.* The reader may attach what weight he pleases to this opinion of the learned antiquary.

In the year 1722, the Prefetto of the Franciscans at Cairo made a journey to Sinai, in company with some missionaries of the Cairo Propaganda. On his way back he passed through the Wady Mukatteb, and gives a description of the writings, much as Cosmas had done. As to the interpretation of them he was totally at a loss. "We had in our company," says he, " persons who were acquainted with the Arabic, Greek, Hebrew, Syriac, Coptic, Latin, Armenian, Turkish, English, Illyrican, German, and Bohemian languages, yet none of them had any knowledge of these characters, which have nevertheless been *cut into the hard rock* with the greatest industry, in a place *where there is neither water nor anything to be gotten to eat.*" His opinion of them is, that "they contain some very secret mysteries, and they were engraved either by the Chaldeans, or *some other persons, long before the coming of Christ.*"

In 1737, Pococke visited the region. His description of these engravings is very brief; but he has copied many of them, and given us two large plates containing what he copied. These are exceedingly valuable, more especially as he gives the exact place and rock from which he copied each.

Shortly after, an English gentleman, Charles Thomson, visited the place, and remarks:—" There are abundance of other inscriptions on the stones about these mountains, but as they are in a very ancient character, void of beauty, and absolutely unintelligible, I thought the pains of copying them might very well be spared."— (*Travels*, vol. iii. p. 363. They were published in 1744).

In the year 1753, Dr Robert Clayton, Bishop of Clogher, translated and published the Journal of the Franciscan Prefetto, already referred to, with remarks on the origin of hieroglyphics. This work seems to have occasioned more speculation, and called up more interest, than any of the preceding, more especially as he offered the sum of £500 to any one who would undertake the journey to Arabia and bring back copies of the inscriptions. He states it as his opinion, that " these characters are the ancient Hebrew characters, which the Israelites having learnt to write at the time of the giving of the law on Mount Sinai, diverted themselves with practising on these mountains during their forty years' abode in the wilderness."

Shortly after, Edward Wortley Montague travelled from Cairo to these regions, and published in 1766, in the *Philosophical Transactions*, " an Account of his Journey from Cairo and Egypt to the Written Mountains in the Desert of Sinai." He ascribes these writings to *Greek* pilgrims from Constantinople or the Morea,—because there happen to be among them one or two brief Greek inscriptions,—as if the fact of these one or two being so distinctly Greek did not prove that they have an entirely different authorship and date from the others.

In 1761, Niebuhr was sent out by the King of Denmark to explore Egypt and Arabia. He examined the inscriptions, and thinks them "of little importance,"—" executed at idle hours by *travellers ;*" —(*Travels*, vol. i. p. 202.) He states, however, one very important fact, " *that even in the third century these inscriptions had been mentioned by a Greek author*,"—(vol. i. p. 200.) We regret that he does not give the name of the Greek author nor his authority for the statement. He seems, however, to have had no doubt of it. And if this be the case, then the theories about pilgrims, travellers, Greeks from Constantinople, cannot be listened to, and even the elaborate theory of Beer, which fixes them to the fourth century, is swept away. He then adds, " they were judged to be neither Jewish nor Arabic, from the appearance of some coarse pieces of sculpture that accompanied them. At last a person who was very well versed in oriental literature, *conjectured that they might be Phœnician, an opinion which is the more probable, as the*

Phœnicians had, at a very remote period, settlements upon the eastern coast of the Arabic gulf."

In the year 1773, Count Gebelin published his *Le Monde Primitif,* in which he endeavours to decipher these writings. With what success we know not, as we have not seen his work.

In 1783, Volney published his travels. He had visited the written valley, but only to sneer at what he saw, and at the attempts of others to unfold the secret. " To these (Greek) pilgrims," he says, " we must attribute the inscriptions and clumsy figures of asses, camels, &c. engraven on these rocks, which have, from these, acquired the name of Djebel Mukatteb or Written Mountain. Mr W. Montague, who travelled a great deal in these countries, and carefully examined these inscriptions, is of this opinion. M. Count de Gebelin, author of *Le Monde Primitif,* has lost his labour, in endeavouring to discover some mysterious meaning."—(*Travels,* vol. ii. pp. 351, 352.)

After this, travels to these regions became more frequent, and as each traveller refers to these inscriptions without casting more light upon their meaning, we need not name them. One important step, however, began to be taken, and that was the copying of them. Messrs Coutelle and Roziere copied seventy-five. Seetzen, Burckhardt, and Henniker, described and copied many. Laborde has given a striking sketch of the whole valley. But the most important work is that of Mr Gray, who, in the Transactions of the Royal Society, published one hundred and eighty-seven inscriptions which he had copied.

In general, the authorship and interpretation of these have been merely the subject of conjecture. Most travellers have contented themselves with *conjecturing* that they must have been the production of pilgrims on their way to or from Mount Sinai. In reference to this we remark as follows:—(1.) There is no other instance on record of pilgrims doing the like, *i. e.* covering miles of rocks and cliffs with their writings. (2.) The *known* resorts of pilgrims and monks, such as Feirân and Sinai, have no inscriptions, or only a very few. (3.) These pilgrims being men of more countries than one. would employ different languages and characters ; whereas these inscriptions are (with very few exceptions, and these manifestly of later date) all of one character, and written by one people. I do not add, at one time and of one generation, as many think, for of this I am by no means convinced. (4.) The supposed pilgrims being Christian, and living between the fourth and sixth centuries, would employ some one of the known languages of the day, whereas the

Mukatteb characters belong to an extinct language. Is it likely, or even possible, that pilgrims of that age would cover miles of rock with inscriptions unknown to the Egyptian merchant; or that a language quite current in the fourth century had become extinct in the sixth? (5.) The number of pilgrims passing through the desert in the fourth century, was nothing when compared with the crowds that passed through it in after ages; why then should the former leave so many vestiges and the latter none? Indeed, Professor Beer resorts very much to conjecture as to the existence of these earlier pilgrimages. (6.) These inscriptions required iron tools, such as hammers, or chisels, or pick-axes, which pilgrims would not think of carrying with them. We certainly carried our hammers with us; but we doubt whether pilgrims did so, though travellers do. Besides, one or two such implements would not do. There must have been *hundreds of chisels and hammers at work on these rocks.* They who wrote the inscriptions were certainly no engravers, but they must have known how to use iron tools; *and they must have had them.*

In 1840, Professor Beer of Leipsic published " a *Century of Sinaitic Inscriptions,*" with an introduction, alphabet, and translations. He denies their extreme antiquity, and, of course, their Jewish origin. Why he and others should have such an aversion to allow them to be Jewish, and, without entering on proof, to treat, as *visionary,* any theory which does so, seems unaccountable. The Jewish theory is the likeliest and the simplest; and I say this all the more decidedly, because I do *not* think it is borne out by actual evidence. But to set a theory aside as *unproved,* is not the same as treating it with contempt, and calling it visionary. Beer's description of Wady Mukatteb is not very accurate; but that is of little moment. The rocks are not "perpendicular as walls," nor do they " afford shelter at midday and in the afternoon from the rays of the sun," as he and Dr Robinson affirm. The inscriptions are *not* found on one side of the valley only, as Mr Gray states; nor do they exist on the " shady side of the valley," for how can a valley of very low rocks *running nearly north and south* have a shady side, save at sunset and sunrise?

Beer maintains that the inscribers must have come from Arabia Petræa; but his proof is summed up in the following sentence:—" I can have no doubt that Arabia Petræa was the region, *since I see no other which can be put in competition with it.*" This is no proof. These Nabathæans of Petra were, as he describes them, " skilled in the arts," yet he admits that the inscriptions are " executed in the rudest style." He says that "the free drawing and bold conjunction of the letters, are such as I find upon the sculptured rocks of no people of that or of an earlier age, evincing the people to whom these inscriptions owe their origin, to have written much and *caligraphically*, and, therefore, to have been highly cultivated and flourishing as a commonwealth." If so, how are the inscriptions so rude? But surely when Professor Beer wrote this sentence, he forgot the Phœnicians, and he forgot the Egyptian hieroglyphics, so beautifully carved on rock, not five miles from Wady Mukatteb. That there are *contractions* in the words is evident;—two letters at least are often thrown into one, but of "bold conjunctions," there is nothing, and of "free drawing" the only proof is in the caricatures of the horns of the goats, which are certainly *free* enough both in sweep and size.

But what had these Nabathæan pilgrims to do at Wady Mukatteb? Were they going to Egypt? No. They would have struck across the country directly by the Haj road, which does not come within sixty or seventy miles of Wady Mukatteb. Were they going to Sinai or Feirân? No. They would not have come near Mukatteb in that case, nor taken up their abode in it. Pilgrims from Petra locating themselves in Wady Mukatteb, either on their way *to* or *from* Sinai! Would an Egyptian pilgrim to Jerusalem go or come by Mount Gilead? Were they going to Serbâl? Yes, it will be said, they were. If so, why did they take such a circuit through such an unwatered region? To go to Serbâl by Mukatteb is to go some forty miles out of the way, without the slightest advantage, nay, with the certainty of perishing with thirst. Nabathæan pilgrims going to Serbâl would go by Feirân, most certainly, where they would find water and shade,—yet these pilgrims have not left a letter upon the rocks of that wady! I admit that those who wrote the inscriptions in Mukatteb, wrote them also in Serbâl, and therefore we must seek for their authorship among a people to whom both of those places would form an object of attraction. Assuredly it was not water, it was not beauty, it was not shade that drew them to Mukatteb, but something else which they were in search of, something which they could find in the neighbourhood of Mukatteb and Serbâl, something in search of which they were willing to endure the want of shade and water. Wady *Magharah* only presented one attraction to Egypt,—her mines and quarries; and the existence of that attraction accounts for the population which once resorted to it and left their mementoes behind to this day. So must we look for some similar attraction to Mukatteb, and setting aside pilgrims and monks, inquire for a people to whom this vast copper region would present an attraction sufficient to make them brave the inhospitalities of the region, and also to provide for themselves, what that region knows nothing of, food and water.

Dr Robinson's note in the last edition of his work (vol. i. p. 592), adds nothing to our information upon the subject, and certainly throws no light upon it. His *facts* are always valuable, but his *reasonings* are not so satisfactory. The contradictory character of this note shews this. The first part of the note approves of Beer's theory, which makes the inscriptions Christian,—the latter part of it approves Professor Tuch's, which makes them Arabic, of date before the Christian era. The Arabic theory rests on conjecture, and is of a much more visionary kind to Mr Forster's. It avoids none of the difficulties already adverted to. It does not account for the resort of Arabic pilgrims to a *waterless* valley; nor does it account for the peculiar character employed. Professor Beer's strong argument, from the *crosses*, as to the Christian origin, has no weight with Professor Tuch, who considers them merely ornamental.

Perhaps it may turn out that Niebuhr's hint about the Phœnicians, may after all be the real key to the puzzle.

MURRAH, 118.

NAKB-EL-BUDRAH, 145.

NAKB-EL-LEGHUM, 146.

NAKB (See Howai and Budrah).—Burckhardt says it means a steep declivity, p. 557. It is generally given as a pass or defile.

NAKHL, or Nukhl;—palm-tree, 191.—Our Arabs used to call both the tree and its fruit by the one word. The name *date*, the fruit of the palm, comes from the Greek δακτυλος, by which word it was classically known. Though the word palm occurs upwards of thirty times in Scripture, *date* does not occur once, save in the margin of 2 Chron. xxxi. 5, where the word "honey" is given "date." Michaelis (the elder) explains the reason of this. Honey was not one of the first-fruits to be offered by the law, so the Rabbis have been in the habit of altering the word "honey" into dates, or date-honey. (Adnot. in Hagiogr. vol. iii. p. 941.) The Talmudical word for dates (or at least unripe dates) is *Hinay*, or *ehinay*. See Simon's Onomast. N. T. p. 42. For a description of date and palm see Kitto's Cyclop. art. Palm, and Röhr's Hist. Geogr. Account of Palestine.

NAKHL, the name of a fort, 270.—The word is given *Nukhl* by Dr

Robinson, not *Nakhl*. The same writer also calls it *Kulat*-en-Nukhl, the *fortress* or castle of Nukhl, whereas it is often called *Khan*, the Inn. It is both a castle and an inn. Our sheikh called it *Kalât-Nakhl*. Wellsted calls the neighbourhood of Nakhl *Batn-Nakhl*, "palm-vale" (vol. ii. p. 458). He seems to mean *Butm*, not *Batn*, at least I can find no word corresponding to the latter. Of the former, I do not know on what authority he makes it to mean *palm*. Robinson quotes authorities which seem decidedly to shew that the *Butm* is the *terebinth*. (Vol. iii. p. 15, 1st edition.)

NEHEYEH, Wady-en-, 308...Inscriptions in, 309.

NILE, Appearance of, 56...Region of, 17.—Homer, in describing Egypt and mentioning the harbourage that vessels find there, speaks of the μέλαν ὕδωρ, with which they supplied themselves. Did he mean this as descriptive of Nile-water, which certainly is dusky? It is curious to notice that he calls the Nile the God-given river of Egypt, Αἰγύπτοιο διϊπετεος ποταμοῖο, Odyss. B. 4, 477—the epithet here reminding us of Acts xix. 35. Why does Ovid call it the *celer Nilus*?

NILOMETER, 53.

NUBK-TREE, 183.—For notices of the Nubk, see Robinson, vol. ii. pp. 210, 292; vol. iii. p. 265, who does not speak of having seen it in the Desert. He calls it "the lote-tree," the "Egyptian Nubk or Sidr," the "Rhamnus Nabeca," called also by the Arabs *Dôm*, "bearing a small acid fruit like a thorn apple." The author of the article Lotus in Knight's "Penny Cyclopædia" gives *Sidr* or *Sidar* as the Arabic name for the tree, and *nabach*, *nibuk*, or *nabk* as the name for the fruit. "This name has been long known as that of a species of Zizyphus, and has been applied by botanists to one species, Zizyphus Napeca. Dr Shaw, in his travels in Barbary, figures a species of Zizyphus which he calls 'Seedra Arabum, quæ et lotus veterum;' it is a prickly branching shrub,* with fruit of the size of a wild plum, and of a sweetish taste and saffron colour." It is only in Egypt, the Desert, and the warmer parts of Palestine that this tree is found. That this should be the tree from which the crown of thorns was made is very unlikely, as it is not found near Jerusalem, and as other shrubs much more prickly grow there plentifully. Haselquist seems to have been the first who suggested the nubk (A.D. 1766, cited by Mr Alford, on Matt. xxvii. 29); tradition having for ages fixed upon a shrub very common both in the Desert

* We found it a *tree* in Wady Feiran.

and round Jerusalem, with long sharp thorns, and known by the name of Spina Christi. Mr Alford suggests some species of cactus, or prickly pear. The prickly pear would never do. It must have been by some slip of pen or memory that Mr Stanley says, speaking of Galilee, "the nabk, that kind of plant of which *tradition* says the crown of thorns was woven" (p. 418). It was not tradition, but the Swedish naturalist that fixed on the nabk. Tradition may be wrong in regard to the Spina, but it at least named a shrub that was in the neighbourhood of Jerusalem.

a shore," has not every creek " a shore?" No. A large part of Malta has no " shore." Like the islands of Shetland, it is girt round with rocky battlements which forbid access. But here the rocks slope down, and end in a shore or beach.

PETRIFIED Forest of Cairo, 66.

PHARAOH'S Highway to Magharâh, 135...Mines, 156.

PHAROS, 23, 24. Homer is the first to mention Pharos. He calls it νῆσος, which no doubt originally it was. He speaks of it as being placed πολυκλύστῳ ἐνι πόντῳ,— an epithet which he probably meant to apply to the whole Mediterranean, and not only to that part of it which is opposite Egypt. The epithet reminds one of the εὐρωκλυδων, which assailed the vessel of the Apostle Paul. He says it is a day's sail from Egypt, which it never could have been, if by that he meant the nearest mainland. See Odyssey, Book iv. 354–359. Pope's translation is quite a misrendering of the passage. Cowper's is more exact—

> There is an isle,
> Amid the billowy flood, Pharos by name,
> In front of Egypt, distant from her shore
> Far as a vessel, by a sprightly gale
> Impelled, may push her voyage in a day.
> The haven there is good, and many a ship
> Finds watering there from rivulets on the coast.

Lucan describes it as " Pellæis proxima muris," b. x. 509. Ovid makes it an " Isle of palms." "Palmiferamque Pharon."

PITS, Use of, 76.

PLOUGH, Eastern, 317...Camel-ploughing, 317.

PORCUPINE.—Two or three specimens of this animal we found. The Arabs call it *Khumfúd*. In the Hebrew it is קִפֹּד from the verb to draw together. Hence it must mean an animal that draws itself together. This, with the Arab cognate, shews that the animal is the hedgehog or porcupine, not the bittern, as our translators render it in the three places where it occurs.—Isa. xiv. 23; xxxiv. 11; Zeph. ii. 14.

POTTERY, Broken, 320, 321, 331, 332.

PRICKLY Plants. 182.—See Akhul.

PYRAMIDS, Cheops, 55...Cephrenes, 55...Myccrenus, 55...Supposed Tombs of Kings, 57...Supposed idea of, 137, *note*...View from, 56, 67. The ancient derivation of the word is thus given by Sandys :—

" The name is derived from a flame of fire, in regard of their shape, broad below and sharp above, like a pointed diamond. By such the ancients did express the original of things, and that formless form-taking substance" (p. 99). The more recent derivations differ from this ; but they also differ from one another, so that it becomes difficult to arrive at a conclusion. The word pyramid does certainly look like Greek, not Egyptian. More than this we shall not say. In Sandys we find the word sometimes given as pyramids, and sometimes as pyramedès. In one place he translates some lines of Propertius,—"not sumptuous pyramids to skies upreared," &c. In another, the lines of Lucan, "When high pyramidès do grace" (Pp. 99, 100). Of the sentiments of their founders he thus writes, —" They, considering the frailty of man, that in an instant buds, blows, and withereth, did endeavour by such sumptuous and magnificent structures, in spite of death, to give unto their fames eternity, but vainly," (p. 100).

Of the antiquity of the pyramids Lepsius thus speaks, when Abraham came to Egypt for the first time he saw these pyramids, which had been built many centuries before his arrival.—*Letters,* p. 20. The number of pyramids in all is estimated at forty.— (*Heeren's Hist. Researches. African Nations,* vol. ii., p. 27.)

We have quoted Job as perhaps referring to the pyramids,—but does not Jeremiah also do this in his Lamentations,—" He has set me in dark places, as the dead of old" (Jer. iii. 6). If, as is said, Jeremiah wrote his Lamentations in Egypt, there is nothing unlikely in this.

QUAILS, 178.

RAHAH, Wady-er-, 210...Traditions of, 211.—Signifies rest, either because it is quite a resting-place in itself, or from Israel's once resting there and taking respite from their toilsome wanderings. There they rested and there Jehovah and his glory rested in the midst of them. The Hebrew word רוֹחָה, relaxation, respite, may correspond with *ráhhât,* the Arabic word for rest.

Was it when Israel was encamped here that the showers came down to which allusion is made in the Psalms, " Thou, O God, didst send a plentiful rain, whereby thou didst confirm thine inheritance when it was weary " (Psa. lxviii. 9) ; and again, " The clouds poured out water, the skies sent out a sound, thine arrows also went abroad" (Psa. lxxvii. 17). If these showers came from " the cloud," they would illustrate the apostle's meaning, " were all baptized into Moses in the cloud " (1 Cor. x. 2).

The existence of such a plain is a strong presumption against *Serbâl* being the real Sinai ; seeing that there is no such open space at the foot of that mountain. I have not entered into the question as to the claims of Serbâl, because it would have required some space, and because after all there is nothing save its own magnificence. and its being probably the resort of Arab pilgrims, in its favour. If grandeur is to settle the point, Serbâl is *facile princeps ;* but such a question is not to be thus determined. As to its being a sacred spot for ages before Christ,—that is very likely, and may be conceded. But the proof on this head is proof which will shew that it was the sacred place of *heathen* worship from time beyond history, —and, therefore, not the spot which would be chosen for the worship of the true God. The two groups stand within sight of each other : on the one the Shekinah-glory resting, on the other the fire of Baal, the mimicry of the divine glory ; at the foot of the one there is the wide plain of Rahah, like the outer court of the temple; at the foot of Serbâl the groves of Baal, the seat of the old idolatry.

RAILWAY to Cairo, 31.

RAIN, 75.—Often in the course of our journeys did our Arabs speak of *mutter, i. e.* rain, reminding us of the Hebrew מָטָר. The distinction between "rain" and "water" in Job v. 10, suggested itself. We had now, as we had afterwards in Palestine, the "rain" coming down on the face of the earth;—whereas in Egypt it was the "water" of the river poured over the face of the fields.

> " Who giveth rain on the face of the earth,
> And sendeth water on the face of the fields."

Job is addressed as one who knew Palestine, for Jordan is named (xl. 23); and as one who knew Egypt, for Behemoth is referred to : and as one who knew the wilderness, for Uz was his native country, and Uz was in the region of Edom (Lam. iv. 21), and Edom was part of the desert. There are besides many references to the wilderness throughout the book of Job.

RAKINEH, the pass of, 255...Ascent of, 256, 257.

RAML, or Ramleh, 254...By some called wady, by others *debbet,* or plain, 255.

RAS, 79.—*Ras* is applied to a bluff headland, as well as to the master of a vessel, just as we use our words *captain* and *cape ;* both from *caput,* the head.

RAS-ATAKAH, 87...Ras Wady Thâl, 132.

RATIONALISM, 85, 105.—If the attempts of rationalists to shut out God from the scenes of Scripture be painful, no less so are the efforts of those who, like Dr Robinson, would compromise matters and reduce a miracle to the very smallest degree of the supernatural. " If we must have a miracle let us have as little of God in it as possible," seems the maxim of some. *Lepsius* has praised the American traveller for his dignified protest against too much of the miraculous in Scripture. But from the lips of rationalism such praise carries no comfort to the conscience of a Christian man. There is danger in trying to stand well with rationalists and literary men. lest we sacrifice the veracity of Scripture to their good opinion. There is danger too in the well-meant efforts of some to win over opponents by making the miraculous as easy and palatable as is consistent with the admission of miracle at all. In neither case do we gain anything; in both we sacrifice the simplicity and truthfulness of the divine record.

RAVEN, 178.—Our Arabs called it Marab.

RED SEA, 82...Appearance of, 94...Passage of, by Israel, miraculous, 98–106...Mr Stanley's idea, 103, *note*...Rosenmuller's, 98...Dr Robinson's, 98.—*Mare Erythræum* of the Greeks and Romans,— *Iam Suph* of the Hebrews, regarding which latter name, Rosenmuller says, " the Hebrew word *Suph* denoted a kind of sea-weed which the ancient Egyptians called *Shari*, and hence the sea obtained among them the name of the Shari Sea." *Bibl. Geogr.* Shaw speaks of the marine vegetation here as very abundant. "In rowing gently over it, such a diversity of madrepores, fucuses, and other marine vegetables presented themselves to the eye, that we could not forbear taking them, as Pliny had done before us, for a forest under water."

The old Portuguese Jesuit, *Jerome Lobo*, gives us the following fact:—" The patriarch and I have frequently amused ourselves with making observations, and could never discover any redness but in the shallows where a kind of reed grew, which they call *Gonesmon*, which redness disappeared as soon as we plucked up the plant. It is observable that St Jerome, confining himself to the Hebrew, calls this sea *Yam-suf; yam* in that language signifies sea, and *suf* is the name of a plant in Æthiopia, from which the *Abyssins* extract a beautiful crimson. Whether this be the same with the *Gonesmon* I know not, but am of opinion that the herb gives to this sea both the colour and the name." (*A Voyage to Abyssinia in* 1622, p. 24.)

In addition to what has been stated in the text, I may notice that the Greek prose hymn, on the ascension of Christ, commences with the Red Sea miracle as its key-note,—" To God the Saviour, who led the people through the sea with feet unwet (ποσὶν ἀβρόχοις) ; and overwhelmed Pharaoh with his whole host, to him alone we sing, because his is the glory." (*Daniel's Thes. Hymnol.* vol. iii. p. 91.)

SAKIEH, or Water Machine, 110...Shadu, 111.—The Arabic word " to water," or " irrigate," corresponds exactly to the Hebrew שָׁקָה, to drink, which is used in the Hiphil for " to irrigate," *i. e.* to cause the earth to drink. See Gen. ii. 6, 10; Deut. xi. 10; Ps. civ. 13; Joel iii. 18. See Robinson, vol. i. p. 28, 541.

SALUTATIONS in the East, 38, 141.

SANDALS, 48.—Our sheikh called his skin-sandals *Enahl*, which word at once recalls the Hebrew נַעַל, shoe or sandal,—something bound round the foot. Deut. xxix. 5,—" Thy shoe (sandal) is not waxen old upon thy foot," spoken of Israel's desert-life. In Ezek. xvi. 10 we have the verb, " I shod thee with badger-skin" (or seal-skin). *Shoes* he called *Marcub*.

SAND Storm, 76.

SARBUT-EL-JEMEL, 132.

SCISTILANS, 249.—The Zistilans, or Scistilans, is not unlike the Hebrew *Habetzel* in appearance, if Gesenius' description be correct (Lex. p. 258). He makes it to be the autumn crocus, of white and violet colour, growing from poisonous bulbs. It is the word translated *rose* in Cant. ii. 1, and Isa. xxxv. 1. See Crocus.

SEBA, Wady, 326, 327, 331.

SEBAIYEH, 223.

SENIEH, Wady, 304.

SERAB, 300.

SERAM, Wady, 294...Inscriptions, 294, 300...Ruins, 295.

SERBAL, 132, 178, 184, 190, 195.—Robinson gives " cloak " as its meaning. It is more likely to be connected with *Sar* prince, and *Bel* or *Bâl* the Phœnician idol,—Bâl being a common termination of names; or it may be from the Arabic sherâ, to glisten, *q.'d.* the splendour of Bâl. Its height is 6300 feet. One or two travellers (Burckhardt and Lepsius) maintained that this is the true " Sinai " and "Paran." Dr Kitto goes very far, however, when he tells us that of this he " entertains *no manner of doubt !*" (*Pictorial Hist. of Pal.* p. 53.) Serbâl was perhaps the sacred mount of the Amalekites. Travellers have generally described Serbâl as visible from Jebel-Mûsa, and to us it seemed so. Dr Robinson denies this. Mr Stanley says, " He (Dr R.) is right and they are wrong. What they took for Serbâl is the double peak of El-Banât," (p. 77). One would like to know the truth in this matter, and to have had Mr Stanley's ground for the above statement. It is strange that almost every traveller has fallen into the above mistake (if it be a mistake)— and their guides also. The two peaks of El-Banât are not likely to be mistaken for the *five* peaks of Serbâl,—those ubiquitous peaks with which one gets so familiar in the desert. It is still more strange, however, if Dr R. be right, that travellers should maintain that they saw *Jebel-Mûsa* from *Serbâl*. Yet Lepsius says so. After mentioning how much concealed Jebel-Mûsa is from most points of view, he adds, "In fact we could never see it from the sea or from any other point of the Peninsula, although we were certainly inquiring for it with impatience, *except from the top of Serbâl* and the foot of its own highest peak." (*Tour*, p. 65.) If Jebel-Mûsa be visible from Serbâl, Serbâl must be visible from Jebel-Mûsa. Burckhardt's description of the view from Serbâl *implies* (though it does not affirm) that he saw Jebel-Mûsa. At the same time, in giving the bearings of some of the neighbouring hills from the top of Serbâl, he does not give that of Jebel-Mûsa. Lepsius, in his "Letters from Egypt" (*Travels*, 342), says, "I could distinguish quite plainly that beyond Jebel-Mûsa the mountains rose higher and higher." He is describing his view from Serbâl. He says, too, that from Jebel-Mûsa, *Um Shomer* was visible. Laborde says the same. Robinson says it "must have been with the mind's eye." Who is right?

I find a more probable derivation of Serbâl quoted from Rödiger by Wellsted. *Serb* means *copia palmarum*, palm-grove, (φοινικων). The word then signifies "the palm-grove of Bâl." Lepsius writes, "The history of the palm-grove of Pharan forms the centre-point of the history of the whole peninsula. . . . It was the *Serb-Bâl*, the palm-grove of Bâl, from which the mountain first obtained its name." (*Letters*, p. 441.) Was it from this that the Amalekites, when they went northward, carried the name of the region which was afterwards called Phœnicia,—the palm-land? This is certainly more likely than Faber's derivation from *Fanax* or Anax = αναξ. "*Eight Dissertations*," vol, ii, p. 155.

SEYALEH, Sayaleh, or Siyaleh, or Seyal, for in all these ways has it been written, a species of acacia, 74, 252.—It is, with the exception of the palm, the largest tree in the Desert. It is not tall, but wide-spreading, with a stem sufficiently thick to furnish the *shittim-wood* for the tabernacle; for there seems little doubt that this is the shittim-wood of Scripture.

SHAVEH, 195.

SHEIKH, 185, 200, 245.—The word *Sheikh* means properly *old*, and from that it came to signify *chief;* just as the Hebrew זָקֵן, *zakâyn*, signifies both an old man and a ruler. *Zakâyn* and *sheikh* are evidently the same word. The elders of Israel are " the sheikhs of Israel." So with *senior* in modern languages,—and *aldermen* or *eldermen*. *Ras* is the Arabic word for the master of a ship, evidently the same as the Hebrew *Rosh*, head or chief; and corresponding to our *captain* from *caput*, the head. (See *Rosenmuller's Biblical Geography, Arabia.*)

SHEKINAH, 78, 188, 205, 233, 238.

SHELLAL, Wady, 142, the "valley of cataracts."—Of this Mr Stanley remarks, that " both in its name and aspect it bears every trace of its wintry caseades," (p. 16).

SHIA Plant, 140.—Burckhardt calls it *Shyh*, and speaks of it as the *Artemisia*, (p. 143). Robinson gives it more fully, *Artemisia Judaica*.

SHORTER CATECHISM, 231.

SHRUBS, Ajram, or Djerum, 195, 234...Ghetâff, 234...Jadheh, 201, 234...Rib'shi, 157...Rim'th, 195...Rittt'm, or Rithem, 195...Zatûr, 201, 234.

SHUBEIKEH, Wady, 132.—Shubeikeh signifies "net" in Arabic, in affinity with the Hebrew שָׂבַךְ, *savach*, or *savacha*, a net. (1 Kings vii. 17.) The feminine form of the word occurs in 1 Kings vii. 18, 20, 41 ; 2 Chron. iv. 12, 13 ; Job xviii. 8; Jer. lii. 22, 23, &c. It is sometimes translated " checker-work," sometimes "net-work," sometimes " wreathen-work," sometimes " a lattice." The eye of the native Arab has caught the *net-work* of mountains here, and given them a name in this wady.

SHUEIB, Wady-esh-, 215.

SICILY, 9.

SIDREH, or Sɪᴅʀɪ, Wady, 146.—This is said to take its name from the thorn-bushes which it contains. If so, perhaps there may be some connection between this and the Hebrew סִיר, *seer*, a thorn. The name *Sihah-Sidreh*, or arid place of Sidreh, recalls the Hebrew verb צָחַח, with its derivations, all meaning to be sunny, or bright, or sun-dried. (See Psal. lxviii. 7 ; Isa. lviii. 11. צְחִיחַ סֶלַע in Ezek. xxiv. 7, is very like Sihah-Sidreh. Our translation makes it

" the top of the rock," or literally "the hot dry place of the rock."
Between *Sihah-Sidhri* and *Mukatteb*, two names of places were given
us by our sheikh, *Tih-Bagh-el-Ran'men* and *Wady-El-Mararah-
Tiguneh*. I do not find these names given by any traveller, and
am not quite sure that I have taken them down accurately.

SIGNS, use of, 186.

SINAI, 210, 211...Traditions of, 212, 213...Convent of, 217, 218...
Service in, 219, 220...Garden of, 221...Library of, 224.—Buxtorf says
it was called Sinai from the tree-fossils found in the rocks, not from
the actual trees, or, as Pococke expresses it, from the "dendrite
stones." Simon gives it as *bush of Jehovah*, and Gesenius as *clayey,
miry*. Robertson, in his *Clavis Pentateuchi*, p. 291, gives as its meaning a blackberry bush, saying, however, that others thought it to be
"spina Ægyptiaca, acacia." The Jews understood it as bush, from
the shrubs, or from the bush that burned. (*Pagninus* in his *Lexicon*
gives the latter.) Most of the old lexicographers take it as meaning
bush, from the bushes there, or some particular shrubs which grew
there. Stockius takes this last, "sic dictus a voce *Seneh*, apud Heb-
ræos et Arabes, spinam, senticetum notante, quia ibi senticetorum
copia dabatur" (*Clavis*, vol. ii. p. 727). Stephanus (*Latin Thesaurus,*
vol. iv. *sub voce*), says, "nomen habet a vepribus et dumetis quibus sep-
tus est; est enim Hebræis Senah arbor spinosa." The word *Seneh,*
signifying bush, occurs only six times, and is not exactly the same as
"Sinai," so that the etymology is not quite certain. Even Jerome,
who is never at a loss for a signification, seems doubtful, for he
gives three meanings, first of *Sin*, and then of *Sinai*, which he
connects together, making the concluding ‫י‬, of Sinai, the pronoun
"my." As to *Sin*, he says it means, (1.) amphora, (2.) tentatio,
(3.) rubus. Of *Sinai* he says it means, (1.) rubus, (2.) amphora
mea, (3.) mensura mea, (4.) mandatum (*De Nom. Heb. Interpr.
de Exodo*). Augustine did not know Hebrew, so that in trying to
spiritualize Sinai, he takes what meaning suits him best,—"in
nominum Hebræorum interpretationibus invenimus Sina interpre-
tari *mandatum*, et alia quædam interpretatur, sed hoc puto præsenti
loco aptius convenire" (On Psa. lxviii. 17). A few sentences farther
on he takes up another figure and adds, "cui sensui congruit et alia
interpretatio quâ interpretatur Sina *mensura*."

One might perhaps suggest that it is cognate with ‫שֵׁן‬, a tooth or
crag. Gesenius, in interpreting the proper name *Seneh* (1 Sam. xiv.
4), suggests that it means *crag* (*Ges. Lex.* p. 591), and that it is the
same as the above word, being derived, not, as is commonly supposed,

from the bushes which might cover it, but from its ruggedness. If this might be entertained, Sinai would mean "the rock," or "the rock of Jehovah," assuming, with Simon, that the   is an abbreviation of the holy name Jah. If this be so, then it would correspond with *Hagar*, which, interpreted by the Arabic, means rock, and not "flight," or "stranger," or "midday," or "night," as lexicographers, looking solely to the Hebrew, have supposed it to mean. Thus the *bondwoman*, and the *bond-mountain*, mean the same thing, *rock*, as the apostle means to imply in Gal. iv. 14.

Of Mount Sinai Josephus says, "This is the highest of all the mountains thereabouts, and the best for pasturage, the herbage being there good; and it had not been before fed upon, *because of the opinion men had that* GOD DWELT THERE, *the shepherds not daring to ascend it*" (*Ant.* b. ii. ch. 12, sect. 1, *Whiston's transl.*). And again, "He (Moses) ascended up to Mount Sinai, which is the highest of all the mountains that are in that country, and is not only very difficult to be ascended by men on account of its vast altitude, but because of the sharpness of its precipices also; nay, indeed, it cannot be looked at without pain of the eyes; and besides this, it was terrible and inaccessible, on account of the rumour that passed about, THAT GOD DWELT THERE" (*Ant.* b. iii. ch. 5, sect. 1). This was of course before Israel visited it, so that it is likely that it has really been in previous ages the place of the manifestation of God, —and so might well be called the " rock or mountain of Jehovah."

The preposition עַל, *upon*, is frequently used in reference to Sinai, but not once in reference to Horeb,—a clear indication that *Sinai* was the *mountain* and *Horeb* the region. In Exod. xvi. 1, we read simply, "lie between Elim and Sinai," which fixes nothing. Exod. xix. 1, 2, has no preposition, but the expressions, "before the mount," and "out of the mountain," evidently point to Sinai. At ver. 11, it is "*upon* Mount Sinai;" ver. 14, "*down from* the mount;" ver. 18, "the Lord descended *upon* it;" ver. 20, "came down *upon* Mount Sinai, *to* (אֶל) the top of the mount;" ver. 23, "come *up to* the mount." In the sixteenth chapter we have the similar use of prepositions; ver. 1, "*come up*;" ver. 4, "*under* the hill;" ver. 12, "come up to me" (אֶל) "to the mountain" (no preposition); ver. 13, "*into* the mountain" (אֶל); ver. 15, do.; ver. 16, "the glory of the Lord, abode *upon* Mount Sinai;" ver. 17, "the sight of the glory of the Lord was like devouring fire on the top of the mount" בְּ, *in* the top, as if the fire were seen coming out of a hollow) ; chap. xxxi. 18, "Communing with him *upon* Mount Sinai" (בְּ, as if in some hollow, either formed by the rock or the surrounding cloud) ; chap. xxxiv. 2, " *Unto* Mount Sinai ;" "*on* (עַל, not *in*, as our translation has it) the top of the mount;" ver, 3. "throughout (Heb. *in*) all the mount ;" ver. 3, "*before* that mount" (in front of); ver. 4, "went up to ;" ver. 29, "came down from" (מִן, twice); ver. 32, "*in* Mount Sinai ;" Lev. vii. 38, "which the Lord commanded Moses *in* Mount Sinai ;" "*in* the wilderness of Sinai ;" xxv. 1, "the Lord spake unto Moses *in* Mount Sinai ;" xxvi. 46, "these are the statutes which the Lord made *in* Mount Sinai ;" xxvii. 34, do. ; Numb. i. 1, "*in* the wilderness of Sinai ;" ver. 19, do.; iii. 1, in Mount Sinai ;" ver. 4, "*in* the wilderness of Sinai ; " ver. 14, "in the wilderness of Sinai ;" ix. 1, do.; ver. 5, do.; x. 12, "out of the wilderness ;" xxvi. 64, "*in* the wilderness of Sinai ;" xxiv. 64, "*in* Mount Sinai ;" xxxiii 15, "in the wilderness of Sinai;" Deut. xxx. 2, "the Lord came *from* Sinai ;" Judges v. 5, " Sinai spoken of as a mountain ; " Neh. ix. 13, "*upon* Mount Sinai ;" Ps. lxviii. 8, "this Sinai," evidently a mountain, from the preceding clause.

The inference from these citations and from those under "Horeb" is, (1.) That Sinai always denotes a mountain, when it is not expressly called a wilderness. (2.) That the preposition *on* is frequently applied to Sinai, but never to Horeb. (3.) That though there are one or two passages in which Horeb *seems* to be spoken of as a mount, yet these are doubtful, and, in general, it is not spoken of as such. Jerome, indeed, makes them to be adjacent mountains (in *Loc. Hebr.*), and speaks of *Pharan* as hard by, "cui jungitur mons et desertum Saracenorum quod vocatur Pharan ;" yet adds that, perhaps Horeb and Sinai were merely different names for one mountain. But Jerome's authority in matters of *desert* topography is not great; and if he could speak of the *desert* of Pharan being near Sinai, he cannot be reckoned on as accurate in other things.

Sinai seems to have been the mountain of Jehovah's true worship, and over against it rose Serbâl, the mountain of Baal's worship,—long before Israel entered the wilderness. After the "God of glory" (the shekinah) appeared to Abraham and led him out of Chaldea into Canaan, did He withdraw that glory to the desert, and take up His abode on Mount Sinai (the hill of Jehovah), and there gather round that sanctuary a band of worshippers, of which Jethro was the representative? And did Bâl the *fire-god* (the imitator of the shekinah) take up his abode on Serbâl and gather his worshippers around him there? Was thus the fire of the false worship set up right in view of the glory of the true? And were the Amalekites there the representatives of Cain's descendants, working in

mines and metals (Gen. iv. 22) ? And was Jethro the representative of Abel, the feeder of sheep, outside the gate of Paradise, where
the flaming sword waved, and from which it passed from place to
place, till it took up its abode in the temple at Jerusalem ?

SOLAF, Wady, 207, 208.—I find no derivation given for this name.
Is it connected with the Hebrew סָלַף to slip away, to be slippery,

to overturn, from the slipperiness of its rocks and debris ?...Inscrip-
tions in, 208, 209.

SOUTHEY, 72.

SPHINX, 55.

SUDHR, Wady, 113, Pococke remarks, " We came to the desert
they called Shedûr, the old Shûr. Vol. i. p. 139.

SUEZ, 86, 89, 90.

SURABIT-EL-KHADIM, 253, a hill.—See Laborde, p. 78–84 ; Robinson, vol. i. p. 77–79, 2d edit.—It is about eight hundred feet high ;
and appears to have been the centre of a great mining district. Dr
Robinson says, " We saw no traces of mines around the place" (vol. i.
p. 80), and mentions, as an "ingenious hypothesis," that the hieroglyphical monuments are the records of the pilgrimages of Egyptian
kings! There is no proof of this any more than for the Arab pilgrimages to Wady Mukatteb ; and it seems strange that such a
hypothesis should be even called ingenious. It is visionary in the
extreme ; all the more so because the " only historical ground for
such an hypothesis" is found in the fact that Moses demanded per-
mission to go three days into the wilderness to sacrifice, " a demand
which seemed to have caused no surprise to the Egyptians, as if it
were something to which they themselves were accustomed!" (Robinson, vol. i. p. 79.) In opposition to what Dr Robinson did not see, we
have what Laborde, Lepsius, and others did see. Lepsius thus writes
—" The Egyptian inscriptions are simply stelæ, to record the working of the copper-mines in the immediate vicinity. Of these stelæ
there were many in the peninsula, certainly more than are known
in the present day, inasmuch as large masses of copper, mixed with
a quantity of iron-ore, were, and still are, found in certain strata of
the sandstone rocks along the skirts of the primeval chain. The
whole country was called after them in hieroglyphics, *Mafkat*, the
copper land, and was under the particular protection of the goddess
Hathor, mistress of Mafkat. The temple of Sarbut-el-Chadem was
also dedicated to her." After speaking of " the *vast mounds of ore*
among which the temple is built," he adds, " the north-eastern hil-

locks, two hundred and fifty yards long and a hundred wide, are *completely covered with a massive crust of iron-ore* six or eight feet thick, and surrounded on all sides by blocks of scoriæ. . . . The ore was conveyed from the more distant works to these airy eminences, which were very advantageously situated for their furnaces, owing to the north-east wind blowing continually on them." (Tour from Thebes, &c. pp. 14–17.) In his "Letters" Lepsius speaks as distinctly on this point. " East and west of the temple are to be seen great slag-hills, which, from their black colour, form a strange contrast to the soil of the neighbourhood. These artificial mounds, the principal of which is two hundred and fifty-six paces long, and from sixty to one hundred paces broad, situated on the tongue of the terrace projecting into the valley, are covered with a massive crest of slag, from four to five feet thick, and thence to their foot from twelve to fifteen feet, sprinkled with single blocks of the same material. . . This free point was chosen only for smelting, on account of the sharp, and, as the Arabs assure me, almost incessant, draught of air," p. 438.

Besides the Egyptian hieroglyphics, there are some " Mukatteb " inscriptions, indicating that the Mukatteb writers had visited, if not dwelt at, Surabît-el-Khadim. (See Forster, p. 138). The distance between the two places is not great, but they lie on quite different roads, the one on the upper and the other on the lower road to Sinai.

I find no interpretations anywhere given of *Surabit-el-Khâdim*, beyond that simply of " Surabit the ancient." But the word Surabit or *Tsurabit* (for it is *sadd* not *sin*, in the original), is nearly the same with the Hebrew *Tsarephath*, or Zarephath, the name of the well-known Phœnician or Sidonian town (1 Kings xvii. 9), and which is interpreted as a "place for melting and refining metals." This corresponds exactly with the description of Surâbit, as given above. If the Phœnicians (or Amalekite-Phœnicians) were the original workers of these mines, this is the name which would be naturally given to the place; and in after times, to distinguish it from Sarepta or Zarephath in the north, it was called Zarephath-the-ancient. Zarephath was the great smelting-place for the mines of the north, and Surabit was the same for the mines of the south ; and the former might take its name from the latter. It is curious to notice the different names in the Phœnician territory which correspond with those in the desert. (1.) *Sin* near Lebanon. The Sinites were among the tribes of Canaan. (Gen. x. 17 ; 1 Chron. i. 15) ; Rosenmuller's Bibl. Geog. *Sin*, the "desert of Sin," (Exod.

xiv. 1; xvii. 1. (2.) *Mearah*, "which is beside the Sidonians," (Josh. xiii. 4). *Wady-Magharah* in the desert. (3.) *Tsur*, or Tyre. *Tsudr* (Wady) in the desert. (4.) *Zarephath*, corresponding to *Surâbit*.

TABERAH, 248.

TAMAR. See Palm.—Both in the Hebrew and Arabic, from the unused root, to stand erect (*Gesenius*).

Virgil's expression is "ardua palma" (*Georg.* b. ii.), and Ovid's "lentæ victoris præmia palmæ" (*Met.* b. x.) It is needless quoting the many references to this tree; but there is a curious one in an old Greek writer, to the effect, that in Egypt the year was figured by a palm (ἐνιαυτον γραφοντες φοινιχα ζωγραφουσι) because the palm brings forth twelve branches in the year, one at every moon —*Horus Apollo. Hierogl.* iii.

Jerome tells us of a Jewish tradition respecting Saul in connection with the palm. He had a vision in which he saw himself placed upon the top of a palm-tree, by which he understood that he was to be king;—" quæ visio signum regale fuit."—*Quest. in Lib. Regum. Works*, vol. i. p. 473. For description of palm, see Paxton's Illustrations of Scripture. Nat. Hist. p. 48–57. In the above work, we are told that the finest palms are to be found "at Jericho and Engeddi." Robinson saw *one* in (1838) at Jericho. I saw none (1856). Mr Stanley says, that the last relic of the ancient palms has disappeared (1853), p. 301.

TAIYEBEH, Wady, 131. Could I have ascertained that this wady went eastward and northward to a considerable extent, I should have been inclined to identify it with "Jotbath" (Numb. xxxiii 33; Deut. x. 7),—both words signifying "goodness" or the "good.' See *Gesenius* on the word.

TARFA-TREE, 146, and elsewhere frequently.

TASET-SUDHR, 113. "The cup of Sûdhr."

TAWARIK, Wady, 73. The author of that interesting and ingenious work, "Israel in Egypt," assumes that Wady Tawârik is the valley through which Israel passed. (P. 404.) This does not seem likely, as the entrance to this wady is by the southern side of Jebel Mukattem, hard by Cairo. In this case Israel would have marched right south, up the Nile, by the *cities* of Egypt, and through its most fruitful and populous territories; nor would they reach the wilderness till they reached Mukattem; whereas they seemed to have struck into the desert at once. Wady Tawârik is quite out of their way; and some reason ought to be given why such a very circuitous route was taken. The only reason urged is, that the wady is said to be called *Wady-et-Tih, i. e.* "the valley of the wanderings." This, however, Robinson denies, and gives authorities (vol. i. p. 546). Israel seems at once to have struck into the desert,— "the way of the wilderness of the Red Sea" (Exod. xiii. 18). This writer assumes that one of the names of the Red Sea was Kolzum or Clysma, *i. e.* the sea of destruction. This would be interesting, if it were proved. That there was a town of that name there is no doubt, its ruins remain near Suez,—that the sea might have had the same name is not unlikely; and that it might have taken that name from the overthrow of Pharaoh, is not improbable. But we should like to see some proof.

TEL-MACLUBA, 9. See Macluba. Tel or Tâl means hill in Arabic, as it does in Hebrew. Tel-âbib, the hill of the ears of corn, Ezek. iii. 15. The Celtic is Tulah, a hill.

TENT, 68...of Kedar, 196.—There are different words for this in the Hebrew, which, though sometimes apparently interchangeable, have the following special significations:—(1.) אֹהֶל, *ohel.* This occurs about three hundred and thirty times in Scripture. It seems to refer to the canvas, or skins, or curtain, or outer covering of the tent. (2.) מִשְׁכָּן, *mishkâhn.* This occurs about one hundred and thirty-six times, and refers to the inner part of the tent,—its boards and framework. The distinction of these words is brought out in such verses as Exod. xxvi. 7, "Thou shalt make curtains of goats' hair to be a covering upon the tabernacle," or literally "to be an *ohel* upon the *mishkâhn.*" Exod. xxxvi. 14, "He made curtains of goats' hair for the *ohel* (which was) over (upon עַל) the *mishkâhn.*" At verse 19, it would seem as if the *ohel* had a covering for itself; and Gesenius says, "When the *ohel* is distinguished from the *mishkâhn, ohel* is the outer covering of the tent, of twelve curtains of goats' hair placed above the *mishkâhn, i. e.* the ten interior curtains which rested on the boards." But may not the verse referred to mean "he made a covering for the *ohel,*" (*i. e.* a covering which constituted the *ohel*) just as it is added (v. 20), "He made boards for the *mishkâhn,*" (*i. e.* boards which constituted the *mishkâhn*). (3.) סֻכָּה, *sûkhah,* and

סֹך, *sokh,* the former occurring about thirty times, and the latter four times. Both mean a hut, or booth, or thicket, or covert,—some shelter made of intertwined branches. They are not used in reference to "the tabernacle," but the former is the word used when the "feast of tabernacles" is spoken of, *Booth* is the word that best expresses the original; and as the root refers to a thicket of trees, so the word is used to denote a hidden retreat for man or a *den* for beasts (Psal. x. 9). In Psal. lxxvi. 2, it is translated "tabernacle," "in Salem is his tabernacle," properly "his den" or secret retreat. Is this the *den* of the lion of the tribe of Judah? (4.) קֻבָּה, *kúbbah*, a tent or bed-chamber, "so called from its arched form," (Gesenius) This form of rooms is very common in the east, at least in Syria, where stone is more plentiful than wood, and so the arch is easier for a roof than joists of wood.

THAL, Wady, 132.—*Tál* in Hebrew is "dew," and in Arabic light rain, from the root "to moisten gently." Abital (2 Sam. iii. 4; 1 Chron. iii. 3) is "the father of dew."

THUB, or Dhob, 144.—The Hebrew word צָב, a species of lizard, corresponds with the Arabic name. There is no difficulty as to the Tsaddi, for that letter in Hebrew is sometimes represented by *dh* in Arabic, as אָרְץ, Hebrew, *Ardh* Arab. German, *Erde*. Scottish, *Yird*. English, *earth*. In Lev. xi. 29 it is translated *tortoise*; but *Ghumphús* was the name which our Arabs applied to the tortoises we used to meet with. (Gumpus is the name for a species of whale.) The *thub* was of a brownish colour, with a scaly skin like a lizard. The largest are said to be a foot and a half long, and the tail forming more than a third. We saw the holes in the sand where it lives, which are said to be open at two ends. The Bedaween make tobacco-pouches of its skin.

TIH, Jebel-et-, 255.—The range of *Et-Tih*, and the inhabitants of that district, the *Tihwayah* tribes, take their name from the Arabic word "to wander." "Et-Tih" is the mountain of the wanderers. Some trace the name to the wanderings of Israel; but this is doubtful. Yet we find here the affinity between the Arabic and Hebrew. The word used for the wanderings in the wilderness is תָּעָה, *tahah*. (Gen. xxi. 14; Psa. cvii. 4; Isa. xvi. 8.) This double mountain-chain, which runs east and west between the two seas, is 4300 feet high at its highest point. In Arabic it is said to be called the wandering desert of the children of Israel. (*Rosenmuller's Bibl. Geogr. Arabia.*)

TOR, or Tur, 240.—A mountain, sometimes applied to Sinai, and sometimes to the group south of Sinai. Tawarah is the adjective formed from this. The Celtic gives *Torr*, a hill. (See "*Derivation of many Classical Proper Names from the Celtic, &c. by T. Stratton, M.D.*

TORTOISE, 312. (See Thub.)

TRADITIONS, Monkish, 211...Superstition of, 212...Sentimental admiration of, 213, 338.

TRAVELLING Equipage, 69.

TURQUOISE, 108.—When Laborde was at Surabit-el-Khadem, he got these stones from the natives; and he mentions that they are found "in great abundance, being brought to the surface by the rains" (Mount Sinai and Petra, p. 84). These he says, "though not to be ranked among the best of precious stones, nevertheless possess a certain value."

USEIT, Wady, 130 131. Called also *Waseit*.

VALLEY (See Wady).—In the Hebrew there are five names for what may be called valleys. (1.) בִּקְעָה, *Bikhâh*, a place opened or levelled by the cleaving of mountains—a plain or a valley—"the plain of Shinar" (Gen. xi. 2). In Deut. xxxiv. 3 it is distinguished from a plain—"the plain of the *valley* of Jericho." It occurs nineteen times. (2.) גַּיְא, *Gahyeh*, a valley into which water may flow, from the unused root, to flow together. It cannot be from גִּיחַ, to break forth, as Mr Stanley suggests, p. 477, because of the omission of the radical *Heth*, specially as the derivatives from that verb retain the radical, *Giah*, 2 Sam. ii. 24; *Gihon*, Gen. ii. 13; 1 Kings i. 33. *Gikhon* and *Gia* cannot be from the same root. It is the word used in reference to the valley of Hinnom (Josh. xv. 8); and out of the fifty-six times in which it occurs, it is used twelve times in reference to that valley. The Scandinavian word, still in use in Shetland, for a ravine or cleft into which the sea flows, is *gioe*. (3.) נַחַל, *Naghal*, a valley watered by a river, or the place hollowed out by a stream; though more generally the stream itself. See Gen. xxvi. 17, 19; Deut. xxi. 4; and Lev. xi. 9; Ezek. xlvii. 5, 6. (4.) עֵמֶק, *Emek*, a low tract of some depth, from the verb to be deep. See Gen. xiv. 3, 8; Josh. vii. 24; Joel iii. 2. (5.) שְׁפֵלָה, *Shephelah*, a low region. This only occurs about twenty times. Deut. ix. 7; Josh. i. 1; 1 Chron. xxvii. 28. *Ghor* is the Arabic word for a long valley between mountains. Respecting these and similar topographical words, the reader ought to consult Mr Stanley's *Appendix* to his "Sinai and Palestine,"—which is perhaps the most valuable part of that able volume.

WADY means a water-course, and in derivation it corresponds to the Hebrew גָּדַד, which signifies to cut away, and hence the noun, " banks of a river" (Josh. iii. 15). It certainly is not used for " river " in Arabic, but always for valley, or bed of a river. This is the chief objection to the Arabic origin of the Spanish names beginning with "guada,"—such as Guadalquiver, which the old geographers and lexicographers interpret by "fluvius magnus," and which modern works of geography set down as undoubtedly from the Arabic *Wady-al-Kebir*, the mighty river. *Nahr-el-Kebir*, is the name now given to the ancient Eleutherus (the most northerly of the rivers of Lebanon).—(*Rosenmuller's Biblical Geogr.*)

It would be interesting to throw together the names of the wadys, with their significations,—even though our information may not enable us entirely to see the aptness of the name. There is the *royal* wady (Wady Sheikh); the *dew* wady (Wady Thal); the the *written* wady (Wady Mukatteb); the *fountain* wady (Wady-el-Ain); the *rest* wady (Wady-er-Rahah); the *cave* wady (Wady Magharah); the *cataract* wady (Wady Shellâl); the *good* wady (Wady Tayibeh); the *wet* wady (Wady Reiyaneh); the *white* wady (Wady Abyad); the *refreshing* wady (Wady Murkhâh); the *concave* wady (Wady Jaifeh); the *sandy* wady (Wady Ramliyeh); the *spacious* wady (Wady Ruhaibeh).

In Psalms i. 3, the words are literally "like a tree planted *upon* the channels of waters." This may refer to what we so often saw,— wadys covered with trees,—the *bed*, not the *brink*, of the river-course being the place of their growth. Regarding the word פֶּלֶג, Gesenius remarks, " it is said properly to signify a *channel* or *water-course*, so called from the idea of dividing." The meaning of the Psalm, however, is the same in either sense; it still points to

> . . . the sweet green saplings of the spring,
> Fresh by the water-courses flourishing.—*Aird.*

WANDERINGS of the Israelites, 138.

WARDAN, Wady, 114.

WATCH, an Eastern, 204.

WATER, Supply of, 111, 143.—Israel got water at Ayun Mûsa naturally, again at Marah miraculously, again at Elim naturally. After this, we only read of the water from the smitten rock, yet they seem to have had water in the " desert of Sin," both at Dophkah and Alush, before they came to Rephidim, which is the first place of which it is said, " there was no water for the people to drink" (Num.

xxxiii 14). Here the miraculous supply began, which seems to have continued during their desert sojourn. The rock, or at least the water, "followed them" (1 Cor. xi. 2), which it would naturally do, for the region round about Sinai is very high, and slopes down in all directions, so that the miraculous fountain from the rock would fill one or more of the wadys down which the Israelites were marching. It is not pleasant to read the following remark in the work of a well-known Christian traveller :—"How they could have obtained a sufficiency of water during their whole stay in the peninsula and their subsequent wanderings in the Desert, even where no want of water is mentioned, *is a mystery which I am unable to solve*, unless we admit the supposition that water was anciently far more abundant in these regions than at present." (Robinson's Biblical Researches, &c. vol. i. p. 106). Dr Robinson might have found equal difficulty in discovering where the *food* came from. Is not the Bible solution the best? Water from the rock and manna from heaven. Take away the *miraculous* from the narrative, and Israel's wanderings become a mere fabulous story of rashness and folly. There is but the choice between a miracle and a fable, or rather a falsehood. For what but a continued miracle can account for the existence of two or three millions in a desert which can barely support a few Arab tribes, and in which no traveller can subsist for a day save by an importation of food or water. If Lepsius had professed himself unable to solve the difficulty, we should not have wondered. But that Robinson should say so is strange. Yet we know how he explains away the miracle of the crossing of the sea. How unwilling are even Christian men, to admit of the direct interference of God.

WATERS of Marah, 118...In the Desert, 143.

WAYMARK, 112.—The word is צִיּוּן, *Tseeyoon*, from the word to "set up." It occurs only three times; 2 Kings xxiii. 17, "What title (or rather "mark") is that that I see?" There had been a special "mark" set up to note the sepulchre of the man of God and to distinguish it from others. This Josiah observed, Ezek. xxxix. 15, "Then shall he set up *a sign* by it," *i.e.* a mark, which was probably a small heap of stones such as those which we used often to see. Jer. xxxi. 21, "Set thee up way-marks." The "landmark," *gevoolah*, was for a different purpose. It did not mark "ways" but lands and fields, from the "cord" or line which measured them. Job xxiv. 2; Deut. xxxii. 8; Ps. lxxiv. 17; Isa. x. 13.

WELLS of Moses, 111...Of Suez, 81...of Ghurandel, 124...of Syria, 323.

HEIGHTS OF MOUNTAINS.

	Feet.
GREAT HERMON,	10,000
ST CATHERINE,	8,063
JEBEL MUSA,	7,033
SERBAL,	6,300
CONVENT OF SINAI,	5,452
WADY FEIRAN,	4,800
JEBEL-ET-TIH.	4,322
DESERT OF ET-TIH,	1,400
HEAD OF WADY EL-ARISH,	2,832
NUKHL,	1,396
ER-RUHAIBEH,	1,032
SURABIT-EL-KHADIM,	800

TEXTS OF SCRIPTURE ILLUSTRATED.

JOEL.

Chap.	Verse.	Page.
i.	12,	192

AMOS.

v.	16,	65
viii.	8,	296
ix.	5,	296

JONAH.

iv.	8,	129, 365

MATTHEW.

xii.	43,	112
xviii.	6,	109
xxi.	12,	49
	24,	109
xxiv.	41,	109

MARK.

v.	38,	65

LUKE.

ii.	8,	330
vi.	48, 49,	301
vii.	37,	43
x.	4,	38
xii.	47,	89
	54,	55, 279

JOHN.

ii.	15,	49
xx.	29,	338

ACTS.

Chap.	Verse.	Page.
iii.	21,	126
xxvii.		6
xxviii.	2,	13

ROMANS.

iii.	20,	21, 229
viii.	19,	123
	22,	265
x.	4,	229
xv.	4,	336

GALATIANS.

i.	17,	214
iv.	25,	214

HEBREWS.

xi.	13,	332
xii.	18,	226
	29,	229

JAMES.

iv.	13,	23

II PETER.

iii.	13,	3

REVELATION.

vii.	9,	194, 220
xviii.	18,	21, 22, 109
xxii.	15.	26
	16,	268

EDINBURGH : PRINTED BY JOHN GREIG & SON.